The District Controller's View
THE MIDLAND & NORTHERN JC

Peterborough - South Lynn - Melton Constable - Yarmouth

It is an irony of history that fifteen years after the LMS relinquished its interest in the M&GN, the standard locomotive of the line should be an LMS engine. Introduced in 1951, the LMS 4MT 2-6-0's took over from a miscellany of LNER classes. Still exhibiting the reporting number of its previous working, the 12.55 Spalding - Bourne, 43088 of Spalding leaves Sutton Bridge with the Saturday 16.20 Nottingham - King's Lynn. (Dr Ian C. Allen/Transport Treasury)

The Midland & Great Northern Joint has been the subject of many books - all informative and some scholarly - and it may be assumed that any further works would have to be a repetition of what has already been written.

Most of these books, however, have been devoted to either the construction history of the line or its locomotives leaving what might be regarded as the most important aspect of the system - its traffic operations - uncovered.

This book therefore hopes to fill this gap and at the same time present the reader with a very clear picture of how the railway operated under British Railways.

Unless stated otherwise, all references in this book are to the 1951/2 period which has been selected because it illustrates the railway when it was still operating on a three-shift basis and before the LMS 2-6-0's completely flooded the motive power field. It should be pointed out that subsequent changes were, by and large, slight and that the book is therefore generally representative of the years between the end of the war and closure.

The M&GN meant different things to different people. To the travelling public the M&GN was a system that ran very few passenger trains whilst those it did run stopped so often that average speeds seemed to run the risk of descending into single figures. To the enthusiast it was a railway that had little to commend itself except on Summer Saturdays when it played host to a dozen or so through trains between the coast and the East Midlands.

A third point of view was that of the railwaymen who ran the system. To them the centre of the firmament was South Lynn and the four corners of the earth Peterborough, Bourne, Cromer and Yarmouth. The rest of the railway system lay below the conscious horizon since the M&GN was a remarkably self-contained railway where contact with other systems was limited to a handful of exchange points.

This isolation was not something to be sneered at since it meant that those in charge could get on with the job - and improvise as needs dictated - without going cap-in-hand to some neighbouring authority.

If any phrase was needed to sum up the M&GN, the Gladstonian expression 'glorious isolation' did rather nicely.

Thanks for assistance with text and illustrations are due to: Ray Meek, A. Cliff, C. Dymock, S. Standbridge, Brian Hunt, Bill King, P. Wilde, W.S.Becket. Chris Hembry, R. Adderson.

To see the railway in a proper perspective, it was necessary to look beyond the passenger timetable and to focus upon the goods traffic which was the real bread-and-butter of the system. The railway brought quite large quantities of coal into the area - even the smallest stations accounted for two or three wagons a day - and took agricultural produce out. Most of the latter was dealt with by a complex series of goods trains but a significant tonnage was conveyed by passenger or parcels service and indeed one of the reasons that passenger trains stopped so frequently was because parcels-rated traffic brought in far more than the sale of passenger tickets.

So heavy was the volume of traffic in some quarters that the evening line occupation west of South Lynn rose to one train for every two route-miles which, by any reckoning, was a staggering statistic - one that many trunk lines would have been hard pressed to match - and shows how far the M&GN was from being the rural backwater many imagined it to be.

What sort of railway was the M&GN? It was a Railwayman's Railway but, more than that, it was one that was greatly respected by its neighbours. Few GN or GE men ever had a bad word to say about the M&GN Joint.

Carriage workings are shown as the working Number followed by the number of vehicles. Thus a train shown as 19/4 is formed by Carriage Working No.19 made up of four vehicles. 2/4+1 indicates Carriage Working No.2/Four coaches plus a parcels van. The full carriage workings are shown in the rear of the book.

The engine and class give the home shed of the engine and its diagram number with the class of engine being shown underneath. Thus the 06.00 empty carriage stock from Melton Constable to North Walsham was worked by Melton Constable No.3 engine, a D16 4-4-0. These details were of the greatest importance and were usually committed to memory by Controllers and other senior operating staff. The full engine diagrams are shown later in the book

Train									05.10				07.35	07.35		06.45			07.55
From									P'boro				Holt	Holt		Melton			Cromer
Class	Goods	ECS	Goods	Pass	Pass	Pass	Goods	Goods	XP	Light	XP	Pass	Pass	Pass	Pass	Goods	Goods	Goods	Pass
Engine	SL2	MC3	Y 2	MC4	MC3	GE	MC5	SL 3	NE1	SL 7	NE1	MC 8	MC6	NOR 1	Yar 3	MC5	SL 2	SL 18	CB 2
Class	LM 4	D16	D16	LM4	D16	F6	LM 4	LM 4	LM4	LM 4	LM4	D16	D16	F6	F6	LM 4	LM 4	J67	F6
Carriage Wkg/Vehicles		27/2		18/4	27/2	2			2/4+1		2/4+1	5/4		19/4	19/4	37/2			23/4
PETERBOROUGH									05.10										
Wisbech Jcn									05/14										
WISBECH SIDINGS																			
Dogsthorpe																			
Eye Green																			
Thorney									05/24										
Wryde									05/27										
MURROW EAST									05.32										
MURROW EAST									05.33										
Wisbech St Mary																			
WISBECH NORTH									05.41										
WISBECH NORTH									05.46										
Horse Shoe Lane																			
Horse Shoe Lane									05/47										
Ferry																			
Tydd									05/53										
Sutton Bge Jcn									05/57										
SUTTON BRIDGE									05.58										
SUTTON BRIDGE									06.01										
Sutton Bridge East									06/02										
Walpole																			
Terrington									06.09										
Clenchwarton																			
West Lynn									06/15										
Single line Jcn									06/16										
Yard	04.00									06.20							07.30		
SOUTH LYNN									06.17		(06.17)								
SOUTH LYNN	04/03								(06.23)	06/21	06.23						07/33		
Yard	*To*							05.32	*To*	*To*	*To*					06.30	*To*		
Hardwick Rd Sdg	*Kings*								*Kings*	*Kings*	*Kings*						*Kings*		
Gayton Rd	*Lynn*							05/40	*Lynn*	*Lynn*	*Lynn*						*Lynn*		
Grimston Rd								05/48								06/52			
Hillington								05/53								06/57			
Massingham								06/09								07/14			
E. Rudham								06/17								07/22			
Raynham Park								06/23								07/27			
FAKENHAM WEST																07/39			
FAKENHAM WEST																07/47			
Langor Bge																			
Thursford																			
MELTON CONSTABLE													07.44	(07.44)		08.21			08.30
MELTON CONSTABLE		06.00		06.36		06.45	06/54					07.17	(07.49)	07.49		(08.45)			
Corpusty				07.01		*To Norwich*						07.26	*To Norwich*		07.40	*To Cromer)*			
AYLSHAM N.						*Norwich*						07.38	*Norwich*		08.01	*Cromer)*			
AYLSHAM N.		06/10										07.39			08.16				
Felmingham		06/25										07.46							
NORTH WALSHAM		06.36										07.51			08.38				
NORTH WALSHAM					06.40							07.52			(10.17)				
Honing					06.46							07.58							
Stalham					06.53							08.05							
Stalham					06.58							08.07							
Catfield					07.03							08.12							
POTTER HEIGHAM					07.08							08.17							
POTTER HEIGHAM					07.09							08.18							
Bridge Halt																			
Martham					07.14							08.23							
Martham					07.18							08.24							
Hemsby					07.24							08.30							
GREAT ORMESBY					07.28							08.34							
GREAT ORMESBY					07.29							08.35							
Scratby																			
California																			
Caister Camp																			
Caister					07.35							08.40							
Newtown																			
Salisbury Rd					07/40							08/45							
LOWESTOFT (CENTRAL)						07.15									08.15				
Lowestoft North						07.22									08.22				
Corton						07.26									08.27				
Hopton-on-Sea						07.31									08.33				
Gorleston Links						07.34									08.38				
Gorleston-on-Sea						07.39									08.41				
White Swan				06.55															
Caister Rd Jcn				06/57											08/49				
YARMOUTH				07.00		07.41						08.46			08.50				
Destination						S. Town									B'ham				

Train				05.30							06.40	06.53		05.40	05.55	06.02		05.50	
From	K' Lynn			K. Lynn							K. Lynn	K. Lynn		Melton	Lynn	Lynn		Melton	
Class	Light	Goods	Goods	Goods	Goods	Goods	Goods	Goods	Goods	Pass	Pass	ECS	Pass	Goods	Goods	Goods	Goods	Goods	Pass
Engine	SL 17	SL 1	SL 4	SL 2	SL 5	SL 6	MC 1	MC 2	Y2	Yar 3	SL 7	NE 1	SL 8	MC 1	SL 5	SL 6	SL 9	MC 2	MC 6
Class	LM 4	K2	K2	LM 4	LM 4	LM 4	LM 4	LM 4	D16	F6	LM 4	LM 4	LM 4	LM 4	LM 4	LM 4	K2	LM 4	D16
Carriage Wkg/Vehicles										37/2	29/3	2/4&1	2/4						19/4
YARMOUTH									06.35	06.45									
Caister Rd Jcn									06/38	06/46									
White Swan									06.40										
Gorleston-on-Sea										06.56									
Gorleston Links										06.59									
Hopton-on-Sea										07.03									
Corton										07.08									
Lowestoft North										07.12									
LOWESTOFT CENTRAL										07.18									
Salisbury Road																			
Newtown																			
Caister																			
Caister Camp																			
California																			
Scratby																			
GREAT ORMESBY																			
GREAT ORMESBY																			
Hemsby																			
Martham																			
Martham																			
Bridge Halt																			
POTTER HEIGHAM																			
POTTER HEIGHAM																			
Catfield																			
Stalham																			
Stalham																			
Honing																			
N. WALSHAM																			
N. WALSHAM																			
Felmingham																			
AYLSHAM N.																			
AYLSHAM N.																			
Corpusty																			
MELTON CONSTABLE																			
MELTON CONSTABLE							05.40	05.50											06.50
Thursford								06.04										06.30	(To
Langor Bridge																			Holt)
FAKENHAM WEST																			06.50
FAKENHAM WEST							06/07												07.10
Raynham Park							06/15												07.23
East Rudham							06/24												
Massingham							06/33												
Hillington																			
Grimston Road							06/47												
Bawsey																			
Gayton Road							06.58							07.13					
Hardwick Rd Sdg																			
Yard														07.28					
SOUTH LYNN	00.22										06.45	06.58							
SOUTH LYNN				05.35							06.50	07.08							
Yard		03.20	05.30	05.40	05.55	06.02												07.30	
Single Line Jcn		03/22	05/34		05/57	06/04					06/51	07/09						07/32	
West Lynn		03/24	05/36		05/59	06.07					06/52	07/10						07/34	
Clenchwharton											06.57								
Terrington						06.18					07.01				07.23				
Walpole											07.06								
Sutton Bridge East		03/47	05/58		06/24												07/39	07/57	
SUTTON BRIDGE					06.24						07.11	07.23				(06.24)	07.40	07.58	
SUTTON BRIDGE		03/48	06/00	(07.30)							07.14	07.25			07.30		(08.03)		
Sutton Bge Jcn		03/50										07/26							
Tydd		03/56										07.34							
Ferry												07.40							
Horse Shoe Lane		04.08																	
Horse Shoe Lane		04.45										07/44							
WISBECH NORTH												07.45							
WISBECH NORTH		04/48										07.46							
Wisbech St. Mary		04/51										07.51							
Murrow East												07.57							
Murrow East		05/00										07.58							
Wryde		05/09										08.04							
Thorney		05/14										08.10							
Eye Green												08.16							
Dogsthorpe																			
WISBECH SIDINGS																			
Wisbech Jcn		05/37										08/23							
Westwood Yard		05.47																	
PETERBOROUGH												08.26							
Destination		Colwick										N'ham				Spalding			

Train		09.05					06.45			07.15	07.40		06.50	06.50	06.45	09.30	09.40	09.50	06.50
From		Holt					P'bro			Crescent	Bourne		W'wd	W'wd	Melton	Crescent	Cromer	P'boro	W'wd
Class	Goods	Pass	Pass	Pass	Pass	Motor	Pass	Motor	Goods	Gds	Pass		Gds	Gds	Gds	Gds	Pass	Goods	Gds
Engine	MC 6	NOR 2	Y 5	GE	NE3	KL11	SL 11	NOR 2	KL11	MC 1	SL 1	SL 7	NE4	NE4	MC5	NE5	MC 7	NE5	NE4
Class	D16	D16	F6		LM 4	C12	LM 4	D16	C12	LM 4	K2	LM 4	LM 4	LM 4	LM 4	LM 4	D16	LM 4	LM 4
Carriage Wkg/Vehicles		15/4	6/4	2	9/4+2	1/2	9/4+2	15/4	1/2		25/3						35/2		
PETERBOROUGH					06.45					07/20									
Wisbech Jcn					06/46					07/27									
WISBECH SIDINGS												07.45		09.50					
Dogsthorpe																10.01		10.11	
Eye Green					06.54								08.01	08.20				10.21	
Thorney					07.01					07/37				08/31					
Wryde					07.05					07/42				08/36					
MURROW EAST					07.11														
MURROW EAST					07.12					07/50				08/44					
Wisbech St Mary					07.18								08.53						10.20
WISBECH NORTH					07.23														
WISBECH NORTH					07.24														10/28
Horse Shoe Lane												08.04							10.30
Horse Shoe Lane					07.25					08.45									
Ferry																			
Tydd					07.35					08/59									
Sutton Bge Jcn					07/39					09/03									
SUTTON BRIDGE					07.40						08.58								
SUTTON BRIDGE					07.42					09/07	09.01								
Sutton Bridge East										09/08									
Walpole					07.48						09.06								
Terrington					07.52						09.10								
Clenchwarton					07.56						09.13								
West Lynn					08/00					09/32	09/17								
Single line Jcn					08/01					09/33	09/18								
Yard										09.34									
SOUTH LYNN					08.02	(08.02)					09.19								
SOUTH LYNN					(08.18)	08.15	08.18	08.45			09.21								
Yard						To		To	09.10	To									
Hardwick Rd Sdg						Kings		Kings		Kings									
Gayton Rd						Lynn	08.25	Lynn		Lynn									
Grimston Rd							08.31		09/32										
Hillington							08.36		09/37										
Massingham							08.46		09.56										
E. Rudham							08.52												
Raynham Park							08.57												
FAKENHAM WEST							09.03												
FAKENHAM WEST							09.06												
Langor Bge																			
Thursford																			
MELTON CONSTABLE	(08.21)	09.14					09.24	(09.14)									10.16		
MELTON CONSTABLE	08.45	(09.37)					09.34	09.37									(To		
Corpusty	To						09.43	To									B'ham)		
AYLSHAM N.	Cromer)						09.55	Norwich											
AYLSHAM N.			09.16				09.57												
Felmingham			09.23				10.04												
NORTH WALSHAM			09.28				10.09								(08.38)				
NORTH WALSHAM			09.30				10.10								10.17				
Honing			09.39				10.16								10/29				
Stalham			09.46				10.23								10.40				
Stalham			09.49				10.24								11.00				
Catfield			09.54				10.29												
POTTER HEIGHAM			09.59				10.34								11.15				
POTTER HEIGHAM			10.00				10.37								11.30				
Bridge Halt																			
Martham			10.05				10.42								11.42				
Martham			10.07				10.43								12.02				
Hemsby			10.13				10.49								12.14				
GREAT ORMESBY			10.17				10.53												
GREAT ORMESBY			10.18				10.54												
Scratby																			
California																			
Caister Camp																			
Caister			10.24				10.59												
Newtown																			
Salisbury Rd			10/29				11/04												
LOWESTOFT (CENTRAL)				10.20															
Lowestoft North				10.27															
Corton				10.31															
Hopton-on-Sea				10.36															
Gorleston Links				10.39															
Gorleston-on-Sea				10.44															
White Swan																			
Caister Rd Jcn																			
YARMOUTH			10.30				11.05												
Destination				S. Town															

WORKING TIMETABLE : 1951/2

Train	05.50				08.00	06.28	07.30	07.50		08.33	05.50	07.30		8.45	07.50		09.44	06.51	07.40
From	Melton				K. Lynn	Norwich	Lynn	Lynn		K. Lynn	Melton	Melton		K. Lynn	Lynn		K. Lynn	Yar	Norwich
Class	Goods	XP	Pass	Goods	Motor	Pass	Goods	Goods	Pass	Motor	Goods	Pass	Pass	Goods	Goods	Pass	Motor	Pass	Pass
Engine	MC 2	MC 7	SL 6	SL 10	KL11	NOR 1	SL 9	SL 10	MC 9	KL11	MC 2	NE 1	SP 1	SL 18	SL 10	Y 4	KL11	NE3	NOR 2
Class	LM 4	D16	LM 4	LM 4	C12	D16	K2	LM 4	LM 4	C12	LM 4	LM 4	LM 4	J67	LM 4	B12	C12	LM 4	D16
Carriage Wkg/Vehicles		GE/4	22/3		1/2	15/4			11/4	1/2		11/4	21/3			4/4	1/2	4/4	15/4
YARMOUTH																		06.51	
Caister Rd Jcn																			
White Swan																			
Gorleston-on-Sea																			
Gorleston Links																			
Hopton-on-Sea																			
Corton																			
Lowestoft North																			
LOWESTOFT CENTRAL																			
Salisbury Road																		06/52	
Newtown																			
Caister																		06.58	
Caister Camp																			
California																			
Scratby																			
GREAT ORMESBY																		07.03	
GREAT ORMESBY																		07.04	
Hemsby																		07.08	
Martham																		07.14	
Martham																		07.15	
Bridge Halt																			
POTTER HEIGHAM																		07.20	
POTTER HEIGHAM																		07.21	
Catfield																		07.28	
Stalham																		07.33	
Stalham																		07.35	
Honing																		07.43	
N. WALSHAM																		07.50	
N. WALSHAM																		07.53	
Felmingham																		07.58	
AYLSHAM N.																		08.03	
AYLSHAM N.																		08.05	
Corpusty																		08.18	
MELTON CONSTABLE						07.19												08.27	08.30
MELTON CONSTABLE		07.05						07.30										08.36	08.32
Thursford		(To						07.37										08.43	(ECS
Langor Bridge		L. St)																	Holt)
FAKENHAM WEST								07.47										08.53	
FAKENHAM WEST								07.49										08.55	
Raynham Park	07.38							07.56										09.02	
East Rudham	07.52							08.02		08.20								09.08	
Massingham								08.09		08.34								09.15	
Hillington								08.18										09.24	
Grimston Road								08.23										09.29	
Bawsey																			
Gayton Road								08.28										09.34	
Hardwick Rd Sdg																			
Yard																			
SOUTH LYNN					08.05			08.35	08.38			(08.35)				09.45	09.49	(09.45)	
SOUTH LYNN									(08.45)			08.45		08/54		(09.55)		09.55	
Yard				07.50											08.55				
Single Line Jcn				07/52								08.46						09/56	
West Lynn				07/54								08.47						09/57	
Clenchwharton				08.01			08.25					08.52							
Terrington							08.34					08.56			09.25				
Walpole												09.01			09.35				
Sutton Bridge East																			
SUTTON BRIDGE						(07.58)						09.06						10.09	
SUTTON BRIDGE				08.03		08.08						09.08	09.15					10.11	
Sutton Bge Jcn												09.09						10.12	
Tydd												09.14						10.16	
Ferry												09.20							
Horse Shoe Lane																			
Horse Shoe Lane												09.24						10.24	
WISBECH NORTH												09.25						10.25	
WISBECH NORTH												09.27						10.27	
Wisbech St. Mary												09.32							
Murrow East												09.38							
Murrow East												09.39						10.38	
Wryde												09.44						10.43	
Thorney												09.50						10.47	
Eye Green																			
Dogsthorpe																			
WISBECH SIDINGS																			
Wisbech Jcn												10/17						11/03	
Westwood Yard																			
PETERBOROUGH												10.21						11.07	
Destination			Spalding				Colwick					Spalding							

Impressive lattice girder bridges were a feature of the M&GN with examples at Sutton Bridge, West Lynn, Potter Heigham, Yarmouth (Bure), Breydon Water, Welland Bank, South Drove and Little Bytham. Not all the structures appear to have been soundly engineered and the bridges at Potter Heigham and West Lynn required expensive modifications. The cost of repairs to the latter or its replacement was the justification for closing the M&GN in 1959. LM4 2-6-0 43094 of South Lynn emerges from Potter Heigham bridge with a Yarmouth - Peterborough passenger train. (Dr Ian C. Allen/Transport Treasury)

ROUTE AVAILABILITY OF ENGINES : M&GN

From / To Loco	Peterborough Sutton Bridge	Sutton Bge South Lynn	South Lynn Yarmouth	Sutton Bridge Saxby*	Melton Cromer B.	Melton Norwich	Yarmouth Lowestoft	Cromer B N&S Jt
A1 4-6-2	X	X	X	X	X	X	X	X
A2 4-6-2	X	X	X	X	X	X	X	X
A3 4-6-2	X	X	X	X	X	X	X	X
A4 4-6-2	X	X	X	X	X	X	X	X
A5 4-6-2T	Y	X	Y	Y	Y	Y	Y	Y
B1 4-6-0	Y	X	Y	Y	Y	Y	Y	Y
B2 4-6-0	Y	X	Y	Y	Y	Y	Y	Y
B12 4-6-0	Y	Y	Y	Y	Y	Y	Y	Y
B17 4-6-0	Y	X	Y	Y	Y	Y	Y	Y
B16 4-6-0	Y	X	Y	Y	Y	Y	Y	X
C12 4-4-2T	Y	X	Y	Y	Y	Y	Y	Y
C13 4-4-2T	Y	X	Y	Y	Y	Y	Y	Y
C14 4-4-2T	Y	X	Y	Y	Y	Y	Y	Y
D9 4-4-0	Y	Y	Y	Y	Y	Y	Y	Y
D15 4-4-0	Y	Y	Y	Y	Y	Y	Y	Y
D16 4-4-0	Y	Y	Y	Y	Y	Y	Y	Y
E4 2-4-0	Y	Y	Y	Y	Y	Y	Y	Y
F3 2-4-2T	Y	Y	Y	Y	Y	Y	Y	Y
F4 2-4-2T	Y	Y	Y	Y	Y	Y	Y	Y
F5 2-4-2T	Y	Y	Y	Y	Y	Y	Y	Y
F6 2-4-2T	Y	Y	Y	Y	Y	Y	Y	Y
G5 0-4-4T	Y	Y	Y	Y	Y	Y	Y	Y
J1 0-6-0	Y	Y	Y	Y	Y	Y	Y	Y
J2 0-6-0	Y	X	Y	Y	Y	Y	Y	Y
J3 0-6-0	Y	Y	Y	Y	Y	Y	Y	Y
J5 0-6-0	Y	Y	Y	Y	Y	Y	Y	Y
J6 0-6-0	Y	Y	Y	Y	Y	Y	Y	Y
J11 0-6-0	Y	Y	Y	Y	Y	Y	Y	Y
J15 0-6-0	Y	Y	Y	Y	Y	Y	Y	Y
J17 0-6-0	Y	Y	Y	Y	Y	Y	Y	Y
J19 0-6-0	Y	Y	Y	Y	Y	Y	Y	Y
J20 0-6-0	Y	Y	Y	Y	Y	Y	Y	Y
J21 0-6-0	Y	Y	Y	Y	Y	Y	Y	Y
J39 0-6-0	Y	EO	Y	Y	Y	Y	Y	Y
J50 0-6-0T	Y	X	Y	Y	Y	Y	Y	X
J52 0-6-0T	Y	X	Y	Y	Y	Y	Y	Y
J63 0-6-0T	Y	Y	Y	Y	Y	Y	Y	Y
J65 0-6-0T	Y	Y	Y	Y	Y	Y	Y	Y
J66 0-6-0T	Y	Y	Y	Y	Y	Y	Y	Y
J67 0-6-0T	Y	Y	Y	Y	Y	Y	Y	Y
J68 0-6-0T	Y	Y	Y	Y	Y	Y	Y	Y
J69 0-6-0T	Y	Y	Y	Y	Y	Y	Y	Y
K1 2-6-0	Y	X	Y	Y	Y	Y	Y	X
K2 2-6-0	Y	Y	Y	Y	Y	Y	Y	Y
K3 2-6-0	X	X	X	X	X	X	X	X
K5 2-6-0	X	X	X	X	X	X	X	X

From / To	Peterborough Sutton Bridge	Sutton Bge South Lynn	South Lynn Yarmouth	Sutton Bridge Saxby*	Melton Cromer B.	Melton Norwich	Yarmouth Lowestoft	Cromer B N. Walsham
L1 2-6-4T	X	X	X	X	X	X	X	X
L3 2-6-4T	X	X	X	X	X	X	X	X
N1 0-6-2T	Y	X	Y	Y	Y	Y	Y	Y
N2 0-6-2T	Y	X	Y	Y	Y	Y	Y	X
N4 0-6--2T	Y	Y	Y	Y	Y	Y	Y	Y
N5 0-6-2T	Y	Y	Y	Y	Y	Y	Y	Y
N7 0-6-2T	Y	Y	Y	Y	Y	Y	Y	Y
O1 2-8-0	Y	X	Y	Y	Y	Y	Y	X
O2 2-8-0	Y	X	Y	Y	Y	Y	Y	X
O3 2-8-0	Y	X	Y	Y	Y	Y	Y	X
O4 2-8-0	Y	X	Y	Y	Y	Y	Y	X
O7 (WD) 2-8-0	Y	X	Y	Y	Y	Y	Y	X
V1 2-6-2T	Y	X	Y	Y	Y	Y	Y	X
V2 2-6-2	X	X	X	X	X	X	X	X
V3 2-6-2T	X	X	X	X	X	X	X	X
V4 2-6-2	Y	Y	Y	Y	Y	Y	Y	Y
W1 4-6-4	X	X	X	X	X	X	X	X
LMS								
LMS 2MT 2-6-2T	Y	Y	Y	Y	Y	Y	Y	Y
LMS 2MT 2-6-0	Y	Y	Y	Y	Y	Y	Y	Y
LMS 3P 2-6-2T	Y	Y	Y	Y	Y	Y	Y	Y
LTS 3P 4-4-2T	Y	X	Y	Y	Y	Y	Y	X
MR 3F 0-6-0	Y	Y	Y	Y	Y	Y	Y	Y
LMS 4P 4-4-0	X	X	X	X	X	X	X	X
LMS 4MT 2-6-0	Y	Y	Y	Y	Y	Y	Y	Y
LMS 4F 0-6-0	Y	Y	Y	Y	Y	Y	Y	Y
LMS 4MT 2-6-4T	Y	X	Y	Y	Y	Y	Y	X
LMS 4MT 2-6-4T	X	X	X	X	X	X	X	X
LMS 4MT 2-6-4T	X	X	X	X	X	X	X	X
LMS 5MT 4-6-0	Y	X	Y	Y	Y	Y	Y	Y
LMS 5MT 2-6-0	X	X	X	X	X	X	X	X
LMS 5XP 4-6-0	X	X	X	X	X	X	X	X
LNWR 7F 0-8-0	Y	X	Y	Y	Y	Y	Y	Y
LMS 7P 4-6-0	X	X	X	X	X	X	X	X
LMS 8F 2-8-0	Y	X	Y	Y	Y	Y	Y	X
BR STANDARD								
BR 2MT 2-6-2T	Y	Y	Y	Y	Y	Y	Y	Y
BR 2MT 2-6-0	Y	Y	Y	Y	Y	Y	Y	Y
BR 3MT 2-6-2T	Y	Y	Y	Y	Y	Y	Y	Y
BR 4MT 2-6-0	Y	Y	Y	Y	Y	Y	Y	Y
BR 4MT 2-6-4T	Y	X	Y	Y	Y	Y	Y	Y
BR 4MT 4-6-0	Y	Y	Y	Y	Y	Y	Y	Y
BR 5MT 4-6-0	X	X	X	X	X	X	X	X
BR 6MT 4-6-2	X	X	X	X	X	X	X	X
BR 7MT 4-6-2	X	X	X	X	X	X	X	X

Y = cleared, X = barred. EO : Emergencies only

* List refers to engines from the M&GN direction. No restriction on LM engines west of Bourne except a ban on unrebuilt 7P 4-6-0's and LM 4-6-2.

* LNER passed for through running only between Saxby and Nottingham or Saxby and Leicester

WORKING TIMETABLE : 1951/2

Station				05.50 Melton	10.13 K. Lynn	05.50 Melton		07.50 Lynn	10.30 K. Lynn	05.50 Melton			07.02 Yar	07.02 Yar	07.50 Lynn	07.20 Yar	09.30 Norwich	08.15 L'toft	08.15 L'toft
Class	Pass	Goods	Goods	Goods	ECS	Goods	Goods	Goods	ECS (PP)	Goods	Goods	Pass	Goods	Goods	Goods	Goods	XP	XP	XP
Engine	CB 2	MC 6	Y 1	MC 2	SL 7	MC 2	YAR 10	SL 10	KL11	MC 2	SL 2	Y 5	Y 1	Y 1	SL 10	YAR 10	NOR 1	MC 3	MC 3
Class	F6	D 16	LM 4	LM 4	LM4	LM 4	J17	LM 4	C12	LM 4	LM 4	F6	LM 4	LM 4	LM 4	J17	D16	D16	D16
Carriage Wkg/Vehicles	17/4			8					1/2		23/4	6/4					18&33/5	37/2	37/5
YARMOUTH		07.02					07.20					07.45					09.00		
Caister Rd Jcn							07/22												
White Swan																			
Gorleston-on-Sea							07.35									08.55			
Gorleston Links																			
Hopton-on-Sea																			
Corton																			
Lowestoft North																09.15			
LOWESTOFT CENTRAL																			
Salisbury Road		07/05										07/46					09/01		
Newtown																			
Caister		07.11										07.52	08.00						
Caister Camp																			
California																			
Scratby																			
GREAT ORMESBY												07.58							
GREAT ORMESBY												07.59	08/10				09.09		
Hemsby												08.04	08.22	08.32					
Martham												08.10		08.43					
Martham												08.11		08.53			09/16		
Bridge Halt																			
POTTER HEIGHAM												08.16		09.03			09.21		
POTTER HEIGHAM												08.19		(09.42)			09.22		
Catfield												08.26							
Stalham												08.30					09.30		
Stalham												08.35					09.32		
Honing												08.43					09/38		
N. WALSHAM												08.50					09.45		
N. WALSHAM												08.51					09.47		
Felmingham												08.56							
AYLSHAM N.												09.01					09.56		
AYLSHAM N.																	09.58		
Corpusty																	10/10		
MELTON CONSTABLE																	10.14	10.20	(10.20)
MELTON CONSTABLE	08.40		08.45								09.35						(10.28)	(10.28)	10.28
Thursford	(To Cromer)		(To Cromer)								(To Cromer)								
Langor Bridge																			
FAKENHAM WEST																			10.42
FAKENHAM WEST																			10.44
Raynham Park																			10/50
East Rudham																			10/53
Massingham				09.25															10/58
Hillington				09.40		10.10													11/04
Grimston Road						10.19				10.34									11/07
Bawsey																			
Gayton Road										10/46									
Hardwick Rd Sdg																			
Yard										10.58									
SOUTH LYNN					10.18				10.35										11.16
SOUTH LYNN																			(11.22)
Yard																			
Single Line Jcn																			
West Lynn																			
Clenchwharton																			
Terrington																			
Walpole								10.28											
Sutton Bridge East								10/38											
SUTTON BRIDGE								10.40							(10.40)				
SUTTON BRIDGE								(11.19)							11.19				
Sutton Bge Jcn															11/21				
Tydd															11.32				
Ferry																			
Horse Shoe Lane																			
Horse Shoe Lane																			
WISBECH NORTH																			
WISBECH NORTH																			
Wisbech St. Mary																			
Murrow East																			
Murrow East																			
Wryde																			
Thorney																			
Eye Green																			
Dogsthorpe																			
WISBECH SIDINGS																			
Wisbech Jcn																			
Westwood Yard																			
PETERBOROUGH																			
Destination																			

Train	09.10	09.18			09.10		11.45	11.45				09.50	11.00	09.40		09.40	10.30	06.40	
From	Lynn	Norwich			Lynn		Low	Low				P'boro	Cromer	Lynn		Lynn	Lynn	Colwick	
Class	Goods	Pass	Goods	Motor	Goods	Pass	Goods	Goods	Goods	Goods	Goods	Goods	Pass	Goods	Motor	Goods	Goods	Goods	Pass
Engine	MC 1	GE	MC 9	KL11	MC 1	Yar 3	YAR 10	YAR 10	YAR 10	SL 13	SL 7	NE5	CB 2	MC 9	KL11	MC 9	SL 13	CC2	Yar 2
Class	LM 4		LM 4	C12	LM 4	F6	J17	J17	J17	LM 4	LM 4	LM 4	F6	LM 4	C12	LM 4	LM 4	K2	D16
Carriage Wkg/Vehicles		20/2		1/2	27/2							23/4			1/2				12/2
PETERBOROUGH																			
Wisbech Jcn																			
WISBECH SIDINGS																			
Dogsthorpe																			
Eye Green												10.30							
Thorney												10.43							
Wryde																			
MURROW EAST																			
MURROW EAST																			
Wisbech St Mary																			
WISBECH NORTH																			
WISBECH NORTH																			
Horse Shoe Lane																			
Horse Shoe Lane																			
Ferry																			
Tydd																			
Sutton Bge Jcn																			
SUTTON BRIDGE																			
SUTTON BRIDGE																		11/23	
Sutton Bridge East																		11/24	
Walpole																			
Terrington																			
Clenchwarton																			
West Lynn																		11/48	
Single line Jcn																		11/49	
Yard											10.30							11.51	
SOUTH LYNN																			
SOUTH LYNN				09.55							10/32				11.22				
Yard		09.40		To						10.30		To			To				
Hardwick Rd Sdg				Kings								Kings			Kings				
Gayton Rd				Lynn								Lynn			Lynn				
Grimston Rd			10/02								10.54						11.35		
Hillington			10/07														11.45		
Massingham	10.04		10/24																
E. Rudham	10/15	10.34												11.10					
Raynham Park	10/20													11.20		11.30			
FAKENHAM WEST																11.45			
FAKENHAM WEST	10.30															12.00			
Langor Bge																12.12			
Thursford																			
MELTON CONSTABLE	11.01	11.05			(11.01)								11.35						
MELTON CONSTABLE	(11.25)				11.25														
Corpusty					(To														
AYLSHAM N.					Norwich)														
AYLSHAM N.																			
Felmingham																			
NORTH WALSHAM																			
NORTH WALSHAM																			
Honing																			
Stalham																			
Stalham																			
Catfield																			
POTTER HEIGHAM																			
POTTER HEIGHAM																			
Bridge Halt																			
Martham																			
Martham																			
Hemsby																			
GREAT ORMESBY																			
GREAT ORMESBY																			
Scratby																			
California																			
Caister Camp																			
Caister																			
Newtown																			
Salisbury Rd																			
LOWESTOFT (CENTRAL)						11.40	11.45												12.33
Lowestoft North						11.47	11.55	12.10											12.40
Corton						11.51		12.15	12.30										12.44
Hopton-on-Sea						11.56			12.35										12.49
Gorleston Links						11.59													12.52
Gorleston-on-Sea						12.04													12.57
White Swan																			
Caister Rd Jcn						12/12													13/05
YARMOUTH						12.13													13.06
Destination																			

Train	11.13	08.15	11.13	07.20		09.25	10.30	11.55	07.02		12.50	10.05	07.02	07.02	13.00	07.50			
From	K. Lynn	L'toft	K. Lynn	Yar		S. Town	Norwich	K. Lynn	Yar		K. Lynn	Yar	Yar	Yar	K. Lynn	Lynn			
Class	Pass	XP	Pass	Goods	Goods	Motor	Pass	Motor	Goods	Pass	Motor	Pass	Goods	Goods	Light	Goods	XP	Goods	Pass
Engine	SL 7	SL 14	MC 3	YAR 10	MC 7	GE	SL 3	KL11	Y1	Y6	KL11	SL 16	Y1	Y1	SP 4	SL 10	GE	MC 8	Yar 3
Class	LM 4	B12	D16	J17	D16		LM 4	C12	LM 4	B12	C12	LM 4	LM 4	LM 4	LM 4	LM 4	D16	D16	F6
Carriage Wkg/Vehicles	38/3	37/6	38/3			2	28/4	1/2		5/4	1/2	5/4					GE/4		27/2
YARMOUTH										10.05							10.30		10.35
Caister Rd Jcn																			10/36
White Swan																			
Gorleston-on-Sea						09.33													10.46
Gorleston Links						09.36													10.49
Hopton-on-Sea						09.40													10.53
Corton						09.45													10.58
Lowestoft North				09.33		09.49													11.02
LOWESTOFT CENTRAL				09.43		09.55													11.08
Salisbury Road										10/06							10/33		
Newtown																			
Caister										10.11									
Caister Camp																			
California																			
Scratby																			
GREAT ORMESBY										10.16								10.46	
GREAT ORMESBY										10.19								10.56	
Hemsby										10.23									
Martham										10.29								11.11	
Martham										10.30								11.41	
Bridge Halt																			
POTTER HEIGHAM								(09.03)		10.35									
POTTER HEIGHAM								09.42		10.36								11/49	
Catfield										10.43								11.56	
Stalham								10.17		10.47		(10.17)							
Stalham								(10.50)		10.48		10.50							
Honing										10.56		11.02	11.15						
N. WALSHAM										11.03			11.32						
N. WALSHAM										11.04			11.45						
Felmingham										11.09			11.54						
AYLSHAM N.										11.14									
AYLSHAM N.										11.16									
Corpusty										11.29									
MELTON CONSTABLE							11.19			11.38									
MELTON CONSTABLE				10.32						11.45						11.50			
Thursford				(To						11.53						(To			
Langor Bridge				Holt)												L. St)			
FAKENHAM WEST										12.03									
FAKENHAM WEST										12.05									
Raynham Park										12.12									
East Rudham										12.18									
Massingham										12.25									
Hillington										12.36									
Grimston Road										12.41									
Bawsey																			
Gayton Road										12.46									
Hardwick Rd Sdg																			
Yard																			
SOUTH LYNN	11.18	(11.16)	(11.18)				12.00			12.53	12.55	(12.53)							
SOUTH LYNN	(11.28)	11.22	11.28							(13.00)	13.00				13/04				
Yard															13.05				
Single Line Jcn		11/23	11/29								13/01								
West Lynn		11/24	11/30								13/02								
Clenchwharton			11.35																
Terrington			11.39																
Walpole			11.44																
Sutton Bridge East																			
SUTTON BRIDGE			11.49								13.13								
SUTTON BRIDGE		11/35	11.51								13.14								
Sutton Bge Jcn			11/52								13/15								
Tydd			11.56								13.20				12.48				
Ferry																			
Horse Shoe Lane															13.03				
Horse Shoe Lane			12/03								13/30				(14.05)				
WISBECH NORTH			12.04								13.31								
WISBECH NORTH			12.06								13.32								
Wisbech St. Mary			12.11																
Murrow East			12.17								13.43								
Murrow East			12.18								13.44								
Wryde			12.24								13/49								
Thorney			12.29								13.53								
Eye Green			12.35																
Dogsthorpe																			
WISBECH SIDINGS																			
Wisbech Jcn			12/42								14/04								
Westwood Yard																			
PETERBOROUGH			12.46								14.08								
Destination		B'ham																	

WORKING TIMETABLE : 1951/2

Train	11.45	10.30	06.45	11.45	12.30	09.40	09.40				10.33		10.30	10.00		09.55		13.35	12.45
From	Low	Lynn	Melton	Low	Holt	Lynn	Lynn				P'bro		Lynn	Spalding		Saxby		Cromer	Lynn
Class	Goods	Goods	Goods	Goods	Goods	Goods	Goods	Goods	Pass	Motor	Pass	Pass	Goods	Goods	Pass	Pass	Goods	Pass	Goods
Engine	YAR 10	SL 13	MC5	YAR 10	MC 7	MC 9	MC 9	SL 15B	SL 8	KL11	Y 4	NOR 1	SL 13	SL 6	GE	SP 4	SL 15A	MC 6	SL 3
Class	J17	LM 4	LM 4	J17	D16	LM 4	LM 4	LM 4	LM 4	C12	B12	D16	LM 4	LM 4	F4	LM 4	LM 4	D16	LM 4
Carriage Wkg/Vehicles									2/4	1/2	2/4	28/4			2	30/3		17/4	
PETERBOROUGH											10.33								
Wisbech Jcn											10/37								
WISBECH SIDINGS																			
Dogsthorpe																			
Eye Green											10.44								
Thorney											10.51								
Wryde											10.56								
MURROW EAST											11.03								
MURROW EAST											11.05								
Wisbech St Mary											11.10								
WISBECH NORTH											11.15								
WISBECH NORTH											11.21								
Horse Shoe Lane																			
Horse Shoe Lane											11/22								
Ferry											11.27								
Tydd											11.33								
Sutton Bge Jcn											11.37								
SUTTON BRIDGE											11.38			(11.07)		12.11			
SUTTON BRIDGE											11.41			11.55		12.13			
Sutton Bridge East														11/57					
Walpole											11.47					12.18			
Terrington											11.50					12.22			
Clenchwarton											11.55					12.26			
West Lynn											11.58			12/18		12/30			
Single line Jcn											11.59			12/19		12/31			
Yard														12.22					
SOUTH LYNN									(12.01)		12.01					12.32			
SOUTH LYNN									(12.14)	12.11	12.14					12.35			
Yard										To					To 12.45				
Hardwick Rd Sdg										Kings					Kings				
Gayton Rd										Lynn	12.21				Lynn				
Grimston Rd											12.26								13/07
Hillington		12.00									12.34								13/12
Massingham		12.22									12.44			12.52					13/29
E. Rudham											12.51			13/03					13/37
Raynham Park											12.56			13/08					13/42
FAKENHAM WEST											13.02			13.20					
FAKENHAM WEST											13.04								13.52
Langor Bge						12.32													
Thursford						12.45	13.01				13.16								
MELTON CONSTABLE					12.45		13.16				13.22						14.23	14.12	(14.23)
MELTON CONSTABLE											13.30	13.32					(14.46)		14.46
Corpusty											13.39	To							To
AYLSHAM N.											13.51	Norwich							Norwich
AYLSHAM N.											13.52								
Felmingham											13.59								
NORTH WALSHAM											14.02								
NORTH WALSHAM											14.05								
Honing											14.12								
Stalham											14.19								
Stalham											14.20								
Catfield											14.25								
POTTER HEIGHAM											14.30								
POTTER HEIGHAM											14.31								
Bridge Halt																			
Martham											14.36								
Martham											14.37								
Hemsby			12.24								14.43								
GREAT ORMESBY			12.33								14.47								
GREAT ORMESBY			13.06								14.48								
Scratby																			
California																			
Caister Camp																			
Caister											14.54								
Newtown																			
Salisbury Rd			13/20								14/59								
LOWESTOFT (CENTRAL)																14.50			
Lowestoft North																14.57			
Corton																15.01			
Hopton-on-Sea	12.58															15.06			
Gorleston Links																15.09			
Gorleston-on-Sea	13.06			13.31												15.14			
White Swan								14.30											
Caister Rd Jcn				13/44				14/33											
YARMOUTH			13.22	13.46				14.35			15.00								
Destination																S. Town			

WORKING TIMETABLE : 1951/2

Train	07.02	10.30	07.02				07.50		13.50	13.50	14.09	14.30	07.50	13.50	07.50			13.21	
From	Yar	Yar	Yar				Lynn		Lynn	Lynn	K. Lynn	K. Lynn	Lynn	Lynn	Lynn			Norwich	
Class	Goods	Goods	Goods	Pass	ECS	Pass	Goods	Goods	Goods	Goods	Motor	Goods	Goods	Goods	Goods	Gds	Pcls	Pass	Pass
Engine	Y 1	MC 8	Y 1	CB 2	SL 7	Yar 2	SL 10	SP 4	SP 4	SP 4	KL11	SL 6	SL 10	SP 4	SL 10	NE 5	NE 1	NOR 2	Y 7
Class	LM 4	D16	LM 4	F6	LM 4	D16	LM 4	LM 4	LM 4	LM 4	C12	LM 4	LM 4	LM 4	LM 4	LM 4	LM 4	D16	D16
Carriage Wkg/Vehicles				28/4	25/3	12/2					1/2					7/4	15/4		6/4+1
YARMOUTH						11.15													12.42
Caister Rd Jcn						11/16													
White Swan																			
Gorleston-on-Sea						11.25													
Gorleston Links						11.28													
Hopton-on-Sea						11.32													
Corton						11.37													
Lowestoft North						11.41													
LOWESTOFT CENTRAL						11.47													
Salisbury Road																			12/43
Newtown																			
Caister																			12.48
Caister Camp																			
California																			
Scratby																			
GREAT ORMESBY																			12.53
GREAT ORMESBY																			12.54
Hemsby																			12.58
Martham																			13.04
Martham																			13.05
Bridge Halt																			
POTTER HEIGHAM																			13.10
POTTER HEIGHAM																			13.11
Catfield		12.06																	13.18
Stalham		12.16																	13.22
Stalham		12.58																	13.23
Honing		13.10																	13.31
N. WALSHAM																			13.38
N. WALSHAM																			13.40
Felmingham	12.05																		13.45
AYLSHAM N.	12.18																		13.50
AYLSHAM N.	12.30																		13.53
Corpusty	12.55		13.10																14.06
MELTON CONSTABLE			13.28														14.09		14.14
MELTON CONSTABLE				13.35															(14.20)
Thursford				(To															
Langor Bridge				Cromer)															
FAKENHAM WEST																			
FAKENHAM WEST																			
Raynham Park																			
East Rudham																			
Massingham																			
Hillington																			
Grimston Road																			
Bawsey																			
Gayton Road																			
Hardwick Rd Sdg																			
Yard																			
SOUTH LYNN											14.14								
SOUTH LYNN						13.40						14/38					14.45		
Yard							13.50					14.40							
Single Line Jcn						13/41	13/52										14/46		
West Lynn						13/42	13/54										14/47		
Clenchwharton						14.03		14.10									14.54		
Terrington								14.15	14.20								15.08		
Walpole									14.25				14.30				15.24		
Sutton Bridge East					14/01								14/37						
SUTTON BRIDGE					14.02								14.38				15.29		
SUTTON BRIDGE													14.50				15.34		
Sutton Bge Jcn													(To				15/35		
Tydd													Long				15.46		
Ferry													Sutton)						
Horse Shoe Lane					(13.03)														
Horse Shoe Lane						14.05										15.50	15/55		
WISBECH NORTH																	15.56		
WISBECH NORTH							14/10									15/55			
Wisbech St. Mary							14.15							14.40			15.59		
Murrow East														14.52	(14.52)				
Murrow East														(15.30)	15.30				
Wryde															15.44				
Thorney																			
Eye Green																			
Dogsthorpe																			
WISBECH SIDINGS																			
Wisbech Jcn																			
Westwood Yard																			
PETERBOROUGH																			
Destination																			

WORKING TIMETABLE : 1951/2

Train	07.15	09.50		09.50		08.15	09.50		12.45		14.35	06.50	15.24		06.50		14.35		11.45
From	Spalding	P'boro		P'boro		Colwick	P'boro		P'bro		S. Lynn	W'wd	Cromer		W'wd		S. Lynn		W'wood
Class	Goods	Goods	Motor	Goods	Goods	Goods	Goods	Pass	Pass	Motor	Goods	Gds	Pass	Pass	Gds	Pass	Goods	Goods	Goods
Engine	SP 3	NE5	KL11	NE5	SL 6	CC 2	NE5	NE 1	SL 8	KL11	MC 2	NE4	GE	NOR 2	NE4	MC 6	MC 2	SL 6	PE6
Class	J6	LM 4	C12	LM 4	LM 4	K2	LM 4	LM 4	LM 4	C12	LM 4	LM 4		D16	LM 4	D16	LM 4	LM 4	LM 4
Carriage Wkg/Vehicles			1/2					4/4	4/4	1/2			15/4	17/4		18/4			
PETERBOROUGH									12.45										
Wisbech Jcn																			
WISBECH SIDINGS									12/49										12.20
Dogsthorpe																			
Eye Green									12.55										12.36
Thorney		11.06							13.02										
Wryde		11.16		11.55					13.07										
MURROW EAST				12.08					13.14										
MURROW EAST				12.20					13.15										
Wisbech St Mary				12.32		13.05			13.21										
WISBECH NORTH							13.20		13.26										
WISBECH NORTH									13.29										
Horse Shoe Lane																			
Horse Shoe Lane									13/33		13.47								
Ferry									13.38										
Tydd									13.44		14.03				14.15				
Sutton Bge Jcn									13.48						14/24				
SUTTON BRIDGE	(12.03)								13.49						14.25				
SUTTON BRIDGE	12.25					13/16			13.51						14.45				
Sutton Bridge East	12/27					13/17									14/56				
Walpole									13.56										
Terrington									14.01										
Clenchwarton									14.05										
West Lynn	12/53					13/40			14.09						15/13				
Single line Jcn	12/54					13/41			14.10						15/14				
Yard	12.55				13.20	13.42									15.15				
SOUTH LYNN									14.11	(14.11)									
SOUTH LYNN				13.05		13/25		(14.19)	14.19	14.20									
Yard				To		To					14.35							15.15	
Hardwick Rd Sdg				Kings		Kings				Kings									
Gayton Rd				Lynn		Lynn			14.26	Lynn	14/48							15.30	
Grimston Rd									14.32		14/58								
Hillington									14.37		15.04						15.14		
Massingham									14.47								15/34		
E. Rudham									14.57								15/43		
Raynham Park									15.02								15/54		
FAKENHAM WEST									15.08										
FAKENHAM WEST									15.10								16/00		
Langor Bge																			
Thursford																			
MELTON CONSTABLE									15.28				15.57				16.29		
MELTON CONSTABLE									15.43					16.02		16.25	(17.34)		
Corpusty									15.52					(To		16.33			
AYLSHAM N.									16.04					Norwich)					
AYLSHAM N.									16.05										
Felmingham									16.12										
NORTH WALSHAM									16.17										
NORTH WALSHAM									16.18										
Honing									16.24										
Stalham									16.31										
Stalham									16.34										
Catfield									16.39										
POTTER HEIGHAM									16.44										
POTTER HEIGHAM									16.45										
Bridge Halt																			
Martham									16.50										
Martham									16.51										
Hemsby									16.57										
GREAT ORMESBY									17.01										
GREAT ORMESBY									17.08										
Scratby																			
California																			
Caister Camp																			
Caister									17.15										
Newtown																			
Salisbury Rd									17/19										
LOWESTOFT (CENTRAL)																			
Lowestoft North																			
Corton																			
Hopton-on-Sea																			
Gorleston Links																			
Gorleston-on-Sea																			
White Swan																			
Caister Rd Jcn																			
YARMOUTH									17.20										
Destination																			

WORKING TIMETABLE : 1951/2

Train	12.42	15.25	12.42							10.30		09.42	16.21	15.58	12.55	12.55	10.30	13.40	14.50
From	Yar	K. Lynn	Yar							Yar		Norwich	K. Lynn	Lynn	Yar	Yar	Yar	S. Town	F. West
Class	Pass	Motor	Pass	Pass	Pcls	Goods	Light	Goods	Pass	Goods	Goods	Goods	Pass	Goods	Pcls	Pcls	Goods	Pass	Goods
Engine	MC 10	KL11	MC 10	MC 11	SL 11	SL 13	SL 1	CC 1	NE 1	MC 8	SL 1	MC 4	SL 12	CC 1	SL 11	NE4	MC 8	GE	SL 13
Class	D16	C12	D16	D16	LM 4	LM 4	K2	K2	LM 4	D16	K2	LM 4	D16	K2	LM 4	LM 4	D16		LM 4
Carriage Wkg/Vehicles	6/4+1	1/2	6/4+1	15/4	9				7/4				30/3		9 vans	9 vans		2	
YARMOUTH					12.55														
Caister Rd Jcn																			
White Swan																			
Gorleston-on-Sea																		13.48	
Gorleston Links																		13.51	
Hopton-on-Sea																		13.55	
Corton																		14.00	
Lowestoft North																		14.04	
LOWESTOFT CENTRAL																		14.19	
Salisbury Road					12/57														
Newtown																			
Caister																			
Caister Camp																			
California																			
Scratby																			
GREAT ORMESBY					13.04														
GREAT ORMESBY					13.07														
Hemsby					13.11														
Martham					13.17														
Martham					13.22														
Bridge Halt																			
POTTER HEIGHAM					13.27														
POTTER HEIGHAM					13.33														
Catfield					13.42														
Stalham					13.47														
Stalham					13.55														
Honing					14.02					13.45			14.13						
N. WALSHAM										14.02			14.20		(14..02)				
N. WALSHAM											(14.38)		14.22			14.38			
Felmingham																			
AYLSHAM N.													14.32						
AYLSHAM N.													14.35		14/52				
Corpusty													14.50		15/12				
MELTON CONSTABLE	(14.14)											14.40	14.59		15.24				
MELTON CONSTABLE	14.20			14.25									15.10						
Thursford	14.28			(To									15.19						
Langor Bridge				Cromer)															
FAKENHAM WEST	14.38												15.29						
FAKENHAM WEST	14.40					14.50							15.36						
Raynham Park	14.47					15/04							15/42						
East Rudham	14.55					15/13							15.48						
Massingham	15.02					15.30							15.56						16.10
Hillington	15.11												16/03						16.25
Grimston Road	15.16												16.08						
Bawsey																			
Gayton Road	15.21																		
Hardwick Rd Sdg																			
Yard																			
SOUTH LYNN	15.28	15.30	(15.28)										16.26		16.30	(16.30)			
SOUTH LYNN	(15.31)		15.31		15.50								16.30		(16.38)	16.38			
Yard						15.58													
Single Line Jcn			15/32			15/52	16/02						16/31			16/39			
West Lynn			15/33			15/53	16/03						16/32			16/40			
Clenchwharton			15.38				16.09						16.37	16.43		16.44			
Terrington			15.42										16.42	16.51					
Walpole			15.47										16.48						
Sutton Bridge East					16/09														
SUTTON BRIDGE			15.52		16.10								16.56						
SUTTON BRIDGE			15.53						16.45				17.02						
Sutton Bge Jcn			15/54						16/47										
Tydd			15/58						16.54										
Ferry																			
Horse Shoe Lane																			
Horse Shoe Lane			16/05																
WISBECH NORTH			16.06																
WISBECH NORTH			16.08						16.25										
Wisbech St. Mary									16.33										
Murrow East									16.39										
Murrow East			16/16						16.42										
Wryde			16/21						16.49										
Thorney			16/25						16.54										
Eye Green									17.01										
Dogsthorpe																			
WISBECH SIDINGS																			
Wisbech Jcn			16/37						17/16										
Westwood Yard																			
PETERBOROUGH			16.40						17.20										
Destination													N'ham						

WORKING TIMETABLE : 1951/2

Train	12.20	12.20		12.20		12.20					14.10		15.40	14.50			16.45	16.30	
From	P'boro	P'boro		P'boro		P'boro					Cromer		P'boro	Pe			Cromer	F'ham	
Class	Goods	Goods	Pass	Goods	Motor	Goods	Light	Goods	Light	Pass	Goods	Pass	Pass	Goods	Pass	Motor	Pass	Pass	Pass
Engine	PE6	PE6	YAR 3	PE6	KL11	PE6	SL 12	SB 18	SP 3	Y7	SL 2	MC 3	SL17	SB 18	MC 8	KL11	MC 11	Y7	GE
Class	LM 4	LM 4	F6	LM 4	C12	LM 4	D16	LM 4	J6	D16	LM 4	D16	LM4	LM 4	D16	C12	D16	D16	
Carriage Wkg/Vehicles			12/2	1/2						10&13/6	5/4	5/4		10/4		1/2	28/4	13/2	2
PETERBOROUGH												15.40							
Wisbech Jcn												15/44							
WISBECH SIDINGS								14.50											
Dogsthorpe								15.01								16.10			
Eye Green	13.06											15.51				16.20			
Thorney	13.16	13.31										15.58							
Wryde		13.41										16.03							
MURROW EAST				14.14								16.10							
MURROW EAST				14.26								16.11							
Wisbech St Mary				14.38		15.30						16.17							
WISBECH NORTH												16.22							
WISBECH NORTH						15/38						16.24							
Horse Shoe Lane						15.40													
Horse Shoe Lane						(17.48)						16/25							
Ferry												16.30							
Tydd												16.36							
Sutton Bge Jcn												16.40							
SUTTON BRIDGE												16.41							
SUTTON BRIDGE												16.46							
Sutton Bridge East																			
Walpole												16.52							
Terrington												16.56							
Clenchwarton												17.00							
West Lynn												17.04							
Single line Jcn												17.05							
Yard																			
SOUTH LYNN												17.06	(17.06)						
SOUTH LYNN					15.40		16.03		16.20		(17.11)		17.11		17.22				
Yard					*To*		*To*		*To*				*To*		*To*				
Hardwick Rd Sdg					*Kings*		*Kings*		*Kings*				*Kings*		*Kings*				
Gayton Rd					*Lynn*		*Lynn*		*Lynn*				*Lynn*		*Lynn*				
Grimston Rd																			
Hillington																			
Massingham																			
E. Rudham																			
Raynham Park																			
FAKENHAM WEST																			
FAKENHAM WEST										16.30									
Langor Bge																			
Thursford										16.42									
MELTON CONSTABLE										16.48	16.50						17.23		
MELTON CONSTABLE										17.02					17.05				
Corpusty										17.12					(To				
AYLSHAM N.										17.24					Norwich)				
AYLSHAM N.										17.25									
Felmingham										17.32									
NORTH WALSHAM										17.37									
NORTH WALSHAM																	18.08		
Honing																	18.14		
Stalham																	18.21		
Stalham																	18.22		
Catfield																	18.27		
POTTER HEIGHAM																	18.32		
POTTER HEIGHAM																	18.33		
Bridge Halt																			
Martham																	18.38		
Martham																	18.40		
Hemsby																	18.46		
GREAT ORMESBY																	18.50		
GREAT ORMESBY																	18.51		
Scratby																			
California																			
Caister Camp																			
Caister																	18.56		
Newtown																			
Salisbury Rd																	19/03		
LOWESTOFT (CENTRAL)			17.30															18.42	
Lowestoft North			17.37															18.49	
Corton			17.41															18.53	
Hopton-on-Sea			17.46															18.58	
Gorleston Links			17.49																
Gorleston-on-Sea			17.54															19.03	
White Swan																			
Caister Rd Jcn			18/02																
YARMOUTH			18.03															19.04	
Destination																			S. Town

14

WORKING TIMETABLE : 1951/2

Train		12.55	13.20				14.50		12.55	15.26	16.20			14.50	07.50	15.50	16.45	12.55	12.55
From		Yar	Vaux				F. West		Yar	Norwich	Melton			F. West	Lynn	Wisbech	S. Bge	Yar	Yar
Class	Goods	Pass	Pcls	Goods	Pcls	Goods	Goods	Pass	Pcls	Goods	Goods	XP	ECS	Goods	Goods	Gds	Goods	Pcls	Pcls
Engine	SL 15	Y7	NE4	SL 6	SP 3	MC 9	SL 13	YAR 3	NE4	MC 1	MC 9	MC 7	MC 6	SL 13	SL 10	NE 5	SL 1	NE4	NE4
Class	LM 4	D16	LM 4	LM 4	J6	LM 4	LM 4	F6	LM 4	LM 4	LM 4	D16		LM 4	LM 4	LM 4	K2	LM 4	LM 4
Carriage Wkg/Vehicles		10&13/6	9 vans		9 vans			12/2	9 vans			GE/4	18/4					9 vans	4 vans
YARMOUTH	14.00							15.25											
Caister Rd Jcn	14/02							15/26											
White Swan	14.05																		
Gorleston-on-Sea								15.36											
Gorleston Links								15.39											
Hopton-on-Sea								15.43											
Corton								15.48											
Lowestoft North								15.52											
LOWESTOFT CENTRAL								15.58											
Salisbury Road																			
Newtown																			
Caister																			
Caister Camp																			
California																			
Scratby																			
GREAT ORMESBY																			
GREAT ORMESBY																			
Hemsby																			
Martham																			
Martham																			
Bridge Halt																			
POTTER HEIGHAM																			
POTTER HEIGHAM																			
Catfield																			
Stalham																			
Stalham																			
Honing																			
N. WALSHAM																			
N. WALSHAM																			
Felmingham																			
AYLSHAM N.																			
AYLSHAM N.																			
Corpusty													16.42						
MELTON CONSTABLE										16.39			16.50						
MELTON CONSTABLE		15.55			16.20							16.45							
Thursford		16.03			16.34							16.44							
Langor Bridge												(To L. St)							
FAKENHAM WEST		16.13						17.04											
FAKENHAM WEST								(17.20)											
Raynham Park																			
East Rudham																			
Massingham																			
Hillington							16.40												
Grimston Road							16.49								17.00				
Bawsey																			
Gayton Road				16.20	(Ex														
Hardwick Rd Sdg					Kings														
Yard				16.55	Lynn)									17.21					
SOUTH LYNN				17.00															
SOUTH LYNN				(17.15)															
Yard																			
Single Line Jcn																			
West Lynn																			
Clenchwharton		16.51																	
Terrington		16.55						17.10											
Walpole								17.15									17.30		
Sutton Bridge East																			
SUTTON BRIDGE																	17.36	(17.36)	
SUTTON BRIDGE																		(17.51)	17.51
Sutton Bge Jcn																			17/52
Tydd																17.27			17.56
Ferry																			
Horse Shoe Lane																17.41			
Horse Shoe Lane																(17.56)			
WISBECH NORTH																			
WISBECH NORTH																			
Wisbech St. Mary																16.55			
Murrow East																17.06			
Murrow East																17.20			
Wryde															17.06	17/31			
Thorney															17.16	17.37			
Eye Green																			
Dogsthorpe																			
WISBECH SIDINGS																			
Wisbech Jcn																			
Westwood Yard																			
PETERBOROUGH																			
Destination																			

Train	14.35	13.45	13.45	13.45				17.08	18.10		17.08	14.35	17.50	17.50	17.50			12.20	17.45
From	S. Lynn	B'ham	B'ham	B'ham				Sutton B	Cromer		Sutton B	S. Lynn	K. Lynn	K. Lynn	K. Lynn			P'boro	Spalding
Class	Goods	XP	XP	XP	XP	Goods	Light	Goods	Pass	Pass	Goods	Goods	Pass	Pass	Pass	Light	ECS	Goods	Pass
Engine	SL 15A	SL 14	Yar 6	Yar 6	NOR 1	SL 7	SL 18	SL 7	MC 6		SL 7	SL 15A	KL 6	MC 3	Y 2	KL 6	MC 1	PE6	SL 5
Class	LM4	B12	B12	B12	D16	LM 4	J67	LM 4	D16		LM 4	LM4	D16	D16	D16	D16	LM 4	LM 4	LM 4
Carriage Wkg/Vehicles		6	5	2	28&32/5				18/4	2			3/4	3/4	3/4		19/4		
PETERBOROUGH																			
Wisbech Jcn																			
WISBECH SIDINGS																			
Dogsthorpe																			
Eye Green																			
Thorney																			
Wryde																			
MURROW EAST																			
MURROW EAST																			
Wisbech St Mary																			
WISBECH NORTH																			
WISBECH NORTH																			
Horse Shoe Lane																		(15.40)	
Horse Shoe Lane																		17.48	
Ferry																			
Tydd																		18/03	
Sutton Bge Jcn																		18/09	
SUTTON BRIDGE																		18.10	**18.25**
SUTTON BRIDGE		17/03				17.08												(18.35)	
Sutton Bridge East						17/10													
Walpole						17.19	17.32												
Terrington								17.41			17.50								
Clenchwarton																			
West Lynn		17/14									18/01								
Single line Jcn		17/15									18/02								
Yard											18.04								
SOUTH LYNN		17.16											17.55	(17.55)					
SOUTH LYNN		(17.24)	17.24			17.30						(18.01)	18.01		18.10				
Yard						(To K. Lynn)										(To K. Lynn)			
Hardwick Rd Sdg																			
Gayton Rd			17/29											18.08					
Grimston Rd			17/34											18.14					
Hillington			17/37											18.19					
Massingham			17/43											18.30					
E. Rudham			17/47											18.36					
Raynham Park			17/53											18.41					
FAKENHAM WEST			17.57											18.46					
FAKENHAM WEST			17.59											18.47			19.00		
Langor Bge																			
Thursford														18.59					
MELTON CONSTABLE	(16.29)		18.12	(18.12)	(18.12)			18.46					19.05	(19.05)			19.16		
MELTON CONSTABLE	17.34		(18.18)	18.18	18.22								(19.15)	19.15					
Corpusty	17/48			18/25	(To									19.24					
AYLSHAM N.	18.08			18.35	Norwich)									19.36					
AYLSHAM N.	18.16			18.36										19.37					
Felmingham														19.44					
NORTH WALSHAM	18.38			18.46							(18.38)			19.51					
NORTH WALSHAM	(19.20)			18.48							19.20			19.53					
Honing				18/52							19/32			19.59					
Stalham				19.00										20.06					
Stalham				19.01							19/41			20.07					
Catfield														20.12					
POTTER HEIGHAM				19.09										20.17					
POTTER HEIGHAM				19.11							19/51			20.18					
Bridge Halt																			
Martham														20.23					
Martham				19/16							19/58			20.24					
Hemsby				19.22										20.30					
GREAT ORMESBY														20.34					
GREAT ORMESBY				19/25							20/10			20.35					
Scratby																			
California																			
Caister Camp																			
Caister														20.41					
Newtown																			
Salisbury Rd				19/33							20/21			20/46					
LOWESTOFT (CENTRAL)									19.40										
Lowestoft North									19.47										
Corton									19.51										
Hopton-on-Sea									19.56										
Gorleston Links									19.59										
Gorleston-on-Sea									20.04										
White Swan																			
Caister Rd Jcn																			
YARMOUTH				19.34							20.23			20.47					
Destination									S. Town										

WORKING TIMETABLE : 1951/2

Train	07.50	16.45	12.55		17.05	13.20	07.50	15.50	16.45	12.55	16.20	15.50	17.50	17.55	12.55	15.58	18.15	16.20	
From	Lynn	S. Bge	Yar		K. Lynn	Vaux	Lynn	Wisbech	S. Bge	Yar	Melton	Wisbech	K.Lynn	K. Lynn	Yar	S.Lynn	K. Lynn	Melton	
Class	Goods	Goods	Pcls	Pass	Motor	Pcls	Goods	Goods	Goods	Pcls	Goods	Gds	Pass	Pass	Pcls	Goods	Goods	Goods	Goods
Engine	SL 10	SL 1	NE4	MC 6	KL11	SP 3	SL 10	NE 5	SL 1	NE4	MC9	NE 5	KL 6	SL 17	NE4	CC 1	SL 18	MC9	SL 15B
Class	LM 4	K2	LM 4	D16	C12	J6	LM 4	LM 4	K2	LM 4	LM 4	LM 4	D16	LM 4	LM 4	K2	J67	LM 4	LM 4
Carriage Wkg/Vehicles			4 vans	18/4	1/2	9 vans			4 vans					3/4	4 vans				
YARMOUTH																			16.00
Caister Rd Jcn																			
White Swan																			
Gorleston-on-Sea																			
Gorleston Links																			
Hopton-on-Sea																			
Corton																			
Lowestoft North																			
LOWESTOFT CENTRAL																			
Salisbury Road																			16/03
Newtown																			
Caister																			
Caister Camp																			
California																			
Scratby																			
GREAT ORMESBY																			
GREAT ORMESBY																			16/12
Hemsby																			
Martham																			
Martham																			16/20
Bridge Halt																			
POTTER HEIGHAM																			
POTTER HEIGHAM																			16/25
Catfield																			
Stalham																			
Stalham																			16/33
Honing																			16/40
N. WALSHAM																			
N. WALSHAM																			16/49
Felmingham																			
AYLSHAM N.																			
AYLSHAM N.																			16/59
Corpusty																			17/11
MELTON CONSTABLE																			17.21
MELTON CONSTABLE				17.05															(17.50)
Thursford				(To															
Langor Bridge				Cromer)															
FAKENHAM WEST											(17.04)								
FAKENHAM WEST											17.20								
Raynham Park											17/31								
East Rudham											17/40								
Massingham											17.50							17.54	
Hillington																		18/07	
Grimston Road																		18/11	
Bawsey																			
Gayton Road																			
Hardwick Rd Sdg																			
Yard																		18.32	
SOUTH LYNN					17.10	(17.00)							17.55	18.00					
SOUTH LYNN						17.15							(18.01)	18.03			18.23		
Yard													(To				18.25		
Single Line Jcn						17/16							Yar	18/04					
West Lynn						17/17							mouth)	18/05					
Clenchwharton						17.28								18.10					
Terrington						17.44								18.14		18.18			
Walpole						18.00								18.19					
Sutton Bridge East																18/34			
SUTTON BRIDGE						18.06								18.24					
SUTTON BRIDGE						(18.49)								18.29		18.35			
Sutton Bge Jcn														18.30		18.37			
Tydd			18.05											18.35		18.43			
Ferry			18.11									18.17		18.41					
Horse Shoe Lane		(17.41)																	
Horse Shoe Lane		17.56										18.21		18.45					
WISBECH NORTH												18.22		18.46	(18.22)				
WISBECH NORTH		18.00										(18.54)		18.51	18.54				
Wisbech St. Mary														18.56	18.58				
Murrow East							18.11					(18.11)		19.02					
Murrow East		(18.38)										18.38		19.03					
Wryde												18.48		19.09					
Thorney	17.52						18.26					18/52		19.15					
Eye Green	18.06						18.36	18.39				19.05		19.21					
Dogsthorpe																			
WISBECH SIDINGS								19.09											
Wisbech Jcn		18.48										19/17		19/34					
Westwood Yard		18.58										19.22							
PETERBOROUGH														19.38					
Destination						Spalding													

17

WORKING TIMETABLE : 1951/2

Train	12.20				16.20	18.10	18.10	19.25				19.35	19.35	17.30	19.45	21.10	18.10		19.15
From	P'boro				Notts	P'boro	P'boro	Cromer				Sutton B	Sutton B	L. St	Lynn	Cromer	P'boro		Norwich
Class	Goods	Pass	Pass	Pass	Pass	Goods	Goods	Pass	Goods	Goods	Goods	Goods	Goods	XP	Goods	Light	Goods	Pass	Pass
Engine	PE6	MC 6	SL 16	Yar 3	SL 12	NE 2	NE 2	MC 7	MC 9	SL 5	SL 7	SL 5	SL 5	MC 11	MC 9	MC 6	NE 2	Y 5	SL 16
Class	LM 4	D16	LM 4	F6	D16	LM 4	LM 4	D16	LM 4	LM 4	LM 4	LM 4	LM 4	D16	LM 4	D16	LM 4	F6	LM 4
Carriage Wkg/Vehicles		18/4	38/3	2	29/3		23/4						GE/4				8/4		10/4+1
PETERBOROUGH			17.55																
Wisbech Jcn			17/59		18/30														
WISBECH SIDINGS																			
Dogsthorpe																			
Eye Green			18.06			18.42	19.02												
Thorney			18.14				19/13												
Wryde			18.19				19/18												
MURROW EAST			18.26																
MURROW EAST			18.28				19/26												
Wisbech St Mary			18.34																
WISBECH NORTH			18.39																
WISBECH NORTH			18.42				19/38												
Horse Shoe Lane			18/43																
Horse Shoe Lane							19/40												
Ferry																			
Tydd			18.54			19.51											20.15		
Sutton Bge Jcn			18/58														20/22		
SUTTON BRIDGE	(18.10)		18.59		19.25														
SUTTON BRIDGE	18.35		19.01		19.29				19.35								20/23		
Sutton Bridge East	18/36								19/36										
Walpole			19.07		19.35				19.48			20.00							
Terrington			19.11		19.39							20.10	20.20						
Clenchwarton					19.43														
West Lynn	19/03		19/18		19/47								20/40			20/48			
Single line Jcn	19/04		19/19		19/48								20/41			20/49			
Yard	19.05										20.05		20.42			20.50			
SOUTH LYNN			19.20		19.49														(21.18)
SOUTH LYNN			19.22		19.52						20/08								21.25
Yard		To			To			19.45			To								To
Hardwick Rd Sdg		Kings			Kings						Kings								Kings
Gayton Rd		Lynn			Lynn						Lynn								Lynn
Grimston Rd								20/07											
Hillington								20/12											
Massingham								20/29											
E. Rudham								20.39							20.47				
Raynham Park															20/55				
FAKENHAM WEST																			
FAKENHAM WEST															21/05				
Langor Bge																			
Thursford																			
MELTON CONSTABLE								20.02						21.32	21.36	21.41			
MELTON CONSTABLE		19.25																	
Corpusty		(To																	
AYLSHAM N.		Norwich)																	
AYLSHAM N.																		(Th	
Felmingham																		Only)	
NORTH WALSHAM																			
NORTH WALSHAM																		22.10	
Honing																		22.16	
Stalham																		22.23	
Stalham																		22.27	
Catfield																		22.32	
POTTER HEIGHAM																		22.37	
POTTER HEIGHAM																		22.38	
Bridge Halt																			
Martham																		23.43	
Martham																		23.44	
Hemsby																		22.50	
GREAT ORMESBY																		22.54	
GREAT ORMESBY																		22.56	
Scratby																			
California																			
Caister Camp																			
Caister																		23.01	
Newtown																			
Salisbury Rd																		23/06	
LOWESTOFT (CENTRAL)				20.50															
Lowestoft North				20.57															
Corton				21.01															
Hopton-on-Sea				21.06															
Gorleston Links																			
Gorleston-on-Sea				21.12															
White Swan																			
Caister Rd Jcn				21/20															
YARMOUTH				21.22														23.07	
Destination																			

18

WORKING TIMETABLE : 1951/2

Train	16.50	16.00	17.30	17.30		13.45		12.55	15.58	17.25	12.55	12.55			19.15			16.00	18.58
From	Norwich	Yar	Norwich	Norwich		B'ham		Yar	Lynn	S. Town	Yar	Yar			Norwich			Yar	S. Town
Class	Pass	Pass	Goods	Pass	Pass	XP	Pass	Pcls	Goods	Pass	Pcls	Pcls	Goods	Pass	Pass	Pass	Pcls	Goods	Motor
Engine	NOR 1	GE	SL 15B	NOR 2	MC 1	MC 11	Y 2	NE4	CC 1	GE	NE4	NE4	SL 2	SL 8	MC 8	MC 6	NE4	SL 15B	GE
Class	D16	D16	LM 4	D16	LM 4	D16	D16	LM 4	K2		LM 4	LM 4	LM 4	LM 4	D16	D16	LM 4	LM 4	
Carriage Wkg/Vehicles	20/2	GE/4		19/4	19/4	18&34/6	9&27/6	4 vans		2	4 vans	4 vans		4&12/6	10/4+1	12/2	4 vans		2
YARMOUTH							16.55							18.15					
Caister Rd Jcn																			
White Swan																			
Gorleston-on-Sea										17.33									19.06
Gorleston Links										17.36									19.09
Hopton-on-Sea										17.40									19.13
Corton										17.45									19.18
Lowestoft North										17.49									19.22
LOWESTOFT CENTRAL										17.55									19.28
Salisbury Road							16/56							18/16					
Newtown																			
Caister							17.01							18.21					
Caister Camp																			
California																			
Scratby																			
GREAT ORMESBY							17.06							18.26					
GREAT ORMESBY							17.07							18.27					
Hemsby							17.11							18.31					
Martham							17.17							18.37					
Martham							17.18							18.38					
Bridge Halt																			
POTTER HEIGHAM							17.23							18.43					
POTTER HEIGHAM							17.24							18.44					
Catfield							17.31							18.51					
Stalham							17.35							18.55					
Stalham							17.41							19.00					
Honing							17.49							19.08					
N. WALSHAM							17.56							19.15					
N. WALSHAM							17.58							19.18					
Felmingham							18.03							19.23					
AYLSHAM N.							18.08							19.28					
AYLSHAM N.							18.10							19.38					
Corpusty							18.23							19.51					
MELTON CONSTABLE	17.43	(17.21)		18.21	(18.21)	(18.12)	18.34							20.00	20.04	(20.00)			
MELTON CONSTABLE		17.50	17.50	(18.24)	18.24	18.25							19.05	(20.07)	(20.10)	20.07			
Thursford			To	18.32		To								To	To				
Langor Bridge			Cromer			Cromer								Kings	Cromer				
FAKENHAM WEST					18.42									Lynn					
FAKENHAM WEST		18/10											19/32						
Raynham Park		18/17											19/40						
East Rudham		18/23											19/49						
Massingham		18/29											19/58						
Hillington		18/37											20.10						
Grimston Road		18/41																	
Bawsey																			
Gayton Road																			
Hardwick Rd Sdg																			
Yard		19.00																(19.00)	
SOUTH LYNN																			
SOUTH LYNN																			
Yard		(19.35)																19.35	
Single Line Jcn																		19/37	
West Lynn																		19/38	
Clenchwharton																			
Terrington																			
Walpole																			
Sutton Bridge East																		19/53	
SUTTON BRIDGE																			
SUTTON BRIDGE																		19/55	
Sutton Bge Jcn																		19/56	
Tydd									18.59									20/01	
Ferry																			
Horse Shoe Lane																			
Horse Shoe Lane									19/11									20/10	
WISBECH NORTH									19/14										
WISBECH NORTH									19.18									20/12	
Wisbech St. Mary							19.10												
Murrow East							19.16												
Murrow East							19.37		19.32									20/20	
Wryde							19.42		19.39		19.55							20/28	
Thorney							19.43		19.59		20.05							20/32	
Eye Green																			
Dogsthorpe																			
WISBECH SIDINGS													20.20				20.25	20.47	
Wisbech Jcn									20/06								20/46		
Westwood Yard							20.17												
PETERBOROUGH																		20.50	
Destination																			

WORKING TIMETABLE : 1951/2

	Pass	Motor	20.25 Crescent Goods	21.15 N. Eng Light	Goods	Pass	23.45 Crescent Goods	23.45 Crescent Goods	23.45 Crescent Goods	23.45 Crescent Goods	23.45 Crescent Goods
Engine	MC 10	KL11	SL 1	CC1	SL 16	SL 17	SL 15B	SL 15B	SL 15B	SL 15B	SL 15B
Class	D16	C12	K2	K2	LM 4	LM 4	LM 4	LM 4	LM 4	LM 4	LM 4
Carriage Wkg/Vehicles	7/4					11/4					
PETERBOROUGH	20.10		20/28			22.45	23/50				
Wisbech Jcn	20/14		20/35	21.20		22/49					
WISBECH SIDINGS							23.55	00.05			
Dogstorpe											
Eye Green	20.21										
Thorney	20.28		20/50			23/00	00/27				
Wryde	20.34		20/55			23/04	00/32				
MURROW EAST	20.41										
MURROW EAST	20.42		21/03	21/45		23/09	00/40				
Wisbech St Mary	20.48					23.15					
WISBECH NORTH	20.53					23.20					
WISBECH NORTH	20.55			22/00		23.22	00/52				
Horse Shoe Lane				21.17			00.54				
Horse Shoe Lane	20/56			21.27		23/23	01.20				
Ferry	21.01										
Tydd	21.07			21/41		23/30	01.36	01.46			
Sutton Bge Jcn	21/11			21/47		23/33		01/55			
SUTTON BRIDGE	21.12			21.48		23.34		01.56			
SUTTON BRIDGE	21.14		22.00	22/20		23.36			02.20		
Sutton Bridge East				22/01					02/21		
Walpole	21.19								02.33	02.43	
Terrington	21.23					23.44				02.53	03.05
Clenchwarton	21.27										
West Lynn	21/31			22/28		23/50					03/20
Single line Jcn	21/32			22/29		23/51					03/21
Yard			22.30		22.45						03.22
SOUTH LYNN	21.33			22.35		23.52					
SOUTH LYNN	21.40	21.45			22/47	23.54					
Yard		To			To	To					
Hardwick Rd Sdg		Kings			Kings	Kings					
Gayton Rd	21.47	Lynn			Lynn	Lynn					
Grimston Rd	21.53										
Hillington	21.58										
Massingham	22.08										
E. Rudham	22.14										
Raynham Park	22.19										
FAKENHAM WEST	22.25										
FAKENHAM WEST	22.27										
Langor Bge											
Thursford	22.39										
MELTON CONSTABLE	22.45										
MELTON CONSTABLE											
Corpusty											
AYLSHAM N.											
AYLSHAM N.											
Felmingham											
NORTH WALSHAM											
NORTH WALSHAM											
Honing											
Stalham											
Stalham											
Catfield											
POTTER HEIGHAM											
POTTER HEIGHAM											
Bridge Halt											
Martham											
Martham											
Hemsby											
GREAT ORMESBY											
GREAT ORMESBY											
Scratby											
California											
Caister Camp											
Caister											
Newtown											
Salisbury Rd											
LOWESTOFT (CENTRAL)											
Lowestoft North											
Corton											
Hopton-on-Sea											
Gorleston Links											
Gorleston-on-Sea											
White Swan											
Caister Rd Jcn											
YARMOUTH											
Destination											

Standard Running Times and Distances

		B12 4-6-0	B12 4-6-0
Engine			
Load		10 Coach	10 Coach
m.ch	Point	Minutes	Minutes
0.00	**PETERBOROUGH NORTH**	0.00	59.00*
6.24	Eye Green	12.00*	48.00
8.38	Thorney	17.00	44.00
10.57	Wryde	20.00	41.00
14.34	Murrow East	25.00	36.00
17.53	Wisbech SM	29.00	32.00
20.05	**WISBECH NORTH**	33.00	28.00
22.44	Ferry	37.00	24.00
25.09	Tydd	41.00	20.00
27.34	Sutton Bridge	45.00	16.00
30.14	Walpole	50.00	11.00
32.14	Terrington	53.00	8.00
33.38	Clenchwarton	55.00	6.00*
36.37	**SOUTH LYNN**	61.00*	0.00
0.00	**SAXBY**	0.00	90.00*
2.33	Edmonthorpe	6.00*	85.00
6.71	South Witham	14.00	78.00
21.16	Castle Bytham	17.00	70.00
13.12	Little Bytham Jcn	23.00	66.00
18.02	**BOURNE**	30.00	57.00
21.75	Twenty	36.00	51.00
23.39	Counter Drain	39.00	49.00
25.26	North Drove	42.00	46.00
26.30	Cuckoo Jcn	44.00	44.00
27.60	Welland Bank Jcn	48.00	41.00
28.11	Clay Lake	49.00	40.00
29.79	Weston	52.00	37.00
31.48	Moulton	55.00	34.00
32.54	Whaplode	57.00	32.00
34.74	Holbeach	60.00	29.00
36.79	Fleet	63.00	26.00
38.23	Gedney	65.00	24.00
39.36	Long Sutton	67.00	22.00
42.38	Dock Junction	72.00	17.00
42.78	Sutton Bridge	73.00	16.00*
52.01	**SOUTH LYNN**	89.00*	0.00
0.00	**SOUTH LYNN**	0.00	48.00*
3.53	Gayton Road	5.00*	42.00
6.40	Grimston Road	9.00	38.00
8.41	Hillington	13.00	35.00
13.20	Massingham	20.00	29.00
16.33	East Rudham	25.00	23.00
18.30	Raynham Park	29.00	19.00
22.11	Fakenham West	34.00	14.00
28.51	Thursford	44.00	6.00*
31.56	**MELTON CONSTABLE**	50.00*	0.00
0.00	**MELTON CONSTABLE**	0.00	67.00*
4.73	Corpusty	7.00*	58.00
11.44	Aylsham North	16.00	48.00
14.69	Felmingham	22.00	44.00
17.13	**NORTH WALSHAM TOWN**	27.00	41.00
20.18	Honing	31.00	34.00
23.75	Stalham	37.00	29.00
26.01	Catfield	40.00	26.00
28.66	**POTTER HEIGHAM**	44.00	22.00
31.46	Martham	48.00	18.00
34.31	Hemsby	52.00	14.00
36.08	Great Ormesby	55.00	11.00
38.68	Caister	59.00	6.00
40.65	Salisbury Road	63.00	1.00*
41.49	**YARMOUTH BEACH**	64.00*	0.00
0.00	**MELTON CONSTABLE**	0.00	30.00*
1.04	Brinington Jcn	2.00*	27.00
5.11	Holt	8.00	20.00
8.55	Weybourne	13.00	13.00
11.30	**SHERINGHAM**	17.00	7.00
13.07	West Runton	20.00	5.00
13.65	Runton West Jcn	22.00	3.00
14.39	Runton East Jcn	23.00	2.00*
15.16	**CROMER BEACH**	25.00*	0.00

The M&GN issued tables of running times for ten coach trains hauled by a B12 or a K2. The up and down timings are shown above (* indicates start to pass or pass to stop: all others are pass to pass). The timings for ordinary trains are shown in the WTT.

WORKING TIMETABLE : 1951/2

Train	16.00	20.25	13.45	19.05		20.50	19.15	21.25	19.45		19.45			20.52	20.52		23.25	23.05
From	Yar	H, Jcn	B'ham	Melton	K. Lynn	Exton	Norwich	K. Lynn	Norwich	K. Lynn	Norwich			Eye G	Eye G		K. Lynn	Lynn
Class	Goods	Goods	XP	Goods	Light	Goods	Pass	Motor	Goods	Light	Goods	Pass	Goods	Goods	Goods	Goods	Goods	Goods
Engine	SL 15B	SL 16	Yar 3	SL 2	SL 7	SL 12	SL 8	KL11	SL 3	SL 16	SL 3	Y 5	SB 18	SB 18	SB 18	NE 2	SL 16	NE 2
Class	LM 4	LM 4	F6	LM 4	LM 4	D16	LM 4	C12	LM4	LM 4	LM 4	F6	LM4	LM4	LM4	LM 4	LM 4	LM 4
Carriage Wkg/Vehicles			36/2				10/4+1	1/2				8/4						
YARMOUTH			19.40									21.00						
Caister Rd Jcn			19/41									(Th						
White Swan												Only)						
Gorleston-on-Sea			19.51															
Gorleston Links																		
Hopton-on-Sea			19.56															
Corton			20.01															
Lowestoft North			20.05															
LOWESTOFT CENTRAL			20.11															
Salisbury Road												21/01						
Newtown																		
Caister												21.06						
Caister Camp																		
California																		
Scratby																		
GREAT ORMESBY												21.11						
GREAT ORMESBY												21.12						
Hemsby												21.16						
Martham												21.22						
Martham												21.23						
Bridge Halt																		
POTTER HEIGHAM												21.28						
POTTER HEIGHAM												21.29						
Catfield												21.35						
Stalham												21.39						
Stalham												21.44						
Honing												21.52						
N. WALSHAM												21.59						
N. WALSHAM																		
Felmingham																		
AYLSHAM N.																		
AYLSHAM N.																		
Corpusty																		
MELTON CONSTABLE						20.52	(20.04)											
MELTON CONSTABLE						21.02	20.10											
Thursford							20.18											
Langor Bridge																		
FAKENHAM WEST							20.28											
FAKENHAM WEST						21.29	20.31											
Raynham Park						21.38	20.38											
East Rudham						21.46	20.45											
Massingham						21.57	20.51				22.13							
Hillington					20.14		21.00				22.25							
Grimston Road					20/21		21.05				22.29							
Bawsey																		
Gayton Road							21.11				22.36							
Hardwick Rd Sdg																		
Yard				20.42							22.46							
SOUTH LYNN							21.18	21.30										
SOUTH LYNN		20/33		20/48	21/00		(21.25)		21/58								23/32	
Yard		20.35		20.50	21.03		To		22.00							23.05	23.35	
Single Line Jcn							Kings											23/07
West Lynn							Lynn											23/09
Clenchwharton																		
Terrington																		
Walpole																		
Sutton Bridge East																		23/32
SUTTON BRIDGE																		
SUTTON BRIDGE																		23/34
Sutton Bge Jcn																		23/36
Tydd																		23/41
Ferry																		
Horse Shoe Lane																		
Horse Shoe Lane																		23/51
WISBECH NORTH																		
WISBECH NORTH																		23/53
Wisbech St. Mary																		
Murrow East																		
Murrow East																		00/03
Wryde																		00/12
Thorney																		00/17
Eye Green													20.52					
Dogsthorpe													21.00	21.20				
WISBECH SIDINGS	20.50												21.30	21.45		00.37		00.50
Wisbech Jcn																		
Westwood Yard	20.57														21.53			01.00
PETERBOROUGH																		
Destination																		

Ironically the busiest signalbox on the M&GN was not an M&GN box at all but was the Great Eastern (GN&GE Joint) box that signalled the level crossing at Murrow West where the South Lynn - Peterborough section of the M&GN crossed the March to Doncaster main line of the GN&GE Joint. The volume of traffic using the crossing was impressive and during the 1950's amounted to 166 trains daily: 134 on the GN&GE Joint and 32 on the M&GN - a train using the crossing every ten minutes on average. LM4 2-6-0 43109 of South Lynn passes the crossing with a Peterborough to King's Lynn service. (Dr Ian C Allen/TRansport Trust).

	00.00	01.00	02.00	03.00	04.00	05.00	06.00
PETERBOROUGH							
Eye Green							
Thorney							
Wryde							
Murrow East							
Wisbech St Mary							
WISBECH (NORTH)							
Ferry							
Tydd							
SUTTON BRIDGE							
Walpole							
Terrington							
Clenchwharton							
SOUTH LYNN							
Gayton Road							
Grimston Road							
Hillington							
Massingham							
East Rudham							
Raynham Park							
FAKENHAM WEST							
Thursford							
MELTON CONSTABLE							

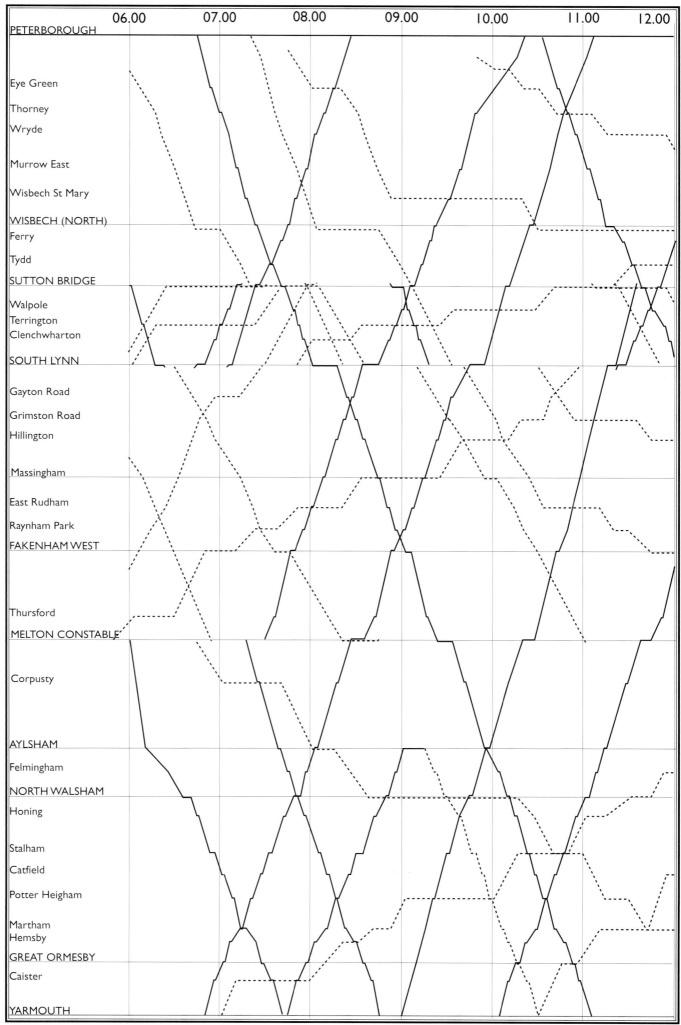

06.00　07.00　08.00　09.00　10.00　11.00　12.00

PETERBOROUGH

Eye Green

Thorney

Wryde

Murrow East

Wisbech St Mary

WISBECH (NORTH)

Ferry

Tydd

SUTTON BRIDGE

Walpole

Terrington

Clenchwharton

SOUTH LYNN

Gayton Road

Grimston Road

Hillington

Massingham

East Rudham

Raynham Park

FAKENHAM WEST

Thursford

MELTON CONSTABLE

Corpusty

AYLSHAM

Felmingham

NORTH WALSHAM

Honing

Stalham

Catfield

Potter Heigham

Martham

Hemsby

GREAT ORMESBY

Caister

YARMOUTH

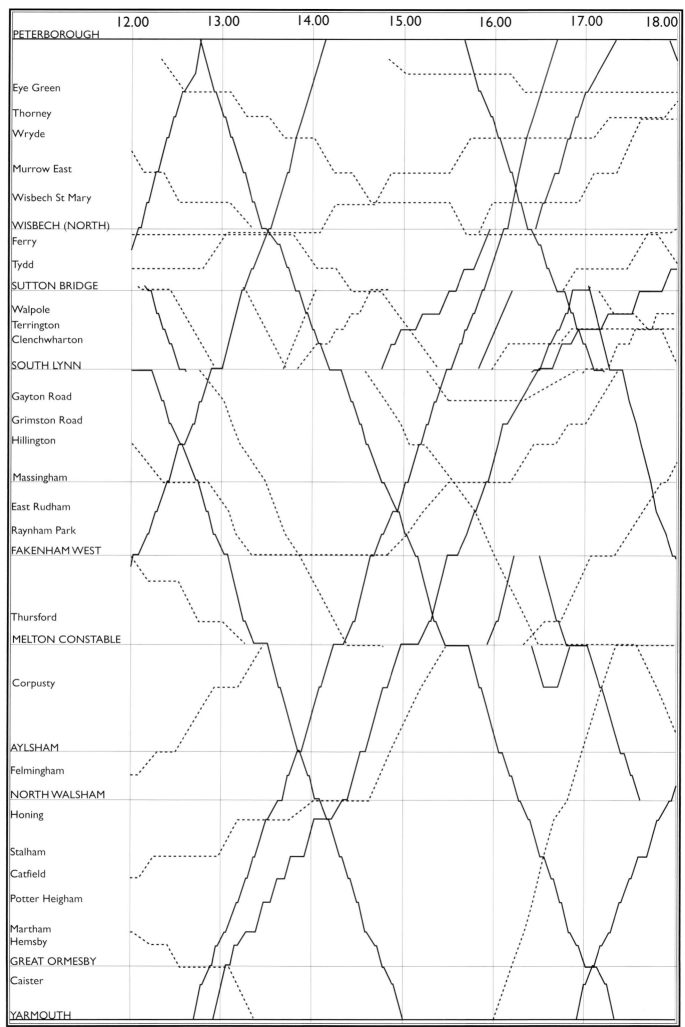

PETERBOROUGH

Eye Green

Thorney

Wryde

Murrow East

Wisbech St Mary

WISBECH (NORTH)

Ferry

Tydd

SUTTON BRIDGE

Walpole
Terrington
Clenchwharton

SOUTH LYNN

Gayton Road

Grimston Road

Hillington

Massingham

East Rudham

Raynham Park

FAKENHAM WEST

Thursford

MELTON CONSTABLE

Corpusty

AYLSHAM

Felmingham

NORTH WALSHAM

Honing

Stalham

Catfield

Potter Heigham

Martham
Hemsby

GREAT ORMESBY

Caister

YARMOUTH

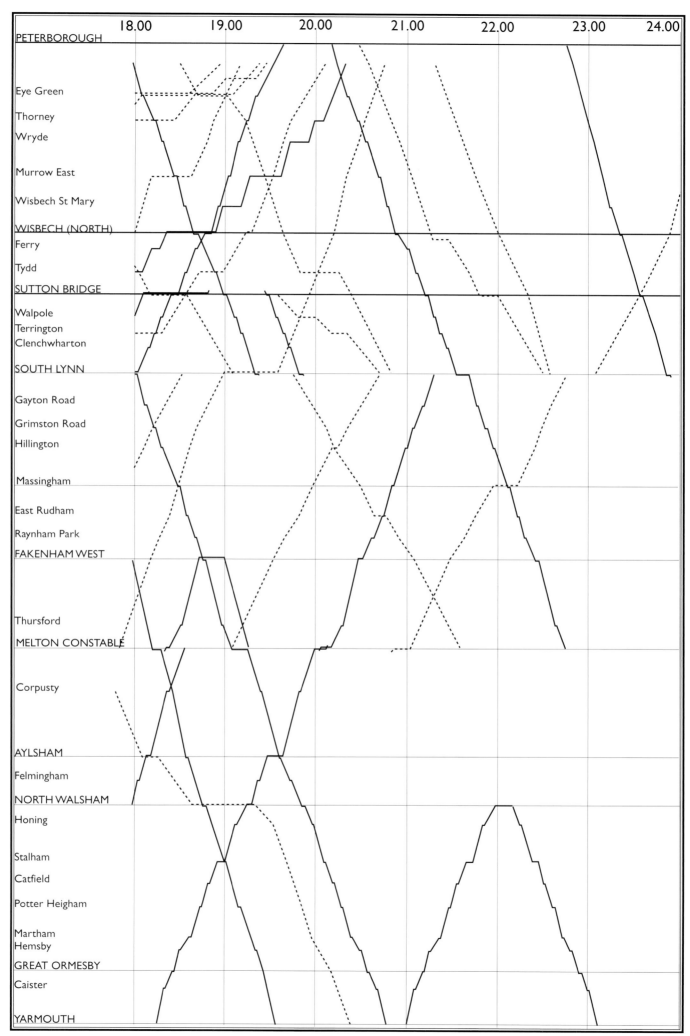

	18.00	19.00	20.00	21.00	22.00	23.00	24.00
PETERBOROUGH							
Eye Green							
Thorney							
Wryde							
Murrow East							
Wisbech St Mary							
WISBECH (NORTH)							
Ferry							
Tydd							
SUTTON BRIDGE							
Walpole							
Terrington							
Clenchwharton							
SOUTH LYNN							
Gayton Road							
Grimston Road							
Hillington							
Massingham							
East Rudham							
Raynham Park							
FAKENHAM WEST							
Thursford							
MELTON CONSTABLE							
Corpusty							
AYLSHAM							
Felmingham							
NORTH WALSHAM							
Honing							
Stalham							
Catfield							
Potter Heigham							
Martham							
Hemsby							
GREAT ORMESBY							
Caister							
YARMOUTH							

25

Although the M&GN finished (or started) at Wisbech Junction, three-quarters of a mile north of the Great Northern Station, by virtue of its joint status its trains ran freely within the GN/Midland areas. M&GN passenger trains started from Peterborough North with the empty stock being berthed on the Wharf at Nene Carriage Sidings whilst goods trains started and terminated from a variety of yards and were governed by the Great Northern Controller at Knebworth: the point from which the route between King's Cross and Grantham (Barkeston) was managed.

Peterborough was a place of contrasts. Its two passenger stations were disreputable, dank and far too small for the traffic they handled. The goods and marshalling yards were, by comparison, the largest on the Great Northern system and stretched for three or four miles. Although people talk about New England as though it was one entity, in fact it consisted of several quite respectably sized yards (West up, East Up, Coal Yard, Westwood, Angle Wharf, etc) whilst outside New England proper there were a variety of other yards, each of which performed a particular function or dealt with a distinct flows of traffic. Departing M&GN goods services generally started from either Peterborough East, Crescent, Westwood or Eastfield, making up their loads at Wisbech Junction (Midland) Yard before getting onto the M&GN proper. It was by no means unusual for sixty or seventy minutes to elapse between the time a train started its journey and touched M&GN metals for the first time. The arrangements for inward trains were similarly elastic although most shed part of their loads at Wisbech Sidings before going terminating at Crescent or New England.

The provision of motive power was primarily the responsibility of New England loco which had a link of twelve M&GN turns and, by the beginning of 1951, twenty-one LMS 4MT 2-6-0's, thirteen of which were used on M&GN turns which included seven engines to cover the needs of the depots at Spalding and Bourne. To even out the motive power responsibilities and ensure that the Midland did its share of the work, M&GN engines working in and out of the Peterborough area within the same shift were serviced not at New England but at Spital Bridge, the former Midland shed at Peterborough. In addition, Spital Bridge had one turn over the M&GN for which it was - somewhat extravagantly - given a pair of 2-6-0's.

The M&GN diagrams for New England are given below and it is interesting to note to none ventured beyond South Lynn save for the odd working to King's Lynn. It cannot be said that the hours worked by the 2-6-0's was excessive and for modern engines that could have remained in traffic for twenty-hours, some of the diagrams amounted to very much less than a good day's work. Indeed, it was unusual for an engine to be prepared for No.6 diagram and instead the engine off No.3 turn would simply be remanned in the shed when it returned after bringing in the 06.51 Yarmouth to Peterborough.

It cannot be said that either Peterborough not the Great Northern displayed much interest in the M&GN after 1948. Before the war the crack M&GN passenger service had been the 15.00 from King's Cross which conveyed through coaches to King's Lynn and Cromer. Whilst the four and a half hours taken to Cromer was easily beaten by the postwar Great Eastern with its Britannia schedules, the three hour timing to King's Lynn was a different matter and had it been developed after the war, the prospects for the M&GN might have improved. Unfortunately matters veered in the opposite direction and when urged in February 1953 to make savings, Liverpool Street responded by closing the line between Peterborough and South Lynn after the passage of the 20.10 Peterborough - Melton Constable. A handful of goods services were rearranged to leave at other times of day whilst the 22.45 Peterborough - King's Lynn passenger was expunged from existence except on Saturdays when the line remained open as formerly. Another victim was the 16.00 Yarmouth - Peterborough express goods - perhaps the most important train in the M&GN timetable - which reached South Lynn too late to proceed via Wisbech. Instead it was rerouted across to the Midland via Bourne and Saxby, taking, more or less, the path of the former 13.50 South Lynn - Saxby which had been altered to terminate at Spalding.

It would be pleasing to record that the Midland regarded this M&GN jewel with its vans of potato crisps and fizzy drinks as something special and had it extended to Nottingham or some other useful destination. Alas, not only did the train languish at Saxby until its wagons were taken up by next morning's workaday locals, but it was downgraded to a class F at Bourne. There are those who believe that tinkering with timetables leads to more productive methods of working and helps to assure longevity. A cynic, however, would suggest that the result is the exact opposite and that history has shown that messing with the railway status quo achieves nothing except to increase deficits and accelerate closures.

NEW ENGLAND LOCO DIAGRAMS : 1952

1: LMS 4MT 2-6-0

New England Loco	04.50	Light	
Peterborough N.	05.10	Pass	
06.17 South Lynn	06.23	Pass	
06.30 Kings Lynn	06.53	ECS	
06.58 South Lynn	07.05	Light	
07.10 S. Lynn loco	08.30	Light	
08.35 South Lynn	08.45	Pass	07.30 ex Melton C.
10.22 Peterborough N.	10.30	ECS	
10.35 Nene CS	10.45	Light	
10.50 Peterborough N. Loco	12.30	Light	
12.35 Peterborough N.	12.45	Pass	Yarmouth
14.11 South Lynn	14.45	Pcls	
15.56 Wisbech North	16.25	Pass	
17.20 Peterborough N.	17.30	ECS	
17.35 Nene CS	17.40	Light	
18.00 New England Loco			

2: LMS 4MT 2-6-0

New England Loco	17.45	Light	
Crescent	18.10	Goods	
20.50 South Lynn	23.05	Goods	
01.00 Crescent	01.10	Light	
01.30 New England Loco			

3: LMS 4MT 2-6-0

New England Loco	06.25	Light	
Peterborough N.	06.45	Pass	Yarmouth
08.02 South Lynn	09.55	Pass	06.51 ex Yarmouth
11.07 Peterborough N.	11.15	ECS	
11.20 Nene CS	11.25	Light	
11.45 New England Loco			

4: LMS 4MT 2-6-0

New England Loco	06.25	Light	
Westwood	06.50	Goods	
10.30 Wisbech (HSL)	13.47	Goods	
15.15 South Lynn	16.38	Pcls	12.55 ex Yarmouth
20.50 Peterborough N.	21.00	ECS	
21.05 Nene CS	21.10	Light	
21.30 New England Loco			

5: LMS 4MT 2-6-0

New England Loco	09.10	Light	
Crescent	09.30	Goods	
13.20 Wisbech (HSL)	15.50	Goods	
19.22 Westwood	19.30	Light	
19.50 New England Loco			

6: LMS 4MT 2-6-0

New England Loco	11.25	Light	
Westwood	11.45	Goods	
15.40 Wisbech (HSL)	17.48	Goods	
19.05 South Lynn	19.10	Light	
19.15 South Lynn loco	(07.50)		

Alternate with South Lynn 10 engine.

BOURNE LOCO DIAGRAMS : 1952

1: LMS 4MT 2-6-0

Bourne Loco	07.30	Light	
Bourne	07.40	Pass	Kings Lynn
08.00 Spalding	08.30	Pass	06.50 K. Lynn - Nottingham
08.51 Bourne	08.53	Pass	06.50 K. Lynn - Nottingham
09.36 Saxby	09.55	Pass	Kings Lynn
10.36 Bourne	10.39	Pass	Kings Lynn
10.59 Spalding	11.45	Pass	Saxby
12.06 Bourne			
		Goods Pilot	
14.26 Bourne	14.26	Pass	13.45 ex-Saxby
14.46 Spalding	16.08	Pilot	Nottingham
16.29 Bourne	18.10	Pass	16.20 ex Nottingham
18.35 Spalding	20.36	Pass	
20.57 Bourne Loco			

2: LMS 4MT 2-6-0

Bourne Loco	12.28	Light	
Bourne	12.38	Pass	11.45 Spalding
13.18 Saxby	13.45	Pass	Spalding
14.22 Bourne	16.35	Pass	
16.56 Spalding	18.05	Pass	Nottingham
18.29 Bourne	18.35	Light	
18.45 Bourne Loco			

SPALDING LOCO DIAGRAMS : 1952

1: LMS 4MT 2-6-0

Spalding Loco	05.15	Light	
Spalding	05.30	Goods	
08.42 Sutton Bridge	09.15	Pass	
09.58 Spalding	12.20	Pass	
13.05 Sutton Bridge	13.35	Pass	
14.20 Spalding	16.00	Pass	
16.40 Sutton Bridge	17.30	Goods	
20.10 Spalding	20.15	Light	
20.30 Spalding Loco			

2: LMS 4MT 2-6-0

Spalding Loco	06.12	Light	
Spalding	06.27	Goods	
06.55 Bourne	08.30	Goods	
09.14 Spalding	09.20	Light	
09.35 Loco	15.00	Light	
15.25 Fleet	16.10	Light	
16.13 Gedney	17.00	Light	
17.03 Long Sutton	17.44	Goods	
20.16 Bourne	21.07	'assenge	Pilot
21.26 Spalding	21.30	Light	
21.45 Spalding Loco			

3: J6 0-6-0

Spalding Loco	07.00	Light	
Spalding	07.15	Goods	
12.55 South Lynn	13.00	Light	
13.10 S. Lynn Loco	16.20	Light	
16.25 Kings Lynn	16.55	Pcls	
19.23 Spalding	19.30	Light	
19.40 Spalding Loco			

4: LMS 4MT 2-6-0

Spalding Loco	11.00	Light	
Spalding	11.15	Pass	09.55 ex Saxby
12.28 South Lynn	12.30	Pass	09.55 ex Saxby
12.40 King's Lynn	13.00	Light	
13.05 South Lynn	13.50	Goods	
15.05 Long Sutton	15.30	Pcls	
16.43 Moulton	18.00	Goods	
18.15 Spalding	18.20	Light	
18.30 Spalding Loco			

5: LMS 4MT 2-6-0

Spalding Loco	13.00	Light	
Spalding	13.15	Goods	
15.48 Sutton Bridge	16.00	Light	
16.10 Long Sutton	16.45	Goods	
18.51 Spalding	18.56	Light	
19.10 Spalding Loco			

6: J6 0-6-0

Spalding Loco	14.15	Light	
14.36 Holbeach	21.00	Light	
21.20 Spalding Loco			

7: J6 0-6-0

Spalding Loco	14.50	Light	
Spalding	15.05	Goods	
17.30 Bourne	18.45	Goods	
20.00 Spalding	20.05	Light	
20.15 Spalding Loco			

8: LMS 4MT 2-6-0

Spalding Loco	15.53	Light	
Spalding	16.08	Pass	
18.06 Nottingham	18.15	ECS	
18.20 Nottingham CS	18.25	Light	
Nottingham	19.42	Pass	
21.26 Spalding	21.30	Light	
21.40 Spalding Loco			

SPITAL BRIDGE LOCO DIAGRAMS : 1952

18: LMS 4MT 2-6-0

Spital Bridge Loco	14.30	Light	
14.35 Wisbech Sidings	14.50	Goods	
16.20 Eye Green	20.52	Goods	
21.53 Westwood Sidings	22.00	Light	
22.05 Spital Bridge Loco			

LOCOMOTIVE ALLOCATION : SOUTH LYNN (31D)

Engine	Class	Aug-50	Sep-50	Oct-50	Nov-50	Dec-50	Jan-51	Feb-51	Mar-51	Apr-51	May-51	Jun-51	Jul-51
64645	5F: J19 0-6-0 (1912)						To Cambs	X	X	X	X	X	X
64646	5F: J19 0-6-0 (1912)						To Cambs	X	X	X	X	X	X
64649	5F: J19 0-6-0 (1912)											To Stratford	X
64653	5F: J19 0-6-0 (1912)						To Cambs	X	X	X	X	X	X
64658	5F: J19 0-6-0 (1912)						To Cambs	X	X	X	X	X	X
64673	5F: J19 0-6-0 (1912)						To Cambs	X	X	X	X	X	X
61533	4P : B12 4-6-0 (1932)												
61537	4P : B12 4-6-0 (1932)												
61540	4P : B12 4-6-0 (1932)												
61547	4P : B12 4-6-0 (1932)												
43090	4MT 2-6-0 (1947)	X	X	X	X	NEW							
43091	4MT 2-6-0 (1947)	X	X	X	X	NEW							
43092	4MT 2-6-0 (1947)	X	X	X	X	NEW							
43093	4MT 2-6-0 (1947)	X	X	X	X	NEW							
43094	4MT 2-6-0 (1947)	X	X	X	X	NEW					To Swindon	X	X
43095	4MT 2-6-0 (1947)	X	X	X	X	NEW							
43104	4MT 2-6-0 (1947)	X	X	X	X	X	X	X	NEW				
43105	4MT 2-6-0 (1947)	X	X	X	X	X	X	X	NEW				
43106	4MT 2-6-0 (1947)	X	X	X	X	X	X	X	X	NEW			
43109	4MT 2-6-0 (1947)	X	X	X	X	X	X	X	X	X	X	NEW	
43110	4MT 2-6-0 (1947)	X	X	X	X	X	X	X	X	X	X	NEW	
43111	4MT 2-6-0 (1947)	X	X	X	X	X	X	X	X	X	X	X	NEW
61738	4F: K2 2-6-0 (1912)									To Colwick	X	X	X
61742	4F: K2 2-6-0 (1912)												
61743	4F: K2 2-6-0 (1912)												
61748	4F: K2 2-6-0 (1912)												
61757	4F: K2 2-6-0 (1912)												
61766	4F: K2 2-6-0 (1912)												
65504	4F: J17 0-6-0 (1901)												
65526	4F: J17 0-6-0 (1901)												
65533	4F: J17 0-6-0 (1901)												
65545	4F: J17 0-6-0 (1901)												
65562	4F: J17 0-6-0 (1901)											To March	X
65579	4F: J17 0-6-0 (1901)											To March	X
65580	4F: J17 0-6-0 (1901)						To Cambs	X	X	X	X	X	X
65582	4F: J17 0-6-0 (1901)												
65588	4F: J17 0-6-0 (1901)						To Cambs	X	X	X	X	X	X
68542	3F: J69 0-6-0T (1902)												
68566	3F: J69 0-6-0T (1902)												
68600	3F: J69 0-6-0T (1902)												
67227	2P: F6 2-4-2T (1911)	X	X	X	Ex K. Lynn								
62534	2P: D16 4-4-0 (1923)									To K. Lynn	X	X	X
62543	2P: D16 4-4-0 (1923)		To Cambs				X	X	X	X	X	X	X
62558	2P: D16 4-4-0 (1923)									To Cambs	X	X	X
62573	2P: D16 4-4-0 (1923)			To Bury			X	X	X	X	X	X	X
62507	2P: D15 4-4-0 (1904)	X	X	X	Ex K. Lynn								To K. Lynn
67356	2P: C12 4-4-2T (1898	X	X	X	X	X	X	X	X	X	X	Ex K. Cross	
68597	2F: J67 0-6-0T (1890)												
68378	2F: J66 0-6-0T (1886)												

LOCOMOTIVE ALLOCATION : MELTON CONSTABLE (32G)

Engine	Class	Aug-50	Sep-50	Oct-50	Nov-50	Dec-50	Jan-51	Feb-51	Mar-51	Apr-51	May-51	Jun-51	Jul-51
65509	4F: J17 0-6-0 (1901)												
65516	4F: J17 0-6-0 (1901)												
65551	4F: J17 0-6-0 (1901)												
65552	4F: J17 0-6-0 (1901)												
65557	4F: J17 0-6-0 (1901)												
65567	4F: J17 0-6-0 (1901)												
65586	4F: J17 0-6-0 (1901)												
69679	3P: N7 0-6-2T (1914)		To Norwich	X	X	X	X	X	X	X	X	X	X
69708	3P: N7 0-6-2T (1914)	X	X	X	X	Ex Norwich							
67224	2P: F6 2-4-2T (1911)		To Norwich	X	X	X	X	X	X	X	X	X	X
67225	2P: F6 2-4-2T (1911)												
67228	2P: F6 2-4-2T (1911)												
62515	2P: D16 4-4-0 (1923)												
62519	2P: D16 4-4-0 (1923)												
62523	2P: D16 4-4-0 (1923)												
62533	2P: D16 4-4-0 (1923)												
62562	2P: D16 4-4-0 (1923)												
62578	2P: D16 4-4-0 (1923)												
62608	2P: D16 4-4-0 (1923)	X	X	X	X	X	X	X	X	X	X	Ex Norwich	
62617	2P: D16 4-4-0 (1923)	X	X	X	X	X	X	X	X	X	X	Ex Norwich	
62620	2P: D16 4-4-0 (1923)												
62509	2P: D15 4-4-0 (1904)												
62520	2P: D15 4-4-0 (1904)												
62528	2P: D15 4-4-0 (1904)											W/D	X
62538	2P: D15 4-4-0 (1904)												
68536	2F: J67 0-6-0T (1890)												
68377	2F: J66 0-6-0T (1886)											W/D	X
68388	2F: J66 0-6-0T (1886)	X	X	X	X	X	X	X	X	X	Ex Norwich		
67152	1P: F4 2-4-2T (1884)												
67162	1P: F4 2-4-2T (1884)												

LOCOMOTIVE ALLOCATION : YARMOUTH BEACH (32F)

Engine	Class	Aug-50	Sep-50	Oct-50	Nov-50	Dec-50	Jan-51	Feb-51	Mar-51	Apr-51	May-51	Jun-51	Jul-51
61971	6F: K3 2-6-0 (1924)	X	X	X	Ex Norwich	To Norwich	X	X	X	X	X	X	X
61520	4P : B12 4-6-0 (1932)												
61530	4P : B12 4-6-0 (1932)		To Ipswich	X	X	X	X	X	X	X	Ex Norwich		
61545	4P : B12 4-6-0 (1932)		To Norwich	X	X	X	X	X	X	X	X	X	X
61545	4P : B12 4-6-0 (1932)	X	X	X	X	X	X	X	X	X	X	Ex Yar (ST)	
61747	4F: K2 2-6-0 (1912)	X	X	Ex New E.		To Norwich	X	X	X	X	X	X	X
65558	4F: J17 0-6-0 (1901)											To L'toft	X
65559	4F: J17 0-6-0 (1901)												
65566	4F: J17 0-6-0 (1901)	X	X	X	X	X	X	X	X	Ex L'toft			
65581	4F: J17 0-6-0 (1901)												
68651	3F: J68 0-6-0T (1912)												
67223	2P: F6 2-4-2T (1911)												
67226	2P: F6 2-4-2T (1911)												
67233	2P: F6 2-4-2T (1911)												
67234	2P: F6 2-4-2T (1911)												
67235	2P: F6 2-4-2T (1911)												
62561	2P: D16 4-4-0 (1923)												
62564	2P: D16 4-4-0 (1923)												
62592	2P: D16 4-4-0 (1923)												
62596	2P: D16 4-4-0 (1923)												
68214	0F: J65 0-6-0T (1889)												

Engine	Class	Aug-51	Sep-51	Oct-51	Nov-51	Dec-51	Jan-52	Feb-52	Mar-52	Apr-52	May-52	Jun-52	Jul-52
64646	5F: J19 0-6-0 (1912)	X	X	X	X	X	X	X	X	X	X	X	Ex Cambridge
61533	4P : B12 4-6-0 (1932)												To Ipswich
61537	4P : B12 4-6-0 (1932)												
61540	4P : B12 4-6-0 (1932)												
61547	4P : B12 4-6-0 (1932)												
43090	4MT 2-6-0 (1947)												
43091	4MT 2-6-0 (1947)												
43092	4MT 2-6-0 (1947)												
43093	4MT 2-6-0 (1947)												
43095	4MT 2-6-0 (1947)												
43104	4MT 2-6-0 (1947)												
43105	4MT 2-6-0 (1947)												
43106	4MT 2-6-0 (1947)												
43109	4MT 2-6-0 (1947)												
43110	4MT 2-6-0 (1947)												
43111	4MT 2-6-0 (1947)												
43142	4MT 2-6-0 (1947)	NEW											
43143	4MT 2-6-0 (1947)	X	NEW										
43144	4MT 2-6-0 (1947)	X	NEW										
43145	4MT 2-6-0 (1947)	X	NEW	To Yarmouth	X	X	X	X	X	X	X	X	X
61742	4F: K2 2-6-0 (1912)												
61743	4F: K2 2-6-0 (1912)			To March	X	X	X	X	X	X	X	X	X
61748	4F: K2 2-6-0 (1912)												
61757	4F: K2 2-6-0 (1912)		To March	X	X	X	X	X	X	X	X	X	X
61766	4F: K2 2-6-0 (1912)												To Boston
65504	4F: J17 0-6-0 (1901)		To March	X	X	X	X	X	X	X	X	X	X
65526	4F: J17 0-6-0 (1901)		To March	X	X	X	X	X	X	X	X	X	X
65533	4F: J17 0-6-0 (1901)			To Cambridge	X	X	X	X	X	X	X	X	X
65545	4F: J17 0-6-0 (1901)		To Cambridge	X	X	X	X	X	X	X	X	X	X
65582	4F: J17 0-6-0 (1901)			To Kings Lynn	X	X	X	X	X	X	X	X	X
68542	3F: J69 0-6-0T (1902)												
68566	3F: J69 0-6-0T (1902)												
68600	3F: J69 0-6-0T (1902)								To Kings Lynn	X	X	X	X
67227	2P: F6 2-4-2T (1911)								To Cambridge	X	X	X	X
62609	2P: D16 4-4-0 (1923)	X	X	X	X	X	X	X	X	X	X	X	Ex Cambridge
67356	2P: C12 4-4-2T (1898)			W/D	X	X	X	X	X	X	X	X	X
68597	2F: J67 0-6-0T (1890)												
68378	2F: J66 0-6-0T (1886)												

Engine	Class	Aug-51	Sep-51	Oct-51	Nov-51	Dec-51	Jan-52	Feb-52	Mar-52	Apr-52	May-52	Jun-52	Jul-52
43145	4MT 2-6-0 (1947)	X	X	X	X	X	X	Ex Yarmouth					
43146	4MT 2-6-0 (1947)	X	NEW										
43147	4MT 2-6-0 (1947)	X	X	NEW									
43148	4MT 2-6-0 (1947)	X	X	NEW									
43149	4MT 2-6-0 (1947)	X	X	NEW									
43150	4MT 2-6-0 (1947)	X	X	NEW									
43151	4MT 2-6-0 (1947)	X	X	NEW									
43152	4MT 2-6-0 (1947)	X	X	NEW									
43153	4MT 2-6-0 (1947)	X	X	X	X	NEW							
43154	4MT 2-6-0 (1947)	X	X	X	X	NEW							
43155	4MT 2-6-0 (1947)	X	X	X	X	NEW							
43156	4MT 2-6-0 (1947)	X	X	X	X	X	NEW	To Yarmouth	X	X	X	X	X
65509	4F: J17 0-6-0 (1901)							To Yarmouth	X	X	X	X	X
65516	4F: J17 0-6-0 (1901)							To Norwich	X	X	X	X	X
65551	4F: J17 0-6-0 (1901)							To Norwich	X	X	X	X	X
65552	4F: J17 0-6-0 (1901)							To Stratford	X	X	X	X	X
65557	4F: J17 0-6-0 (1901)												
65567	4F: J17 0-6-0 (1901)					To Norwich	X	X	X	X	X	X	X
65574	4F: J17 0-6-0 (1901)	X	Ex Norwich		To Norwich	X	X	X	X	X	X	X	X
65586	4F: J17 0-6-0 (1901)				To Norwich	X	X	X	X	X	X	X	X
69708	3P: N7 0-6-2T (1914)		To Norwich	X	X	X	X	X	X	X	X	X	X
68623	3F: J69 0-6-0T (1902)	X	X	X	X	X	X	X	X	X	X	Ex Norwich	
67224	2P: F6 2-4-2T (1911)	X	Ex Norwich										
67225	2P: F6 2-4-2T (1911)												
67228	2P: F6 2-4-2T (1911)												
67229	2P: F6 2-4-2T (1911)	X	X	X	X	X	X	X	X	X	X	X	Ex Norwich
62515	2P: D16 4-4-0 (1923)												
62519	2P: D16 4-4-0 (1923)												
62523	2P: D16 4-4-0 (1923)												
62533	2P: D16 4-4-0 (1923)								To Norwich	X	X	X	X
62562	2P: D16 4-4-0 (1923)										To Norwich	X	X
62578	2P: D16 4-4-0 (1923)												
62608	2P: D16 4-4-0 (1923)					To Norwich	X	X	X	X	X	X	X
62610	2P: D16 4-4-0 (1923)	Ex Norwich			To Norwich	X	X	X	X	X	X	X	X
62617	2P: D16 4-4-0 (1923)												
62620	2P: D16 4-4-0 (1923)												
62509	2P: D15 4-4-0 (1904)								To Norwich	X	X	X	X
62520	2P: D15 4-4-0 (1904)		W/D	X	X	X	X	X	X	X	X	X	X
62538	2P: D15 4-4-0 (1904)								To Norwich	X	X	X	X
68536	2F: J67 0-6-0T (1890)												
68388	2F: J66 0-6-0T (1886)									W/D	X	X	X
67152	1P: F4 2-4-2T (1884)							W/D	X	X	X	X	X
67162	1P: F4 2-4-2T (1884)		To Yar (V)	X	X	X	X	X	X	X	X	X	X

Engine	Class	Aug-51	Sep-51	Oct-51	Nov-51	Dec-51	Jan-52	Feb-52	Mar-52	Apr-52	May-52	Jun-52	Jul-52
61520	4P : B12 4-6-0 (1932)												
61530	4P : B12 4-6-0 (1932)												
61545	4P : B12 4-6-0 (1932)												
43145	4MT 2-6-0 (1947)	X	X	Ex S. Lynn				To Melton	X	X	X	X	X
43156	4MT 2-6-0 (1947)	X	X	X	X	X	X	Ex Melton	X	X	X	X	X
43157	4MT 2-6-0 (1947)	X	X	X	X	X	X	X	X	X	X	X	NEW
43158	4MT 2-6-0 (1947)	X	X	X	X	X	X	X	X	X	X	X	NEW
65509	4F: J17 0-6-0 (1901)	X	X	X	X	X	X	Ex Melton					
65559	4F: J17 0-6-0 (1901)	X	To L'toft	X	X	X	X	X	X	X	X	X	X
65566	4F: J17 0-6-0 (1901)								To Plaistow	X	X	X	X
65581	4F: J17 0-6-0 (1901)												
68651	3F: J68 0-6-0T (1912)												
67223	2P: F6 2-4-2T (1911)												
67226	2P: F6 2-4-2T (1911)												
67233	2P: F6 2-4-2T (1911)												
67234	2P: F6 2-4-2T (1911)												
67235	2P: F6 2-4-2T (1911)												
62561	2P: D16 4-4-0 (1923)												
62564	2P: D16 4-4-0 (1923)												
62592	2P: D16 4-4-0 (1923)												
62596	2P: D16 4-4-0 (1923)												
68214	0F: J65 0-6-0T (1889)												

LOCOMOTIVE ALLOCATION : SOUTH LYNN (31D)

Engine	Class	Aug-52	Sep-52	Oct-52	Nov-52	Dec-52	Jan-53	Feb-53	Mar-53	Apr-53	May-53	Jun-53	Jul-53
64646	5F: J19 0-6-0 (1912)												
61533	4P : B12 4-6-0 (1932)	X	X	Ex Ipswich							To S. Town	X	X
61537	4P : B12 4-6-0 (1932)												
61540	4P : B12 4-6-0 (1932)												
61547	4P : B12 4-6-0 (1932)												
43090	4MT 2-6-0 (1947)												
43091	4MT 2-6-0 (1947)												
43092	4MT 2-6-0 (1947)												
43093	4MT 2-6-0 (1947)												
43094	4MT 2-6-0 (1947)	X	X	Ex Spital B									
43095	4MT 2-6-0 (1947)												
43104	4MT 2-6-0 (1947)												
43105	4MT 2-6-0 (1947)												
43106	4MT 2-6-0 (1947)												
43109	4MT 2-6-0 (1947)												
43110	4MT 2-6-0 (1947)												
43111	4MT 2-6-0 (1947)												
43142	4MT 2-6-0 (1947)												
43143	4MT 2-6-0 (1947)												
43144	4MT 2-6-0 (1947)								To Neasden	X	X	X	X
61742	4F: K2 2-6-0 (1912)		To March	X	X	X	X	X	X	X	X	X	X
61748	4F: K2 2-6-0 (1912)												
65517	4F: J17 0-6-0 (1901)	X	X	X	X	X	X	X	X	X	X	X	Ex Cambridge
65520	4F: J17 0-6-0 (1901)	X	X	X	X	X	X	X	X	X	X	X	Ex Cambridge
65562	4F: J17 0-6-0 (1901)	X	X	X	X	X	X	Ex Cambridge					
65579	4F: J17 0-6-0 (1901)	X	X	X	X	X	X	Ex March					
68542	3F: J69 0-6-0T (1902)												
68566	3F: J69 0-6-0T (1902)												
62568	2P: D16 4-4-0 (1923)	X	Ex Cambridge	To Spital B	X	X	X	X	X	X	X	X	X
62609	2P: D16 4-4-0 (1923)												
68494	2F: J67 0-6-0T (1890)	X	X	X	X	X	X	X	X	X	X	X	Ex Norwich
68515	2F: J67 0-6-0T (1890)	X	Ex K. Lynn										To Melton
68597	2F: J67 0-6-0T (1890)												To Norwich
68623	2F: J67 0-6-0T (1890)	X	X	X	X	X	X	X	X	X	X	X	Ex Melton
68378	2F: J66 0-6-0T (1886)												

LOCOMOTIVE ALLOCATION : MELTON CONSTABLE (32G)

Engine	Class	Aug-52	Sep-52	Oct-52	Nov-52	Dec-52	Jan-53	Feb-53	Mar-53	Apr-53	May-53	Jun-53	Jul-53
43145	4MT 2-6-0 (1947)												
43146	4MT 2-6-0 (1947)												
43147	4MT 2-6-0 (1947)												
43148	4MT 2-6-0 (1947)												
43149	4MT 2-6-0 (1947)												
43150	4MT 2-6-0 (1947)												
43151	4MT 2-6-0 (1947)												
43152	4MT 2-6-0 (1947)												
43153	4MT 2-6-0 (1947)												
43154	4MT 2-6-0 (1947)												
43155	4MT 2-6-0 (1947)												
65557	4F: J17 0-6-0 (1901)												
68623	3F: J69 0-6-0T (1902)												To S. Lynn
67224	2P: F6 2-4-2T (1911)												
67225	2P: F6 2-4-2T (1911)												
67228	2P: F6 2-4-2T (1911)												
67229	2P: F6 2-4-2T (1911)												To L'toft
62515	2P: D16 4-4-0 (1923)												
62519	2P: D16 4-4-0 (1923)												
62533	2P: D16 4-4-0 (1923)												
62578	2P: D16 4-4-0 (1923)												
62592	2P: D16 4-4-0 (1923)	X	X	X	X	X	X	X	X	X	X	X	Ex Norwich
62617	2P: D16 4-4-0 (1923)												
62620	2P: D16 4-4-0 (1923)												
68515	2F: J67 0-6-0T (1890)	X	X	X	X	X	X	X	X	X	X	X	Ex S. Lynn
68536	2F: J67 0-6-0T (1890)												

LOCOMOTIVE ALLOCATION : YARMOUTH BEACH (32F)

Engine	Class	Aug-52	Sep-52	Oct-52	Nov-52	Dec-52	Jan-53	Feb-53	Mar-53	Apr-53	May-53	Jun-53	Jul-53
61520	4P: B12 4-6-0 (1932)												
61530	4P: B12 4-6-0 (1932)												
61545	4P: B12 4-6-0 (1932)												
61568	4P: B12 4-6-0 (1932)	X	X	X	X	X	X	X	X	X	X	X	Ex Norwich
43156	4MT 2-6-0 (1947)												
43157	4MT 2-6-0 (1947)												
43158	4MT 2-6-0 (1947)												
43159	4MT 2-6-0 (1947)	NEW											
43160	4MT 2-6-0 (1947)	NEW											
43161	4MT 2-6-0 (1947)	X	NEW						To Neasden	X	X	X	X
65509	4F: J17 0-6-0 (1901)												To Norwich
65581	4F: J17 0-6-0 (1901)												
65586	4F: J17 0-6-0 (1901)	X	X	X	X	X	X	X	X	X	X	X	Ex Norwich
68651	3F: J68 0-6-0T (1912)												
67223	2P: F6 2-4-2T (1911)												
67226	2P: F6 2-4-2T (1911)												
67233	2P: F6 2-4-2T (1911)												
67234	2P: F6 2-4-2T (1911)												
67235	2P: F6 2-4-2T (1911)												
62561	2P: D16 4-4-0 (1923)		To Norwich	X	X	X	X	X	X	X	X	X	X
62564	2P: D16 4-4-0 (1923)		To Norwich	X	X	X	X	X	X	X	X	X	X
62592	2P: D16 4-4-0 (1923)		To Norwich	X	X	X	X	X	X	X	X	X	X
62596	2P: D16 4-4-0 (1923)		To Norwich	X	X	X	X	X	X	X	X	X	X
68214	0F: J65 0-6-0T (1889)												

Engine	Class	Aug-53	Sep-53	Oct-53	Nov-53	Dec-53	Jan-54	Feb-54	Mar-54	Apr-54	May-54	Jun-54	Jul-54
64646	5F: J19 0-6-0 (1912)												
61537	4P : B12 4-6-0 (1932)												
61540	4P : B12 4-6-0 (1932)											To Norwich	X
61547	4P : B12 4-6-0 (1932)												
43068	4MT 2-6-0 (1947)	X	X	X	X	X	X	X	X	X	X	X	Ex Neasden
43090	4MT 2-6-0 (1947)												
43091	4MT 2-6-0 (1947)												
43092	4MT 2-6-0 (1947)												
43093	4MT 2-6-0 (1947)												
43094	4MT 2-6-0 (1947)												
43095	4MT 2-6-0 (1947)												
43104	4MT 2-6-0 (1947)												
43105	4MT 2-6-0 (1947)												
43106	4MT 2-6-0 (1947)												
43107	4MT 2-6-0 (1947)	X	X	X	X	X	X	X	X	X	X	X	Ex Neasden
43109	4MT 2-6-0 (1947)												
43110	4MT 2-6-0 (1947)												
43111	4MT 2-6-0 (1947)												
43142	4MT 2-6-0 (1947)												
43143	4MT 2-6-0 (1947)												
43144	4MT 2-6-0 (1947)	X	X	X	X	X	X	X	X	X	X	X	Ex Neasden
61748	4F: K2 2-6-0 (1912)			To Lincoln	X	X	X	X	X	X	X	X	X
65517	4F: J17 0-6-0 (1901)												
65520	4F: J17 0-6-0 (1901)								To Cambridge	X	X	X	X
65562	4F: J17 0-6-0 (1901)								To March	X	X	X	X
65579	4F: J17 0-6-0 (1901)												
68494	3F: J69 0-6-0T (1902)												
68542	3F: J69 0-6-0T (1902)												
68566	3F: J69 0-6-0T (1902)												
68567	3F: J69 0-6-0T (1902)	X	X	X	Ex Cambridge				To Cambridge	X	X	X	X
68623	3F: J69 0-6-0T (1902)												

Engine	Class	Aug-53	Sep-53	Oct-53	Nov-53	Dec-53	Jan-54	Feb-54	Mar-54	Apr-54	May-54	Jun-54	Jul-54
43145	4MT 2-6-0 (1947)												
43146	4MT 2-6-0 (1947)												
43147	4MT 2-6-0 (1947)												
43148	4MT 2-6-0 (1947)												
43149	4MT 2-6-0 (1947)												
43150	4MT 2-6-0 (1947)												
43151	4MT 2-6-0 (1947)												
43152	4MT 2-6-0 (1947)												
43153	4MT 2-6-0 (1947)												
43154	4MT 2-6-0 (1947)												
43155	4MT 2-6-0 (1947)												
65509	4F: J17 0-6-0 (1901)	X	X	X	X	X	Ex Norwich						
65551	4F: J17 0-6-0 (1901)	X	X	X	X	X	X	X	X	X	Ex Norwich		
65557	4F: J17 0-6-0 (1901)						To Norwich	X	X	X	X	X	X
67224	2P: F6 2-4-2T (1911)												
67225	2P: F6 2-4-2T (1911)												
67228	2P: F6 2-4-2T (1911)												
62515	2P: D16 4-4-0 (1923)												
62519	2P: D16 4-4-0 (1923)												
62533	2P: D16 4-4-0 (1923)												
62564	2P: D16 4-4-0 (1923)	X	X	X	X	X	X	X	X	X	Ex Norwich	To Norwich	X
62578	2P: D16 4-4-0 (1923)												
62592	2P: D16 4-4-0 (1923)			To Norwich	X	X	X	X	X	X	X	X	X
62596	2P: D16 4-4-0 (1923)	X	X	X	X	Ex Norwich	To Norwich	X	X	X	X	X	X
62617	2P: D16 4-4-0 (1923)												
62620	2P: D16 4-4-0 (1923)												
68515	2F: J67 0-6-0T (1890)												
68536	2F: J67 0-6-0T (1890)												

Engine	Class	Aug-53	Sep-53	Oct-53	Nov-53	Dec-53	Jan-54	Feb-54	Mar-54	Apr-54	May-54	Jun-54	Jul-54
61520	4P : B12 4-6-0 (1932)												
61530	4P : B12 4-6-0 (1932)			To Norwich	X	X	X	X	X	X	X	X	X
61530	4P : B12 4-6-0 (1932)	X	X	X	X	X	X	X	X	X	Ex Norwich		
61545	4P : B12 4-6-0 (1932)											To Yar (ST)	X
61568	4P : B12 4-6-0 (1932)			To Yar (ST)	X	X	X	X	X	X	X	X	X
61568	4P : B12 4-6-0 (1932)	X	X	X	X	X	X	X	X	X	Ex Ipswich	To Ips	X
43156	4MT 2-6-0 (1947)												
43157	4MT 2-6-0 (1947)												
43158	4MT 2-6-0 (1947)												
43159	4MT 2-6-0 (1947)												
43160	4MT 2-6-0 (1947)												
43161	4MT 2-6-0 (1947)	X	X	X	X	X	X	X	X	X	X	X	Ex Nesden
65581	4F: J17 0-6-0 (1901)												
65586	4F: J17 0-6-0 (1901)												
68651	3F: J68 0-6-0T (1912)												
67223	2P: F6 2-4-2T (1911)				To L'toft	X	X	X	X	X	X	X	X
67226	2P: F6 2-4-2T (1911)				To L'toft	X	X	X	X	X	X	X	X
67233	2P: F6 2-4-2T (1911)			To L'toft	X	X	X	X	X	X	X	X	X
67234	2P: F6 2-4-2T (1911)				To L'toft	X	X	X	X	X	X	X	X
67235	2P: F6 2-4-2T (1911)			To Yar (ST)	X	X	X	X	X	X	X	X	X
68214	0F: J65 0-6-0T (1889)												

LOCOMOTIVE ALLOCATION : SOUTH LYNN (31D)

Engine	Class	Aug-54	Sep-54	Oct-54	Nov-54	Dec-54	Jan-55	Feb-55	Mar-55	Apr-55	May-55	Jun-55	Jul-55
64646	5F: J19 0-6-0 (1912)						To Cambridge	X	X	X	X	X	X
61537	4P : B12 4-6-0 (1932)	To Ipswich	X	X	X	X	X	X	X	X	X	X	X
61547	4P : B12 4-6-0 (1932)			To Norwich	X	X	X	X	X	X	X	X	X
43068	4MT 2-6-0 (1947)												
43090	4MT 2-6-0 (1947)												
43091	4MT 2-6-0 (1947)												
43092	4MT 2-6-0 (1947)												
43093	4MT 2-6-0 (1947)												
43094	4MT 2-6-0 (1947)												
43095	4MT 2-6-0 (1947)												
43104	4MT 2-6-0 (1947)												
43105	4MT 2-6-0 (1947)												
43106	4MT 2-6-0 (1947)												
43107	4MT 2-6-0 (1947)												
43109	4MT 2-6-0 (1947)												
43110	4MT 2-6-0 (1947)												
43111	4MT 2-6-0 (1947)												
43142	4MT 2-6-0 (1947)												
43143	4MT 2-6-0 (1947)												
43144	4MT 2-6-0 (1947)												
65503	4F: J17 0-6-0 (1901)	X	X	X	X	X	X	X	X	X	Ex March		
65506	4F: J17 0-6-0 (1901)	X	X	X	X	X	Ex Cambridge						
65517	4F: J17 0-6-0 (1901)										W/D	X	X
65579	4F: J17 0-6-0 (1901)				W/D	X	X	X	X	X	X	X	X
68494	3F: J69 0-6-0T (1902)												
68542	3F: J69 0-6-0T (1902)												
68555	3F: J69 0-6-0T (1902)	X	X	Ex Cambridge					To Cambridge	X	X	X	X
68566	3F: J69 0-6-0T (1902)												
68623	3F: J69 0-6-0T (1902)												

LOCOMOTIVE ALLOCATION : MELTON CONSTABLE (32G)

Engine	Class	Aug-54	Sep-54	Oct-54	Nov-54	Dec-54	Jan-55	Feb-55	Mar-55	Apr-55	May-55	Jun-55	Jul-55
64900	5F: J39 0-6-0 (1926)	X	X	X	Ex Norwich				To Norwich	X	X	X	X
43145	4MT 2-6-0 (1947)												
43146	4MT 2-6-0 (1947)												
43147	4MT 2-6-0 (1947)												
43148	4MT 2-6-0 (1947)												
43149	4MT 2-6-0 (1947)												
43150	4MT 2-6-0 (1947)												
43151	4MT 2-6-0 (1947)												
43152	4MT 2-6-0 (1947)												
43153	4MT 2-6-0 (1947)												
43154	4MT 2-6-0 (1947)												
43155	4MT 2-6-0 (1947)												
65509	4F: J17 0-6-0 (1901)												
65551	4F: J17 0-6-0 (1901)												
67224	2P: F6 2-4-2T (1911)												
67225	2P: F6 2-4-2T (1911)												
67228	2P: F6 2-4-2T (1911)												
62515	2P: D16 4-4-0 (1923)												
62519	2P: D16 4-4-0 (1923)												
62533	2P: D16 4-4-0 (1923)												
62578	2P: D16 4-4-0 (1923)												
62592	2P: D16 4-4-0 (1923)	X	X	X	X	X	Ex Norwich	To Yarmouth	X	Ex Yarmouth	To Norwich	X	X
62617	2P: D16 4-4-0 (1923)												
62620	2P: D16 4-4-0 (1923)												
68515	2F: J67 0-6-0T (1890)												
68536	2F: J67 0-6-0T (1890)												
68214	0F: J65 0-6-0T (1889)	X	X	X	Ex Yarmouth	To Yarmouth	X	X	X	X	X	X	X

LOCOMOTIVE ALLOCATION : YARMOUTH BEACH (32F)

Engine	Class	Aug-54	Sep-54	Oct-54	Nov-54	Dec-54	Jan-55	Feb-55	Mar-55	Apr-55	May-55	Jun-55	Jul-55
61520	4P : B12 4-6-0 (1932)								To Norwich	X	X	X	X
61530	4P : B12 4-6-0 (1932)												
61545	4P : B12 4-6-0 (1932)	X	X	X	X	X	Ex Norwich						
43156	4MT 2-6-0 (1947)												
43157	4MT 2-6-0 (1947)												
43158	4MT 2-6-0 (1947)												
43159	4MT 2-6-0 (1947)												
43160	4MT 2-6-0 (1947)												
43161	4MT 2-6-0 (1947)												
65581	4F: J17 0-6-0 (1901)												
65586	4F: J17 0-6-0 (1901)												
68651	3F: J68 0-6-0T (1912)												
62564	2P: D16 4-4-0 (1923)	X	X	X	X	X	Ex Norwich			To Norwich	X	X	X
62592	2P: D16 4-4-0 (1923)	X	X	X	X	X	X	Ex Melton		To Melton	X	X	X
68214	0F: J65 0-6-0T (1889)				To Melton	X	Ex Melton						

31

LOCOMOTIVE ALLOCATION : SOUTH LYNN (31D)

Engine	Class	Aug-55	Sep-55	Oct-55	Nov-55	Dec-55	Jan-56	Feb-56	Mar-56	Apr-56	May-56	Jun-56	Jul-56
43068	4MT 2-6-0 (1947)												
43090	4MT 2-6-0 (1947)												
43091	4MT 2-6-0 (1947)												
43092	4MT 2-6-0 (1947)												
43093	4MT 2-6-0 (1947)												
43094	4MT 2-6-0 (1947)												
43095	4MT 2-6-0 (1947)												
43104	4MT 2-6-0 (1947)												
43105	4MT 2-6-0 (1947)												
43106	4MT 2-6-0 (1947)											To W. Halse	X
43107	4MT 2-6-0 (1947)												
43109	4MT 2-6-0 (1947)												
43110	4MT 2-6-0 (1947)												
43111	4MT 2-6-0 (1947)												
43142	4MT 2-6-0 (1947)												
43143	4MT 2-6-0 (1947)												
43144	4MT 2-6-0 (1947)												
65503	4F: J17 0-6-0 (1901)				To March	X	X	X	X	X	X	X	X
65506	4F: J17 0-6-0 (1901)										To Cambridge	X	X
65584	4F: J17 0-6-0 (1901)	X	X	X	Ex March								
68494	3F: J69 0-6-0T (1902)												
68542	3F: J69 0-6-0T (1902)												
68566	3F: J69 0-6-0T (1902)												
68567	3F: J69 0-6-0T (1902)	X	Ex Cambridge				To Cambridge	X	X	X	X	X	X
68623	3F: J69 0-6-0T (1902)												

LOCOMOTIVE ALLOCATION : MELTON CONSTABLE (32G)

Engine	Class	Aug-55	Sep-55	Oct-55	Nov-55	Dec-55	Jan-56	Feb-56	Mar-56	Apr-56	May-56	Jun-56	Jul-56
64913	5F: J39 0-6-0 (1926)	X	X	X	X	X	X	X	X	Ex Norwich			
43145	4MT 2-6-0 (1947)												
43146	4MT 2-6-0 (1947)												
43147	4MT 2-6-0 (1947)												
43148	4MT 2-6-0 (1947)												
43149	4MT 2-6-0 (1947)												
43150	4MT 2-6-0 (1947)												
43151	4MT 2-6-0 (1947)												
43152	4MT 2-6-0 (1947)												
43153	4MT 2-6-0 (1947)												
43154	4MT 2-6-0 (1947)												
43155	4MT 2-6-0 (1947)												
65509	4F: J17 0-6-0 (1901)												
65514	4F: J17 0-6-0 (1901)	X	X	X	Ex Norwich								
65551	4F: J17 0-6-0 (1901)												
65567	4F: J17 0-6-0 (1901)	X	Ex Norwich										
68625	3F: J69 0-6-0T (1902)	X	X	X	X	Ex Cambridge							
67224	2P: F6 2-4-2T (1911)					To L'toft	X	X	X	X	X	X	X
67225	2P: F6 2-4-2T (1911)				To Stratford	X	X	X	X	X	X	X	X
67228	2P: F6 2-4-2T (1911)					To Stratford	X	X	X	X	X	X	X
62515	2P: D16 4-4-0 (1923)												
62519	2P: D16 4-4-0 (1923)												
62533	2P: D16 4-4-0 (1923)												
62561	2P: D16 4-4-0 (1923)	X	Ex Norwich										
62578	2P: D16 4-4-0 (1923)												
62617	2P: D16 4-4-0 (1923)												
62620	2P: D16 4-4-0 (1923)				W/D	X	X	X	X	X	X	X	X
68515	2F: J67 0-6-0T (1890)												
68536	2F: J67 0-6-0T (1890)												

LOCOMOTIVE ALLOCATION : YARMOUTH BEACH (32F)

Engine	Class	Aug-55	Sep-55	Oct-55	Nov-55	Dec-55	Jan-56	Feb-56	Mar-56	Apr-56	May-56	Jun-56	Jul-56
64802	5F: J39 0-6-0 (1926)	X	X	X	X	X	X	X	X	X	X	Ex Norwich	
61530	4P : B12 4-6-0 (1932)												
61545	4P : B12 4-6-0 (1932)												
43156	4MT 2-6-0 (1947)												
43157	4MT 2-6-0 (1947)												
43158	4MT 2-6-0 (1947)												
43159	4MT 2-6-0 (1947)												
43160	4MT 2-6-0 (1947)												
43161	4MT 2-6-0 (1947)												
65557	4F: J17 0-6-0 (1901)	X	X	X	X	X	X	X	X	X	X	Ex Norwich	
65581	4F: J17 0-6-0 (1901)												
65586	4F: J17 0-6-0 (1901)												
68651	3F: J68 0-6-0T (1912)												
62564	2P: D16 4-4-0 (1923)		X	X	Ex Norwich	To Norwich	X	X	X	X	X	X	X
68214	0F: J65 0-6-0T (1889)												

LOCOMOTIVE ALLOCATION : SOUTH LYNN (31D)

Engine	Class	Aug-56	Sep-56	Oct-56	Nov-56	Dec-56	Jan-57	Feb-57	Mar-57	Apr-57	May-57	Jun-57	Jul-57
43068	4MT 2-6-0 (1947)												
43090	4MT 2-6-0 (1947)												
43091	4MT 2-6-0 (1947)												
43092	4MT 2-6-0 (1947)												
43093	4MT 2-6-0 (1947)												
43094	4MT 2-6-0 (1947)												
43095	4MT 2-6-0 (1947)												
43104	4MT 2-6-0 (1947)												
43105	4MT 2-6-0 (1947)												
43107	4MT 2-6-0 (1947)												
43109	4MT 2-6-0 (1947)												
43110	4MT 2-6-0 (1947)											To K. Lynn	X
43111	4MT 2-6-0 (1947)												
43142	4MT 2-6-0 (1947)												
43143	4MT 2-6-0 (1947)												
43144	4MT 2-6-0 (1947)												
65584	4F: J17 0-6-0 (1901)												
68494	3F: J69 0-6-0T (1902)												
68542	3F: J69 0-6-0T (1902)												
68566	3F: J69 0-6-0T (1902)												
68623	3F: J69 0-6-0T (1902)												

LOCOMOTIVE ALLOCATION : MELTON CONSTABLE (32G)

Engine	Class	Aug-56	Sep-56	Oct-56	Nov-56	Dec-56	Jan-57	Feb-57	Mar-57	Apr-57	May-57	Jun-57	Jul-57
64802	5F: J39 0-6-0 (1926)	X	X	X	X	X	X	Ex Norwich					
64913	5F: J39 0-6-0 (1926)			To Norwich	X	X	Ex Norwich	To Norwich	X	X	X	X	X
64968	5F: J39 0-6-0 (1926)	X	X	X	X	X	X	X	X	X	Ex Norwich		To Norwich
43086	4MT 2-6-0 (1947)	X	X	X	X	X	X	X	X	X	X	Ex New E.	
43089	4MT 2-6-0 (1947)	X	X	X	X	X	X	X	X	X	X	Ex Spital B	
43145	4MT 2-6-0 (1947)												
43146	4MT 2-6-0 (1947)												
43147	4MT 2-6-0 (1947)												
43148	4MT 2-6-0 (1947)												
43149	4MT 2-6-0 (1947)												
43150	4MT 2-6-0 (1947)												
43151	4MT 2-6-0 (1947)												
43152	4MT 2-6-0 (1947)												
43153	4MT 2-6-0 (1947)												
43154	4MT 2-6-0 (1947)												
43155	4MT 2-6-0 (1947)												
65509	4F: J17 0-6-0 (1901)												
65514	4F: J17 0-6-0 (1901)								To Stratford	X	X	X	X
65551	4F: J17 0-6-0 (1901)												
65557	4F: J17 0-6-0 (1901)	X	X	Ex Yarmouth					To Norwich	X	X	X	X
65567	4F: J17 0-6-0 (1901)												
65588	4F: J17 0-6-0 (1901)	X	X	X	X	X	X	X	Ex Norwich				
68625	3F: J69 0-6-0T (1902)												
62515	2P: D16 4-4-0 (1923)												
62519	2P: D16 4-4-0 (1923)						W/D	X	X	X	X	X	X
62533	2P: D16 4-4-0 (1923)												
62561	2P: D16 4-4-0 (1923)												
62578	2P: D16 4-4-0 (1923)												
62597	2P: D16 4-4-0 (1923)	X	X	X	X	X	X	X	X	X	Ex Yarmouth		
62617	2P: D16 4-4-0 (1923)										W/D	X	X
68515	2F: J67 0-6-0T (1890)						W/D	X	X	X	X	X	X
68536	2F: J67 0-6-0T (1890)												

LOCOMOTIVE ALLOCATION : YARMOUTH BEACH (32F)

Engine	Class	Aug-56	Sep-56	Oct-56	Nov-56	Dec-56	Jan-57	Feb-57	Mar-57	Apr-57	May-57	Jun-57	Jul-57
64802	5F: J39 0-6-0 (1926)	To Norwich	X	X	X	X	X	X	X	X	X	X	X
61530	4P : B12 4-6-0 (1932)												
61540	4P : B12 4-6-0 (1932)	X	X	X	X	X	Ex Norwich						
61545	4P : B12 4-6-0 (1932)						W/D	X	X	X	X	X	X
43156	4MT 2-6-0 (1947)												
43157	4MT 2-6-0 (1947)												
43158	4MT 2-6-0 (1947)												
43159	4MT 2-6-0 (1947)												
43160	4MT 2-6-0 (1947)												
43161	4MT 2-6-0 (1947)												
65557	4F: J17 0-6-0 (1901)			To Melton	X	X	X	X	X	X	X	X	X
65581	4F: J17 0-6-0 (1901)												
65586	4F: J17 0-6-0 (1901)												
68651	3F: J68 0-6-0T (1912)												
62517	2P: D16 4-4-0 (1923)	Ex Yar (V)											
62597	2P: D16 4-4-0 (1923)	X	X	Ex Yar (ST)							To Melton	X	X
68214	0F: J65 0-6-0T (1889)		W/D	X	X	X	X	X	X	X	X	X	X

33

LOCOMOTIVE ALLOCATION : SOUTH LYNN (31D)

Engine	Class	Aug-57	Sep-57	Oct-57	Nov-57	Dec-57	Jan-58	Feb-58	Mar-58	Apr-58	May-58	Jun-58	Jul-58
43068	4MT 2-6-0 (1947)												
43090	4MT 2-6-0 (1947)												
43091	4MT 2-6-0 (1947)												
43092	4MT 2-6-0 (1947)												
43093	4MT 2-6-0 (1947)												
43094	4MT 2-6-0 (1947)												
43095	4MT 2-6-0 (1947)												
43104	4MT 2-6-0 (1947)												
43105	4MT 2-6-0 (1947)												
43107	4MT 2-6-0 (1947)												
43110	4MT 2-6-0 (1947)	Ex K. Lynn											
43111	4MT 2-6-0 (1947)												
43142	4MT 2-6-0 (1947)												
43143	4MT 2-6-0 (1947)												
43144	4MT 2-6-0 (1947)												
65503	4F: J17 0-6-0 (1901)	X	X	X	X	X	X	X	X	X	X	X	Ex March
65584	4F: J17 0-6-0 (1901)												
68494	3F: J69 0-6-0T (1902)									W/D	X	X	X
68499	3F: J69 0-6-0T (1902)	X	X	X	X	X	X	X	X	X	Ex K. Lynn		
68542	3F: J69 0-6-0T (1902)												
68545	3F: J69 0-6-0T (1902)	X	X	X	X	X	X	X	X	X	Ex K. Lynn	To K. Lynn	X
68556	3F: J69 0-6-0T (1902)	X	X	X	X	X	X	X	X	X	Ex K. Lynn	To New E.	X
68566	3F: J69 0-6-0T (1902)												
68623	3F: J69 0-6-0T (1902)											To Barrow H	X
D2016	0F: Diesel 0-6-0	X	X	X	X	X	X	X	X	X	Ex Cambridge		
D2017	0F: Diesel 0-6-0	X	X	X	X	X	X	X	X	X	Ex Cambridge		

LOCOMOTIVE ALLOCATION : MELTON CONSTABLE (32G)

Engine	Class	Aug-57	Sep-57	Oct-57	Nov-57	Dec-57	Jan-58	Feb-58	Mar-58	Apr-58	May-58	Jun-58	Jul-58
64726	5F: J39 0-6-0 (1926)	X	X	X	X	X	X	X	X	X	X	X	Ex Ipswich
64802	5F: J39 0-6-0 (1926)		To Norwich	X	X	X	X	X	X	X	X	X	X
43086	4MT 2-6-0 (1947)		To New E.	X	X	X	X	X	X	X	X	X	X
43089	4MT 2-6-0 (1947)		To Cambridge	X	X	X	X	X	X	X	X	X	X
43145	4MT 2-6-0 (1947)												
43146	4MT 2-6-0 (1947)												
43147	4MT 2-6-0 (1947)												
43148	4MT 2-6-0 (1947)												
43149	4MT 2-6-0 (1947)												
43150	4MT 2-6-0 (1947)												
43151	4MT 2-6-0 (1947)												
43152	4MT 2-6-0 (1947)												
43153	4MT 2-6-0 (1947)												
43154	4MT 2-6-0 (1947)												
43155	4MT 2-6-0 (1947)												
65509	4F: J17 0-6-0 (1901)			To Norwich	X	X	X	X	X	X	X	X	X
65551	4F: J17 0-6-0 (1901)												
65567	4F: J17 0-6-0 (1901)												
65588	4F: J17 0-6-0 (1901)												
68625	3F: J69 0-6-0T (1902)												To Yar (ST)
62515	2P: D16 4-4-0 (1923)									W/D	X	X	X
62533	2P: D16 4-4-0 (1923)		W/D	X	X	X	X	X	X	X	X	X	X
62561	2P: D16 4-4-0 (1923)							W/D	X	X	X	X	X
62578	2P: D16 4-4-0 (1923)			W/D	X	X	X	X	X	X	X	X	X
62597	2P: D16 4-4-0 (1923)												
68536	2F: J67 0-6-0T (1890)							W/D	X	X	X	X	X
11170	0F: Diesel 0-6-0	X	X	X	X	X	X	Ex Norwich					
11172	0F: Diesel 0-6-0	X	X	X	X	X	X	X		X	Ex Norwich		To Norwich
11176	0F: Diesel 0-6-0	X	X	X	X	X	X	Ex Norwich					

LOCOMOTIVE ALLOCATION : YARMOUTH BEACH (32F)

Engine	Class	Aug-57	Sep-57	Oct-57	Nov-57	Dec-57	Jan-58	Feb-58	Mar-58	Apr-58	May-58	Jun-58	Jul-58
61530	4P : B12 4-6-0 (1932)												
61533	4P : B12 4-6-0 (1932)	X	X	Ex Ipswich									
61540	4P : B12 4-6-0 (1932)			W/D	X	X	X	X	X	X	X	X	X
43156	4MT 2-6-0 (1947)												
43157	4MT 2-6-0 (1947)												
43158	4MT 2-6-0 (1947)												
43159	4MT 2-6-0 (1947)												
43160	4MT 2-6-0 (1947)												
43161	4MT 2-6-0 (1947)												
65581	4F: J17 0-6-0 (1901)												
65586	4F: J17 0-6-0 (1901)												
68651	3F: J68 0-6-0T (1912)										W/D	X	X
62517	2P: D16 4-4-0 (1923)												
62524	2P: D16 4-4-0 (1923)	X	X	X	X	X	X	X	X	X	X	X	Ex Yar (V)
11174	0F: Diesel 0-6-0	X	X	X	X	Ex Norwich							

34

LOCOMOTIVE ALLOCATION : SOUTH LYNN (31D)

Engine	Class	Aug-58	Sep-58	Oct-58	Nov-58	Dec-58	Jan-59	Feb-59	Mar-59	Apr-59	May-59	Jun-59	Jul-59
43068	4MT 2-6-0 (1947)							To Boston	X	X	X	X	X
43090	4MT 2-6-0 (1947)							To K. Lynn	X	X	X	X	X
43091	4MT 2-6-0 (1947)							To Boston	X	X	X	X	X
43092	4MT 2-6-0 (1947)							To Boston	X	X	X	X	X
43093	4MT 2-6-0 (1947)							To Boston	X	X	X	X	X
43094	4MT 2-6-0 (1947)							To K. Lynn	X	X	X	X	X
43095	4MT 2-6-0 (1947)							To Boston	X	X	X	X	X
43104	4MT 2-6-0 (1947)							To Boston	X	X	X	X	X
43105	4MT 2-6-0 (1947)							To Stratford	X	X	X	X	X
43107	4MT 2-6-0 (1947)							To Boston	X	X	X	X	X
43110	4MT 2-6-0 (1947)							To Boston	X	X	X	X	X
43111	4MT 2-6-0 (1947)							To Boston	X	X	X	X	X
43142	4MT 2-6-0 (1947)							To Boston	X	X	X	X	X
43143	4MT 2-6-0 (1947)							To Boston	X	X	X	X	X
43144	4MT 2-6-0 (1947)							To Stratford	X	X	X	X	X
65503	4F: J17 0-6-0 (1901)			To March	X	X	X	X	X	X	X	X	X
65584	4F: J17 0-6-0 (1901)			To March	X	X	X	X	X	X	X	X	X
68499	3F: J69 0-6-0T (1902)	To K. Lynn	X	X	X	X	X	X	X	X	X	X	X
68542	3F: J69 0-6-0T (1902)	To K. Lynn	X	X	X	X	X	X	X	X	X	X	X
68566	3F: J69 0-6-0T (1902)							To Cambridge	X	X	X	X	X
D2016	0F: Diesel 0-6-0							To Cambridge	X	X	X	X	X
D2017	0F: Diesel 0-6-0							To Cambridge	X	X	X	X	X

LOCOMOTIVE ALLOCATION : MELTON CONSTABLE (32G)

Engine	Class	Aug-58	Sep-58	Oct-58	Nov-58	Dec-58	Jan-59	Feb-59	Mar-59	Apr-59	May-59	Jun-59	Jul-59
64726	5F: J39 0-6-0 (1926)			To L'toft	X	X	X	X	X	X	X	X	X
43145	4MT 2-6-0 (1947)							To Norwich	X	X	X	X	X
43146	4MT 2-6-0 (1947)							To Norwich	X	X	X	X	X
43147	4MT 2-6-0 (1947)							To Boston	X	X	X	X	X
43148	4MT 2-6-0 (1947)							To Stratford	X	X	X	X	X
43149	4MT 2-6-0 (1947)							To Stratford	X	X	X	X	X
43150	4MT 2-6-0 (1947)							To Stratford	X	X	X	X	X
43151	4MT 2-6-0 (1947)							To Stratford	X	X	X	X	X
43152	4MT 2-6-0 (1947)							To Col'ter	X	X	X	X	X
43153	4MT 2-6-0 (1947)							To Col'ter	X	X	X	X	X
43154	4MT 2-6-0 (1947)							To Boston	X	X	X	X	X
43155	4MT 2-6-0 (1947)							To Boston	X	X	X	X	X
65551	4F: J17 0-6-0 (1901)								To Norwich	X	X	X	X
65567	4F: J17 0-6-0 (1901)			To L'toft	X	X	X	X	X	X	X	X	X
65588	4F: J17 0-6-0 (1901)			To L'toft	X	X	X	X	X	X	X	X	X
62597	2P: D16 4-4-0 (1923)								To Norwich	X	X	X	X
11170	0F: Diesel 0-6-0								To Norwich	X	X	X	X
11176	0F: Diesel 0-6-0								To Norwich	X	X	X	X

LOCOMOTIVE ALLOCATION : YARMOUTH BEACH (32F)

Engine	Class	Aug-58	Sep-58	Oct-58	Nov-58	Dec-58	Jan-59	Feb-59	Mar-59	Apr-59	May-59	Jun-59	Jul-59
61530	4P : B12 4-6-0 (1932)						To Norwich	X	X	X	X	X	X
61533	4P : B12 4-6-0 (1932)						To Norwich	X	X	X	X	X	X
43156	4MT 2-6-0 (1947)							To Norwich	X	X	X	X	X
43157	4MT 2-6-0 (1947)							To Norwich	X	X	X	X	X
43158	4MT 2-6-0 (1947)							To Boston	X	X	X	X	X
43159	4MT 2-6-0 (1947)							To Norwich	X	X	X	X	X
43160	4MT 2-6-0 (1947)							To Norwich	X	X	X	X	X
43161	4MT 2-6-0 (1947)							To Norwich	X	X	X	X	X
65581	4F: J17 0-6-0 (1901)								To Norwich	X	X	X	X
65586	4F: J17 0-6-0 (1901)								To Norwich	X	X	X	X
62517	2P: D16 4-4-0 (1923)						To Norwich	X	X	X	X	X	X
62524	2P: D16 4-4-0 (1923)						To Norwich	X	X	X	X	X	X
11174	0F: Diesel 0-6-0							To Yar (ST)	X	X	X	X	X

It is unlikely that any part of British Railways - with the possible exception of the London, Tilbury and Southend - came close to the degree of motive power standardisation achieved by the M&GN. The extent of locomotive uniformity was all the more surprising since the rag-bag of engines that had been employed during and immediately after the war formed such a tangle of museum pieces that the task of clearing them out in favour of a single modern type seemed a task of monumental proportions. The majority of passenger trains were worked by B12 4-6-0's and D16 4-4-0's whilst a sizeable fleet of GER J17 0-6-0's took care of most of the goods traffic. The Great Northern was represented by a batch of K2 2-6-0's.

The need for change was, however, pressing since the fleet inherited from the LNER had not been specifically designed for the M&GN and at times showed signs of difficulty - age and maintenance - with the basic service, let alone the Summer Saturday service which saw seven heavy trains running in both directions between Yarmouth and the East Midlands. To add to the difficulty any replacement engine would not only have to be sufficiently powerful to handle 350-ton express services between Yarmouth and South Lynn but would also be light enough to work over the heavily restricted section between South Lynn and Sutton Bridge.

These rather exacting demands were met by the LMS 4MT 2-6-0 which arrived on the system in late 1950 and very quickly accounted for half the M&GN motive power fleet. In addition to the thirty-plus example divided between the three M&GN sheds, a further twenty were allocated to the two Peterborough sheds with the result that by the mid-fifties it became difficult to find a passenger service that was not worked at some stage of its journey by one of the class.

It was not obvious from the public timetable that South Lynn and King's Lynn stations served the same town and to emphasise the fact that South Lynn was two miles from the town centre, the M&GN placed both stations in its timetables; a connecting service operating between the two. For many years this connection was operated by conventional trains but in 1951 a pair of C12 4-4-2T's and a push and pull set - redundant from the King's Cross - Alexandra Palace shuttle - arrived at King's Lynn and commenced work on the reasonably frequent service between the two stations. The service over the connecting line remained a rather cosmopolitan affair; the push and pull train being worked by GN locomotives despite being based at King's Lynn whilst M&GN LMS 2-6-0's worked the through trains to and from King's Lynn. C12 4-4-2T 67374 leaves King's Lynn for South Lynn with the push & pull in May 1957. (R.C. Riley/Transport Treasury)

There can be no question about South Lynn's importance to the M&GN: it was very much the focal point of the system and in many respects the point at which East met West. Very little traffic went through South Lynn without being remarshalled and the volume of trade was sufficient to keep two pilot engines busy in both its goods yards. The West Yard was - by a small margin - the busier of the two and received daily six trains from Peterborough and two each from Spalding, Sutton Bridge and Colwick. These thirteen trains were broken up on arrival (and added to traffic that had been tripped in from the Great Eastern via King's Lynn) to form thirteen departures for Norwich and Melton Constable which had three each and one each for Cromer, Fakenham and Gayton Road. The balance was completed by five trips to King's Lynn. It is interesting to note that while there were through services to Cromer and Norwich, there were none to Yarmouth, a fact that said something about the dearth of commercial activity on the eastern reaches of the system. (In fairness to Yarmouth, it has to be said that it generated the only true express goods that the M&GN operated. Smith's Crisps, Birds Eye frozen foods, Corona lemonades and several other well known brands filled the wagons of the 16.00 goods to Peterborough although few of their raw materials came in by rail).

The East Yard dealt with up road traffic and received nine main line trains and seven trips from King's Lynn. The majority of these services came from Melton Constable whilst Norwich, Fakenham and Yarmouth contributed one each. The last mentioned was actually a through service to Peterborough but called for half an hour in order to put off a Great Eastern section for King's Lynn. Not only was it the most important train on the M&GN but with a running time of four hours and fifty minutes from Yarmouth to Wisbech Sidings, it was faster than some of the Yarmouth - Peterborough passenger trains.

There were ten departures from the East Yard, five for Peterborough, two for Colwick and one each for Spalding, Sutton Bridge and Long Sutton. A noticeable omission was Saxby where the M&GN came into contact with the Midland system via the Kettering - Nottingham main line but most of the traffic for the Midland was routed via Peterborough whilst any that had to go via Bourne was sent down to Sutton Bridge which was the junction point for the Saxby route.

Next to the 16.00 ex Yarmouth, the most important M&GN services were the trains that ran to and from Colwick; a huge marshalling yard on the eastern periphery of Nottingham which dealt largely although not exclusively with the Great Northern's share of coal traffic from the Nottinghamshire coalfield. The number of services from Colwick varied but usually the timetable catered for two trains a day; both leaving Colwick at about the time their opposite numbers with empty wagons would pull out of South Lynn. The Lynn men signed the road as far as Sleaford where up and down trains would meet and exchange crews. Crew changeovers of this sort were a favoured way of Great Northern operating, especially in Lincolnshire where trains between New England and Doncaster would swap crews at dark and lonely places such as Woodhall Junction and Bardney.

So far as the onlooker was concerned the Colwick trains were of significance because they were jointly worked by South Lynn and Colwick with engines from each shed alternating daily and bringing the prospect of strangers from a far-off land spending the night in South Lynn Loco. The trains did introduce an operating problem for the GN since the section between Sutton Bridge and South Lynn was barred to half the engines allocated to Colwick and if one of the booked 'Ragtimer' 2-6-0's was not available, the choice of alternatives was severely limited. A J6 - which Colwick had in abundance - would be a considerable reduction in load whilst a J39 was barred on account of weight. (Strictly speaking, a J39 could pass between Sutton Bridge and South Lynn in an emergency but the Controller at Cambridge was hardly likely to regard the presence of a J39 on the 08.15 Colwick - South Lynn as sufficient

1: K2 2-6-0

Arr	Location	Dep	Working
	Loco	03.10	Light
	South Lynn	03.20	Goods
05.47	Westwood	05.55	Light
06.05	Spital Bridge Loco	07.00	Light
	Crescent Yard	07.15	Goods
09.34	South Lynn	09.45	Light
09.55	Loco	15.40	Light
	South Lynn	15.50	ECS
16.10	Sutton Bridge	16.45	Goods
19.06	Wisbech Jcn	19.10	Light
	Spital Bridge Loco	20.10	Light
	Crescent Yard	20.25	Goods
22.30	South Lynn	22.35	Light
22.40	Loco		

2: LMS 4MT 2-6-0

Arr	Location	Dep	Working
	Loco	03.50	Light
	South Lynn	04.00	Goods
04.10	King's Lynn	05.30	Goods
05.40	South Lynn	06.30	Goods
08.21	Melton C.	09.35	Passenger
10.15	Cromer B.	10.20	Light
10.25	Beach Loco	14.00	Light
14.05	Cromer B.	14.10	Goods
16.40	Melton C.	19.05	Goods
20.42	South Lynn	20.50	Light
21.00	Loco		

3: LMS 4MT 2-6-0

Arr	Location	Dep	Working
	Loco	05.22	Light
	South Lynn	05.32	Goods
08.05	Norwich City	10.30	Pass
11.19	Melton C	11.25	Light
11.30	Melton Loco	14.36	
	Melton C	14.46	Goods
16.08	Norwich City	19.45	Goods
20.53	Melton C	21.02	Goods
22.42	South Lynn		
23.00	Loco		

3: LMS 4MT 2-6-0

Arr	Location	Dep	Working
	Loco	05.22	Light
	South Lynn	05.32	Goods
08.05	Norwich City	10.30	Pass
11.19	Melton C	14.46	Goods
16.08	Norwich City	19.45	Goods
22.42	South Lynn		
23.00	Loco		

4: K2 2-6-0

Arr	Location	Dep	Working
	Loco	05.20	Light
	South Lynn	05.30	Goods
10.30	Colwick		
10.40	Colwick Loco	(08.00)	

Alternate with Colwick 1 engine.

5: LMS 4MT 2-6-0

Arr	Location	Dep	Working
	Loco	05.45	Light
	South Lynn	05.55	Goods
12.48	Spalding	12.55	Light
13.00	Spalding loco	17.35	Light
	Spalding	17.45	Pass
18.25	Sutton Bridge	19.35	Goods
20.42	South Lynn		
20.55	Loco		

6: LMS 4MT 2-6-0

Arr	Location	Dep	Working
	Loco	05.52	Light
	South Lynn	06.02	Goods
06.18	Terrington	07.23	Goods
07.40	Sutton Bridge	08.00	Pass
08.41	Spalding	10.00	Goods
12.22	South Lynn	13.20	Goods
13.30	King's Lynn	14.28	Goods
14.38	South Lynn	15.15	Goods
15.30	Gayton Road	16.20	Goods
16.55	South Lynn		
17.10	Loco		

7: LMS 4MT 2-6-0

Arr	Location	Dep	Working
	Loco	06.10	Light
06.25	King's Lynn	06.40	Passenger
06.45	South Lynn	06.50	Passenger
07.56	Spalding	08.15	Passenger
09.16	South Lynn	09.19	Passenger
09.25	King's Lynn	10.13	ECS
10.18	Sputh Lynn	10.30	Light
10.35	King's Lynn	11.13	Passenger
11.18	South Lynn	11.20	Light
11.25	Loco	13.40	Light
14.02	Sutton Bridge	14.15	Goods
14.20	Dock Jcn	14.30	Goods
14.35	Sutton Bridge	17.08	Goods
18.04	South Lynn	20.05	Goods
20.15	King's Lynn	20.40	Light
20.45	Loco		

8 LMS 4MT 2-6-0

Arr	Location	Dep	Working
	Loco	06.35	Light
	South Lynn	07.08	Passenger
08.28	Peterborough N.	08.35	ECS
08.40	Nene CS	08.50	Light
08.55	Spital Bridge loco	10.20	Light
10.25	Peterborough N.	10.33	Yarmouth
12.01	South Lynn	12.05	Light
12.10	Loco	14.09	Light
	South Lynn	14.19	12.45 Peterborough
17.20	Yarmouth B	18.15	Passenger
20.00	Melton C	20.10	Passenger
21.18	South Lynn	21.20	Light
21.30	Loco		

9: K2 2-6-0

Arr	Location	Dep	Working
	Loco	07.20	Light
	South Lynn	07.30	Goods
12.32	Colwick	(08.15)	

Alternate with Colwick 2 engine.

10 LMS 4MT 2-6-0

Arr	Location	Dep	Working
	Loco	07.40	Light
	South Lynn	07.50	Goods
12.58	Wisbech (HSL)	14.05	Goods
14.52	Murrow East	15.30	Goods
18.58	Westwood Yard	19.05	Light
19.15	New England Loco	(11.45)	

Alternate with New England 6 engine.

11 LMS 4MT 2-6-0

Arr	Location	Dep	Working
	Loco	08.08	Light
	South Lynn	08.18	06.45 ex Peterborough
11.05	Yarmouth B.	12.55	Pcls
16.30	South Lynn	16.35	Light
16.45	Loco		

12: D16 4-4-0

Arr	Location	Dep	Working
	Loco	15.40	Light
16.08	King's Lynn	16.21	Passenger
16.26	South Lynn	16.30	Passenger
17.50	Spalding	18.47	16.20 ex Nottingham
19.49	South Lynn	19.52	Passenger
20.00	King's Lynn	20.10	Light
20.15	Exton Road	20.53	Goods
21.03	South Lynn	21.10	Light
21.20	Loco		

13 LMS 4MT 2-6-0

Arr	Location	Dep	Working
	Loco	10.20	Light
	South Lynn	10.30	Goods
13.20	Fakenham West	14.50	Goods
17.24	South Lynn		
17.30	Loco		

14: B12 4-6-0

Arr	Location	Dep	Working
	Loco	11.10	Light
	South Lynn	11.22	09.00 Yarmouth - Birmingham
13.40	Leicester	15.15	13.45 Birmingham - Yarmouth
17.16	South Lynn	17.20	Light
17.30	Loco		

15A: LMS 4MT 2-6-0

Arr	Location	Dep	Working
	Loco	12.35	Light
	South Lynn	12.45	Goods
14.23	Melton C	17.34	Goods
20.23	Yarmouth Beach	20.25	Light
20.30	Yarmouth Loco	(13.50)	

15B: LMS 4MT 2-6-0

Arr	Location	Dep	Working
	Yarmouth Loco	13.50	Light
	Yarmouth Beach	14.00	Goods
14.05	White Swan Yard	14.30	Goods
14.35	Yarmouth Beach	16.00	Goods
17.21	Melton Constable.	17.50	Goods
19.00	South Lynn	19.35	Goods
21.27	Westwood Yard	21.35	Light
21.45	Spital Bridge Loco	23.35	Light
	Crescent Yard	23.45	Goods
03.22	South Lynn	03.25	Light
03.35	Loco		

16: LMS 4MT 2-6-0

Arr	Location	Dep	Working
	Loco	12.40	Light
	South Lynn	13.00	10.05 ex Yarmouth
14.08	Peterborough	14.15	ECS
14.20	Nene CS	14.30	Light
14.35	Spital Bridge Loco	17.30	Light
17.35	Nene CS	17.45	ECS
17.50	Peterborough	17.55	Passenger
19.20	South Lynn	19.22	Passenger
19.27	King's Lynn	20.15	Light
20.20	Harbour Jcn	20.30	Goods
20.35	South Lynn	21.25	Passenger
21.30	King's Lynn	21.55	Light
22.00	South Lynn	22.45	Goods
22.55	King's Lynn	23.25	Goods
23.35	South Lynn	23.40	Light
23.50	Loco		

17: LMS 4MT 2-6-0

Arr	Location	Dep	Working
	Loco	17.01	Light
	South Lynn	17.11	15.40 ex Peterborough
17.18	King's Lynn	17.55	Passenger
18.00	South Lynn	18.03	Passenger
19.38	Peterborough	19.45	ECS
19.50	Nene CS	19.55	Light
20.00	Spital Bridge Loco	22.20	Light
22.25	Spital Bridge Loco	22.35	ECS
22.40	Peterborough	22.45	Passenger
23.52	South Lynn	23.54	Passenger
23.59	King's Lynn	00.20	Light
00.25	Loco		

18: J67 0-6-0T

Arr	Location	Dep	Working
	Loco	22.15	Light
	West Yard		Pilot & Trips
21.30	Loco		

19: J69 0-6-0T

Arr	Location	Dep	Working
	Loco	12.00	Light
	East Yard		Pilot & Trips
04.00	Loco		

COLWICK (NOTTINGHAM) LOCO DIAGRAMS : 1952

1: K2 2-6-0

Arr	Location	Dep	Working
	Loco	06.20	Light
	Colwick	06.40	Goods
11.51	South Lynn	11.55	Light
12.00	S. Lynn Loco	15.48	Light
	South Lynn	15.58	Goods
20.17	Westwood Yard	21.15	Light
22.35	S. Lynn Loco		

2: K2 2-6-0

Arr	Location	Dep	Working
	Loco	08.00	Light
	Colwick	08.15	Goods
13.42	South Lynn	13.45	Light
13.50	S. Lynn Loco		

justification for bending the rules. He would almost certainly cancel the train at Spalding and send a Lynn engine and guard out for it later in the day).

Most of the M&GN's energies went into moving goods traffic which had an excitement of its own but the passenger side of the business at South Lynn was impressive and, thanks to the M&GN's method of working trains, busy. There were times of the day at South Lynn when a spectator had difficulty in keeping up with the number of trains yet move ten miles down the line towards Melton Constable and it was difficult to believe you were on the same railway.

Much of South Lynn's activity arose because the M&GN believed in staging its engines which meant that almost every train that called, changed engines. The intention was to keep engines within arm's reach of their owning depot and, as a result, reduce maintenance costs and the incidence of failure.

One by-product of this policy was to ensure that Peterborough engines were never seen in Yarmouth (nor, indeed, east of South Lynn) and that Yarmouth engines did not visit Peterborough. In fact only Melton and Lynn engines visited both extremities of the system whilst the latter had the added kudos of running its engines to Nottingham and Leicester.

Another was to make South Lynn a much busier place than it might otherwise have been been: witness the events that took place between eight and nine each morning.

At 08.02 the 06.45 Peterborough - Yarmouth arrived, its BR4

SOUTH LYNN YARD (1952)

Train	Arrive	Loco	Diagram	Depart	Destination
		K2 2-6-0	South Lynn 1	03.20	Peterborough
23.45 Peterborough	03.22	LM4 2-6-0	South Lynn 15B		
		LM4 2-6-0	South Lynn 2	04.00	King's Lynn
		K2 2-6-0	South Lynn 4	05.30	Colwick
		LM4 2-6-0	South Lynn 3	05.32	Norwich City
05.30 King's Lynn	05.40	LM4 2-6-0	South Lynn 2		
		LM4 2-6-0	South Lynn 5	05.55	Spalding
		LM4 2-6-0	South Lynn 6	06.02	Sutton Bridge
		LM4 2-6-0	South Lynn 2	06.30	Cromer Beach
05.40 Melton C.	07.28	LM4 2-6-0	Melton C. 1		
		K2 2-6-0	South Lynn 9	07.30	Colwick
		J67 0-6-0T	South Lynn 18	07.30	King's Lynn
		LM4 2-6-0	South Lynn 10	07.50	Peterborough
08.45 King's Lynn	08.55	J67 0-6-0T	South Lynn 18		
		LM4 2-6-0	Melton C. 1	09.10	Norwich City
07.15 Peterborough	09.34	K2 2-6-0	South Lynn 1		
		LM4 2-6-0	Melton C. 9	09.40	Melton C.
		LM4 2-6-0	South Lynn 13	10.30	Fakenham W.
05.50 Melton C.	10.58	LM4 2-6-0	Melton C. 2		
06.40 Colwick	11.51	K2 2-6-0	Colwick2		
10.00 Spalding	12.22	LM4 2-6-0	South Lynn 6		
		LM4 2-6-0	South Lynn 15A	12.45	Norwich
07.15 Spalding	12.55	J6 0-6-0	Spalding 3		
13.00 King's Lynn	13.05	LM4 2-6-0	Spalding 4		
		LM4 2-6-0	South Lynn 6	13.20	King's Lynn
08.15 Colwick	13.42	K2 2-6-0	Colwick2		
		LM4 2-6-0	Spalding 4	13.50	Long Sutton
		LM4 2-6-0	Melton C. 2	14.35	Melton C.
14.30 King's Lynn	14.38	LM4 2-6-0	South Lynn 6		
		LM4 2-6-0	South Lynn 6	15.15	Gayton Road
07.45 Peterborough	15.15	LM4 2-6-0	New England 4		
		K2 2-6-0	Colwick1	15.58	Peterborough
16.20 Gayton Road	16.55	LM4 2-6-0	South Lynn 6		
14.50 Fakenham West	17.21	LM4 2-6-0	South Lynn 13		
17.08 Sutton Bridge	18.04	LM4 2-6-0	South Lynn 4		
16.20 Melton C.	18.32	LM4 2-6-0	Melton C. 9		
16.00 Yarmouth	19.00	LM4 2-6-0	South Lynn 15B	(19.35)	
12.20 Peterborough	19.05	J6 0-6-0	New England 6		
	(19.00)	LM4 2-6-0	South Lynn 15B	19.35	Peterborough
		LM4 2-6-0	Melton C. 9	19.45	Melton C.
		LM4 2-6-0	South Lynn 7	20.05	King's Lynn
20.25 Harbour Jcn	20.35	LM4 2-6-0	South Lynn 16		
19.02 Melton C.	20.42	LM4 2-6-0	South Lynn 2		
19.35 Sutton Bridge	20.42	LM4 2-6-0	South Lynn 5		
18.10 Peterborough	20.50	LM4 2-6-0	New England 2		
20.50 Exton Road	21.03	D16 4-4-0	South Lynn 12		
20.25 Peterborough	22.30	K2 2-6-0	South Lynn 1		
19.45 Norwich City	22.46	LM4 2-6-0	South Lynn 3		
22.45 King's Lynn	22.55	LM4 2-6-0	South Lynn 16		
		LM4 2-6-0	New England 2	23.05	Peterborough
		LM4 2-6-0	South Lynn 16	23.25	King's Lynn

SOUTH LYNN - 1952

Train	Arrive	Loco	Shed	Stock	Depart	Destination
05.10 Peterborough	06.17	LM4 2-6-0	New Eng 1	2/4+1	06.23	King's Lynn
06.40 King's Lynn	06.45	LM4 2-6-0	S. Lynn 7	37/2	06.50	Nottingham
06.53 King's Lynn ECS	06.58	LM4 2-6-0	New Eng 1	2/4+1	(07.08)	(Change engine)
(Change engine)	(06.58)	LM4 2-6-0	S. Lynn 8	2/4	07.08	Peterborough
06.45 Peterborough	08.02	LM4 2-6-0	New Eng 3	9/4 + 2	(08.18)	(Change engine)
08.00 King's Lynn	08.05	C12 4-4-2T	K. Lynn 1	1/2 (PP)	08.15	King's Lynn
(Change engine)	(08.02)	LM4 2-6-0	S. Lynn 11	9/4 + 2	08.18	Yarmouth
07.30 Melton Constable	08.35	LM4 2-6-0	Melton C. 9	11/4	(08.45)	(Change engine)
08.33 King's Lynn	08.38	C12 4-4-2T	K. Lynn 1	1/2 (PP)	08.45	King's Lynn
(Change engine)	(08.35)	LM4 2-6-0	New Eng 1	11/4	08.45	Peterborough
07.40 Bourne	09.19	LM4 2-6-0	S. Lynn 7	25/3	09.21	King's Lynn
06.51 Yarmouth	09.45	B12 4-6-0	Yarmouth 4	4/4	(09.55)	(Change engine)
09.44 King's Lynn	09.49	C12 4-4-2T	K. Lynn 1	1/2 (PP)	09.55	King's Lynn
(Change engine)	(09.45)	LM4 2-6-0	New Eng 3	4/4	09.55	Peterborough
10.13 King's Lynn ECS	10.18	LM4 2-6-0	S. Lynn 7	5		For 11.22/14.45
	(10.18)	LM4 2-6-0	S. Lynn 7		10.30	Light to Kings Lynn
10.30 King's Lynn ECS	10.35	C12 4-4-2T	K. Lynn 1	1/2 (PP)	(11.22)	
08.15 Lowestoft	11.16	D16 4-4-0	Melton C. 3	37/5	(11.22)	(Change engine)
11.13 King's Lynn	11.18	LM4 2-6-0	S. Lynn 7	38/3	(11.28)	(Change engine)
(Change engine)	(11.16)	B12 4-6-0	S. Lynn 14	37/6	11.22	Birmingham NS
	(10.35)	C12 4-4-2T	K. Lynn 1	1/2 (PP)	11.28	King's Lynn
	(11.18)	D16 4-4-0	Melton C. 3	38/3	11.28	Peterborough
11.55 King's Lynn	12.00	C12 4-4-2T	K. Lynn 1	1/2 (PP)	(12.11)	
10.33 Peterborough	12.01	LM4 2-6-0	S. Lynn 8	2/4	(12.14)	(Change engine)
	(12.00)	C12 4-4-2T	K. Lynn 1	1/2 (PP)	12.11	King's Lynn
(Change engine)	(12.01)	B12 4-6-0	Yarmouth 4	2/4	12.14	Yarmouth
09.55 Saxby	12.32	LM4 2-6-0	Spalding 4	30/3	12.35	King's Lynn
10.05 Yarmouth	12.53	B12 4-6-0	Yarmouth 6	5/4	(13.00)	(Change engine)
12.50 King's Lynn	12.55	C12 4-4-2T	K. Lynn 1	1/2 (PP)	(13.05)	
(Change engine)	(12.53)	LM4 2-6-0	S. Lynn 16	5/4	13.00	Peterborough
	(12.55)	C12 4-4-2T	K. Lynn 1	1/2 (PP)	13.05	King's Lynn
12.45 Peterborough	14.11	LM4 2-6-0	New Eng 1	4/4	(14.19)	(Change engine)
14.09 King's Lynn	14.14	C12 4-4-2T	K. Lynn 1	1/2 (PP)	(14.20)	
(Change engine)	(14.11)	LM4 2-6-0	S. Lynn 8	4/4	14.19	Yarmouth
	(14.14)	C12 4-4-2T	K. Lynn 1	1/2 (PP)	14.20	King's Lynn
	(10.18)	LM4 2-6-0	New Eng 1	7/4	14.45	Pcls Wisbech North
12.42 Yarmouth	15.28	D16 4-4-0	Melton C. 10	6/4 + 1	(15.31)	
15.25 King's Lynn	15.30	C12 4-4-2T	K. Lynn 1	1/2 (PP)	(15.40)	
	(15.28)	D16 4-4-0	Melton C. 10	6/4 + 1	15.31	Peterborough
	(15.30)	C12 4-4-2T	K. Lynn 1	1/2 (PP)	15.40	King's Lynn
16.21 King's Lynn	16.26	D16 4-4-0	S. Lynn 12	30/3	16.30	Nottingham
12.55 Yarmouth (Pcls)	16.30	LM4 2-6-0	S. Lynn 11	Vans	(16.38)	(Change engine)
(Change engine)	(16.30)	LM4 2-6-0	S. Lynn 11	Vans	16.38	Peterborough
13.20 Yarmouth V (Pcls)	17.00	J6 0-6-0	Spalding 3	5/4	(17.15)	
15.40 Peterborough	17.06	D16 4-4-0	Melton C. 3	5/4	(17.11)	(Change engine)
17.05 King's Lynn	17.10	C12 4-4-2T	K. Lynn 1	1/2 (PP)	(17.22)	
	(17.06)	LM4 2-6-0	S. Lynn 17	5/4	17.11	King's Lynn
	(17.00)	J6 0-6-0	Spalding 3	Vans	17.15	Spalding
13.45 Birmingham	17.16	B12 4-6-0	S. Lynn 14	37/6	(17.24)	(Change engine)
	(17.10)	C12 4-4-2T	K. Lynn 1	1/2 (PP)	17.22	King's Lynn
	(17.16)	B12 4-6-0	Yarmouth 6	37/5	17.24	Lowestoft
17.50 King's Lynn	17.55	LM4 2-6-0	S. Lynn 17	3/4	(18.01)	(Change engine)
17.55 King's Lynn	18.00	LM4 2-6-0	S. Lynn 17	3/4	(18.03)	
(Change engine)	(17.55)	D16 4-4-0	Melton C. 3	3/4	18.01	Yarmouth
	(18.00)	LM4 2-6-0	S. Lynn 17	3/4	18.03	Peterborough
17.55 Peterborough	19.20	LM4 2-6-0	S. Lynn 16	38/3	19.22	King's Lynn
16.20 Nottingham	19.49	D16 4-4-0	S. Lynn 12	29/3	19.52	King's Lynn
19.15 Norwich	21.18	LM4 2-6-0	S. Lynn 8	10/4 + 1	(21.25)	(Change engine)
(Change engine)	(21.18)	LM4 2-6-0	S. Lynn 16	10/4 + 1	21.25	King's Lynn
21.25 King's Lynn	21.30	C12 4-4-2T	K. Lynn 1	1/2 (PP)		
20.10 Peterborough	21.33	D16 4-4-0	Melton C. 10	7/4	21.40	Melton Constable
	(21.30)	C12 4-4-2T	K. Lynn 1	1/2 (PP)	21.45	King's Lynn
22.45 Peterborough	23.52	LM4 2-6-0	S. Lynn 17	11/4	23.54	King's Lynn

2-6-0 being uncoupled and run to the shed to turn for the 06.51 Yarmouth - Peterborough. At 08.05 the push and pull from King's Lynn ran in with its C12 4-4-2T and a few minutes later an LM4 2-6-0 arrived from the shed to work the Yarmouth train forward. At 08.15 the push and pull returned to King's Lynn and at 08.18 the 06.45 ex Peterborough pulled out of the station. The pattern was then repeated a quarter of an hour later (and many times a day after that) with the arrival of the 07.30 Melton Constable - Peterborough.

With trains of only three and four coaches for the most part, double-heading was not a regular feature of M&GN operations although it was freely permitted over the M&GN except for crossing of the Ouse bridge which lay a short distance to the West of South Lynn station. In the event of an up train needing assistance, the pilot had to run light to West Lynn on the far side of the Ouse and wait at the advance starter. The train then followed (as best it could) with a shunter on board to draw up clear of the level crossing at West Lynn. at which point the

SOUTH LYNN FOOTPLATEMEN'S TURNS OF DUTY (1950/1)

SOUTH LYNN 1

On Duty	02.10			
Prepare				SL1/K2
S. Lynn Loco	03.10	Light		SL1/K2
South Lynn (E. Yard)	03.20	Goods		SL1/K2
05.47	P'boro (Westwood)	05.55	Light	SL1/K2
06.05	Spital Bridge Loco	07.00	Light	SL1/K2
	Crescent Yard	07.15	Goods	SL1/K2
09.34	South Lynn (W. Yard)	09.45	Light	SL1/K2
09.55	S. Lynn Loco			
10.10	Off Duty			

SOUTH LYNN 2

On Duty	02.50			
Prepare				SL2/LM4
S. Lynn Loco	03.50	Light		SL2/LM4
South Lynn (W. Yard)	04.00	Goods		SL2/LM4
04.10	King's Lynn	05.30	Goods	SL2/LM4
05.40	South Lynn (W. Yard)	06.30	Goods	SL2/LM4
08.21	Melton C.	08.36		Pass
09.45	South Lynn			
10.50	Off Duty			

SOUTH LYNN 3

On Duty	05.20			
Prepare				SL7/LM4
S. Lynn Loco	06.10	Light		SL7/LM4
06.25	King's Lynn	06.40	Passenger	SL7/LM4
06.45	South Lynn	06.50	Passenger	SL7/LM4
07.56	Spalding	08.15	Passenger	SL7/LM4
09.16	South Lynn	09.19	Passenger	SL7/LM4
09.25	King's Lynn	10.13	ECS	SL7/LM4
10.18	Sputh Lynn	10.30	Light	SL7/LM4
10.35	King's Lynn	11.13	Passenger	SL7/LM4
11.18	South Lynn			
	Prepare			SL7/LM4
13.20	Off Duty			

SOUTH LYNN 4

On Duty	04.20			
Prepare				SL4/K2
S. Lynn Loco	06.10	Light		SL4/K2
South Lynn (E. Yard)	05.30	Goods		SL4/K2
08.40	Sleaford	09.00	Goods	CC1/K2
11.51	South Lynn (W. Yard)	11.55	Light	CC1/K2
12.00	S. Lynn Loco			
12.20	Off Duty			

SOUTH LYNN 5

On Duty	04.52			
Prepare				SL6/LM4
S. Lynn Loco	05.52	Light		SL6/LM4
South Lynn (E. Yard)	06.02	Goods		SL6/LM4
06.18	Terrington	07.23	Goods	SL6/LM4
07.40	Sutton Bridge	08.00	Pass	SL6/LM4
08.41	Spalding	10.00	Goods	SL6/LM4
12.22	South Lynn (W. Yard)		Relieved	
12.52	Off Duty			

SOUTH LYNN 6

On Duty	05.07			
Prepare				SL3/LM4
S. Lynn Loco	05.22	Light		SL3/LM4
South Lynn (E. Yard)	05.32	Goods		SL3/LM4
08.05	Norwich City	10.30	Pass	SL3/LM4
11.19	Melton C	11.25	Light	SL3/LM4
11.30	Melton Loco	11.45		Pass
12.53	South Lynn			
13.07	Off Duty			

SOUTH LYNN 7

On Duty	06.55			
Prepare				SL11/LM4
S. Lynn Loco	08.08	Light		SL11/LM4
08.13	South Lynn	08.18		Pass
08.46	Massingham	09.25	Goods	MC2/LM4
10.58	South Lynn (E. Yard)			
	As Required			
14.55	Off Duty			

SOUTH LYNN 8

On Duty	05.30			
S. Lynn Loco	05.45	Light		SL5/LM4
South Lynn	05.55	Goods		SL5/LM4
10.02	Fleet	10.25	Goods	SP3/J6
12.55	South Lynn (W. Yard)	13.00	Light	SP3/J6
13.10	S. Lynn Loco			
13.30	Off Duty			

SOUTH LYNN 9

On Duty	05.35			
Prepare				SL8/LM4
S. Lynn Loco	06.35	Light		SL8/LM4
South Lynn	07.08	Passenger		SL8/LM4
08.28	Peterborough N.	08.35	ECS	SL8/LM4
08.40	Nene CS	08.50	Light	SL8/LM4
08.55	Spital Bridge loco	10.20	Light	SL8/LM4
10.25	Peterborough N.	10.33	Yarmouth	SL8/LM4
12.01	South Lynn	12.05	Light	SL8/LM4
12.10	S. Lynn Loco			
13.35	Off Duty			

SOUTH LYNN 10

On Duty	05.35			
Prepare				SL9/K2
S. Lynn Loco	07.20	Light		SL9/K2
South Lynn (E. Yard)	07.30	Goods		SL9/K2
10.22	Spalding	10.40	Goods	CC2/K2
13.42	South Lynn (W. Yard)	13.45	Light	CC2/K2
13.50	S. Lynn Loco			
14.00	Off Duty			

SOUTH LYNN 11

On Duty	06.40			
Prepare				SL10/LM4
S. Lynn Loco	07.40	Light		SL10/LM4
South Lynn (E. Yard)	07.50	Goods		SL10/LM4
13.03	Horse Shoe Lane		Relieved	
	Wisbech North	13.29		Pass
14.11	South Lynn			
14.40	Off Duty			

SOUTH LYNN 12

On Duty	07.58			
South Lynn	08.18	Passenger		SL11/LM4
11.05	Yarmouth B.	12.55	Parcels	SL11/LM4
16.30	South Lynn	16.35	Light	SL11/LM4
16.45	S. Lynn Loco			
16.55	Off Duty			

SOUTH LYNN 13

On Duty	09.20			
Prepare				SL13/LM4
S. Lynn Loco	10.20	Light		SL13/LM4
South Lynn (W. Yard)	10.30	Goods		SL13/LM4
13.20	Fakenham West	14.50	Goods	SL13/LM4
17.24	South Lynn (E. Yard)	17.25	Light	SL13/LM4
17.30	S. Lynn Loco			
17.40	Off Duty			

SOUTH LYNN 14

On Duty	10.10			
Prepare				SL14/B12
S. Lynn Loco	11.10	Light		SL14/B12
South Lynn	11.22	Passenger		SL14/B12
13.40	Leicester (LR)	15.15	Passenger	SL14/B12
17.16	South Lynn	17.20	Light	SL14/B12
17.30	S. Lynn Loco			
18.10	Off Duty			

SOUTH LYNN 15

On Duty	11.08			
South Lynn	11.28			Pass
12.04	Wisbech North			
	Horse Shoe Lane	13.47	Goods	NE4/LM4
15.15	South Lynn (W. Yard)			
	South Lynn	16.38		Pass
17.56	Tydd	18.03	Goods	NE6/LM4
19.05	South Lynn (W. Yard)	19.10	Light	NE6/LM4
19.15	S. Lynn Loco			
19.25	Off Duty			

SOUTH LYNN 16

On Duty	11.35			
Prepare				SL15A/LM4
S. Lynn Loco	12.35	Light		SL15A/LM4
South Lynn (W. Yard)	12.45	Goods		SL15A/LM4
14.23	Melton Constable	17.50	Goods	SL15B/LM4
19.00	South Lynn (W. Yard)		Relieved	
19.35	Off Duty			

SOUTH LYNN 17

On Duty	11.40			
Prepare				SL16/LM4
S. Lynn Loco	12.40	Light		SL16/LM4
South Lynn	13.00	Passenger		SL16/LM4
14.08	Peterborough	14.15	ECS	SL16/LM4
14.20	Nene CS	14.30	Light	SL16/LM4
14.35	Spital Bridge Loco	17.30	Light	SL16/LM4
17.35	Nene CS	17.45	ECS	SL16/LM4
17.50	Peterborough	17.55	Passenger	SL16/LM4
19.20	South Lynn		Relieved	
19.40	Off Duty			

SOUTH LYNN 18

On Duty	12.05			
South Lynn (W. Yard)	13.20	Goods		SL6/LM4
13.30	King's Lynn	14.28	Goods	SL6/LM4
14.38	South Lynn (E. Yard)		Light	SL6/LM4
	South Lynn (W. Yard)	15.15	Goods	SL6/LM4
15.30	Gayton Road	16.20	Goods	SL6/LM4
16.55	South Lynn (E. Yard)	17.00	Light	SL6/LM4
17.10	S. Lynn Loco			
	As required			
20.05	Off Duty			

SOUTH LYNN 19

On Duty	13.09			
Prepare				SL8/LM4
12.10	S. Lynn Loco	14.09	Light	SL8/LM4
14.14	South Lynn	14.19	Passenger	SL8/LM4
17.20	Yarmouth B	18.15	Passenger	SL8/LM4
20.00	Melton C	20.10	Passenger	SL8/LM4
21.18	South Lynn		Relieved	
21.28	Off Duty			

SOUTH LYNN 20

On Duty	13.25			
	S. Lynn Loco	13.40	Light	SL7/LM4
14.02	Sutton Bridge	14.15	Goods	SL7/LM4
14.20	Dock Jcn	14.30	Goods	SL7/LM4
14.35	Sutton Bridge	17.08	Goods	SL7/LM4
18.04	South Lynn	20.05	Goods	SL7/LM4
20.15	King's Lynn	20.40	Light	SL7/LM4
20.45	S. Lynn Loco			
21.25	Off Duty			

SOUTH LYNN 21

On Duty	13.25			
Prepare				MC2/LM4
S. Lynn Loco	14.25	Light		MC2/LM4
14.30	South Lynn (E. Yard)	14.35	Goods	MC2/LM4
16.29	Melton Constable	19.05	Goods	SL2/LM4
20.42	South Lynn	20.50	Light	SL2/LM4
21.00	Loco			
21.25	Off Duty			

SOUTH LYNN 22

On Duty	14.40			
Prepare				SL1/K2
S. Lynn Loco	15.40	Light		SL1/K2
15.45	South Lynn	15.50	ECS	SL1/K2
16.10	Sutton Bridge	16.45	Goods	SL1/K2
19.06	Wisbech Jcn	19.10	Light	SL1/K2
19.15	Spital Bridge Loco	20.10	Light	SL1/K2
20.15	Crescent Yard	20.25	Goods	SL1/K2
22.30	South Lynn	22.35	Light	SL1/K2
22.40	Loco			
22.50	Off Duty			

SOUTH LYNN FOOTPLATEMEN'S TURNS OF DUTY (1950/1)

SOUTH LYNN 23

Arr	Location	Dep	Work	Engine
	On Duty	15.03		
	Prepare			SL12/D16
	S. Lynn Loco	15.40	Light	SL12/D16
16.08	King's Lynn	16.21	Passenger	SL12/D16
16.26	South Lynn	16.30	Passenger	SL12/D16
17.50	Spalding	18.47	Passenger	SL12/D16
19.49	South Lynn	19.52	Passenger	SL12/D16
20.00	King's Lynn	20.10	Light	SL12/D16
20.15	Exton Road	20.53	Goods	SL12/D16
21.03	South Lynn	21.10	Light	SL12/D16
21.20	Loco			
23.03	Off Duty			

SOUTH LYNN 24

Arr	Location	Dep	Work	Engine
	On Duty	15.20		
	Prepare			SP3/J6
13.10	S. Lynn Loco	16.20	Light	SP3/J6
16.25	Kings Lynn	16.55	Pcls	SP3/J6
18.06	Sutton Bridge	19.35	Goods	SL5/LM4
20.42	South Lynn	20.45	Light	SL5/LM4
20.55	Loco			
23.20	Off Duty			

SOUTH LYNN 25

Arr	Location	Dep	Work	Engine
	On Duty	15.33		
12.00	S. Lynn Loco	15.48	Light	CC1/K2
	South Lynn (E. Yard)	15.58	Goods	CC1/K2
20.17	Westwood Yard	21.15	Light	CC1/K2
22.35	S. Lynn Loco			
23.33	Off Duty			

SOUTH LYNN 26

Arr	Location	Dep	Work	Engine
	On Duty	15.55		
	Prepare			SL17/LM4
	S. Lynn Loco	17.01	Light	SL17/LM4
	South Lynn	17.11	Passenger	SL17/LM4
17.18	King's Lynn	17.55	Passenger	SL17/LM4
18.00	South Lynn	19.22	Passenger	SL16/LM4
19.27	King's Lynn	20.15	Light	SL16/LM4
20.20	Harbour Jcn	20.30	Goods	SL16/LM4
20.35	South Lynn (E. Yard)	20.40	Light	SL16/LM4
20.45	South Lynn	21.25	Passenger	SL16/LM4
21.30	King's Lynn	21.55	Light	SL16/LM4
22.00	South Lynn	22.45	Goods	SL16/LM4
22.55	King's Lynn	23.25	Goods	SL16/LM4
23.35	South Lynn	23.40	Light	SL16/LM4
23.50	S. Lynn Loco			
00.00	Off Duty			

SOUTH LYNN 27

Arr	Location	Dep	Work	Engine
	On Duty	16.46		
	South Lynn	18.01	Pass	MC3/D16
19.05	Melton Constable	19.07	Light	MC3/D16
19.15	Melton Loco			
	Melton Constable	21.02	Goods	SL3/LM4
22.46	South Lynn (E. Yard)	22.50	Light	SL3/LM4
23.00	S. Lynn Loco			
00.46	Off Duty			

SOUTH LYNN 28

Arr	Location	Dep	Work	Engine
	On Duty	17.40		
	South Lynn	18.03	Passenger	SL17/LM4
19.38	Peterborough	19.45	ECS	SL17/LM4
19.50	Nene CS	19.55	Light	SL17/LM4
20.00	Spital Bridge Loco	22.20	Light	SL17/LM4
22.25	Spital Bridge Loco	22.35	ECS	SL17/LM4
22.40	Peterborough	22.45	Passenger	SL17/LM4
23.52	South Lynn	23.54	Passenger	SL17/LM4
23.59	King's Lynn	00.20	Light	SL17/LM4
00.25	S. Lynn Loco			
01.40	Off Duty			

SOUTH LYNN 29

Arr	Location	Dep	Work	Engine
	On Duty	19.10		
19.00	South Lynn (E. Yard)	19.35	Goods	SL29/LM4
21.27	Westwood Yard	21.35	Light	SL29/LM4
21.45	Spital Bridge Loco	23.35	Light	SL29/LM4
23.40	Crescent Yard	23.45	Goods	SL29/LM4
03.22	South Lynn (W. Yard)	03.25	Light	SL29/LM4
03.35	S. Lynn Loco			
03.45	Off Duty			

SOUTH LYNN 30A

Arr	Location	Dep	Work	Engine
	On Duty	05.30		
	West Yard Pilot			SL18/J67
13.30	Off Duty			

SOUTH LYNN 30B

Arr	Location	Dep	Work	Engine
	On Duty	13.00		
	West Yard Pilot			SL18/J67
21.00	Off Duty			

SOUTH LYNN 30C

Arr	Location	Dep	Work	Engine
	On Duty	20.30		
	West Yard Pilot			SL18/J67
04.30	Off Duty			

SOUTH LYNN 31A

Arr	Location	Dep	Work	Engine
	On Duty	11.45		
	S. Lynn Loco	12.00	Light	SL19/J69
	East Yard Pilot			SL19/J69
19.45	Off Duty			

SOUTH LYNN 31B

Arr	Location	Dep	Work	Engine
	On Duty	20.00		
	East Yard Pilot	03.45	Light	SL19/J69
03.50	S. Lynn Loco			SL19/J69
04.00	Off Duty			

---

pilot engine backed down and coupled up under the direction of the shunter. In the opposite direction, double-headed trains stopped at West Lynn for the pilot to be uncoupled and to run ahead light to South Lynn. The alternative method of providing two engines on a train - banking - where the assisting engine pushed at the rear was prohibited throughout the M&GN except for the short section (Sutton Bridge Junction to Sutton Bridge Station boxes) through Sutton Bridge station.

The motive power element of South Lynn was no less interesting than the working of traffic and, for the LNER, had a high degree of standardisation thanks to the arrival in 1950 of a batch of LMS 4MT 2-6-0's. The arrival of these modern engines - of strange appearance with their edges and corners until one grew used to them - had the effect of bringing South Lynn into the grouping since up to the arrival of the LMS engines, the allocation had consisted entirely of pre-grouping engines. In late 1950, for example, the passenger work had been covered by four B12 4-6-0 and four D16 'Claud' 4-4-0's whilst goods traffic had been handled by nine J17 0-6-0's with the heavier work being shouldered by K2 2-6-0's and J19 0-6-0's. Shunting duties and the local passenger service to King's Lynn had been handled by equally venerable museum pieces.

Two years later the picture had changed completely although not all the imports were brand new! Someone decided that the local service between King's Lynn and South Lynn would be suitable for push and pull operation and duly arranged for the two-coach set that had been used on the short-lived Marylebone - Ruislip service to come to King's Lynn to take over the working. Accompanying the set were a pair of elderly C12 4-4-2's that had been engaged on the Alexandra Palace motor train.

Such matters could not hide the difference that the LMS 2-6-0's made to the South Lynn allocation and by October 1952 the D16 4-4-0's, the K2 2-6-0's and the J19's were down to one each whilst the J17's had disappeared altogether. Melton Constable, Yarmouth Beach and the M&GN element of New England were similarly re-equipped with the result that the M&GN, for so long a poor relative, suddenly

---

LOCAL SERVICE : SOUTH LYNN - KING'S LYNN (1952)

Train			05.10					07.40					09.55		
From			P'boro					Bourne					Saxby		
Class	Goods	Light	Pass	Goods	Motor	Motor	Pass	Motor	Light	Motor	Motor	Pass	Motor	Goods	Motor
Engine	SL2	SL7	NE1	SL18	KL11	KL11	SL7	KL11	SL7	KL11	KL11	SP4	KL11	SL6	KL11
Class	LM4	LM4	LM4	J67	C12	C12	LM4	C12	LM4	C12	C12	LM4	C12	LM4	C12
SOUTH LYNN	04.00	06.20	06.23	07.30	08.15	08.45	09.21	09.55	10.30	11.22	12.11	12.35	13.05	13.20	14.20
KING'S LYNN	04.10	06.25	06.28	07.40	08.20	08.50	09.26	10.00	10.35	11.27	12.16	12.40	13.10	13.30	14.25

Train															
From															
Class	Light	Goods	Pass	ECS	Motor	Motor	Goods	Motor	ECS	PP(ECS)	Pass	Motor	Motor	Light	Motor
Egine	SL17	SL2	SL7	NE1	KL11	KL11	SL18	KL11	SL7	KL11	SL7	KL11	KL11	SP4	KL11
Shed	LM4	LM4	LM4	LM4	C12	C12	J67	C12	LM4	C12	LM4	C12	C12	LM4	C12
KING'S LYNN	00.17	05.30	06.40	06.53	08.00	08.33	08.45	09.44	10.13	10.30	11.13	11.55	12.50	13.00	14.09
SOUTH LYNN	00.22	05.40	06.45	06.58	08.05	08.38	08.55	09.49	10.18	10.35	11.18	12.00	12.55	13.05	14.14
Destination	Loco		Notts								P'bro				

Train			15.40			17.55	16.20		19.15				22.45	
From			P'boro			P'boro	Notts		Norwich				P'bro	
Class	Motor	Light	Light	Pass	Motor	Light	Light	Pass	Pass	Goods	Pass	Motor	Goods	Pass
Engine	KL11	SL12	SP3	SL17	KL11	SL18	KL6	SL16	SL12	SL7	SL16	KL11	SL16	SL17
Class	C12	D16	J6	LM4	C12	J67	D16	LM4	D16	LM4	LM4	C12	LM4	LM4
SOUTH LYNN	15.40	16.03	16.20	17.11	17.22	17.30	18.10	19.22	19.52	20.05	21.25	21.45	22.45	23.54
KING'S LYNN	15.45	16.08	16.25	17.16	17.27	17.35	18.15	19.27	19.57	20.15	21.30	21.50	22.55	23.59

Train			13.20											
From			Vaux											
Class	Goods	Motor	Pass	Pcls	Motor	Pass	Pass	Goods	Goods	Light	Goods	Motor	Light	Goods
Egine	SL6	KL11	SL12	SP3	KL11	KL6	SL17	SL18	SL16	SL7	SL12	KL11	SL16	SL16
Shed	LM4	C12	D16	J6	C12	D16	LM4	J67	LM4	LM4	LM4	C12	LM4	LM4
KING'S LYNN	14.30	15.25	16.21	16.55	17.05	17.50	17.55	18.15	20.25	20.40	20.50	21.25	21.55	23.25
SOUTH LYNN	14.40	15.30	16.26	17.00	17.10	17.55	18.00	18.25	20.35	20.50	21.00	21.30	22.00	23.35
Destination			Notts			Yar	P'bro							

J6 0-6-0 64198 (New England) pulls away from the East Yard and enters South Lynn station with the 08.25 to Peterborough, Westwood Yard, on Saturday 7th August 1954. Normally such trains were worked by K2 or 4MT 2-6-0's but on Saturdays when engines were at a premium, trains of empty wagons tended to take whatever could be spared. (V. R. Webster / Kidderminster Railway Museum).

became the most modern railway - at least in motive power terms - in East Anglia. This did not mean that the old order was swept away entirely since Melton and Yarmouth retained their D16 4-4-0's and B12 4-6-0's for their passenger workings and the late afternoon at South Lynn had a distinct LNER - if not GER - atmosphere well into the 1950's.

Even without the engine-changing, the passenger service at South Lynn was of considerable interest. The station consisted of two island platforms, the outer faces dealing with up and down services whilst the centre road - convenient for both up and down connections - was used mainly by the push and pull to King's Lynn. A handful of Peterborough trains ran to King's Lynn instead of Yarmouth but one, the 15.40 from Peterborough, managed to do both by arriving at King's Lynn at 17.15 and forming the 17.55 to Yarmouth. The associated engine working was interesting since the same D16 4-4-0 that worked the service from Peterborough to South Lynn, worked it from South Lynn to Melton Constable whilst an LM4 2-6-0 worked the *interregnum* to King's Lynn and back.

The working of the day was the Leicester which changed from D16 to B12 in the morning and then from B12 to B12 on the return journey in the afternoon. As described elsewhere, the D16 that worked the morning train from Yarmouth was later superseded by a B12 which for a couple of years from mid-1952 made the Leicester the sole domain of B12's; a connection broken in October 1954 when South Lynn lost its allocation of B12's.

The South Lynn B12's did not spend all their time wallowing in the glory of the Leicester since in early 1952 the working of

the 18.02 South Lynn to Yarmouth (17.55 ex King's Lynn) was transferred from Melton to South Lynn. Casting around for an engine to work the train, the Leicester engine, which only worked a six-hour day - presented itself as an obvious candidate and perforce was made to leave South Lynn with the Yarmouth train, which it worked as far as Melton Constable, three-quarters of an hour after arriving with the Leicester.

It was pleasant to stand at Massingham and see two B12 4-6-0's pass through in the space of an hour but less satisfying was the sight of one on the 19.45 Norwich - South Lynn goods; the return working of the 18.02 from South Lynn. The Great North of Scotland may have used the class on all sorts of strange workings but to the M&GN, the B12's were special.

In addition to being worked by B12 4-6-0's, the Leicester was unique in that it conveyed a buffet car which was attached to the train at South Lynn and ran as far as Leicester, returning later in the day with the eastbound service. On Fridays the car continued forward to Yarmouth and worked from Yarmouth to Leicester and back until the down service on Monday when it reverted to South Lynn. In the summer of 1956, by which time the train was in the hands of LMS 2-6-0's, the service was revised in that it was diverted to call at Spalding where the change of engines took place during the reversal. The engine to work the train came in with the 09.33 stopping train from King's Lynn. To avoid further complications, the dining car working was reallocated from South Lynn to Yarmouth and worked from Yarmouth to Leicester and back each day of the week. The car used was E668E which had been built as a

First Class Restaurant car by the Great Eastern and had been rebuilt by the LNER circa 1934.

Next to the B12's, perhaps the most noticeable engines at South Lynn were the Great Northern K2 2-6-0's which had arrived in 1947 as a stop-gap until something more suitable - and more modern - could be found. Their principal duties included the two day diagram that covered the 16.00 Yarmouth - Peterborough express goods and the South Lynn - Colwick services upon which they worked turn and turn about with a pair of Colwick engines.

This was one of the few instances where local engines went beyond the reach of M&GN control for any period of time and the working always carried the risk that some *contretemps* in Nottingham would result in the South Lynn engine being used on a train to Manchester or York whilst something even worse than a Ragtimer was sent back in the diagram to South Lynn.

The arrival of the LMS 2-6-0's saw the K2's gradually drift away from the area and the last left South Lynn for Lincoln in October 1953.

Another instance of a shared working was the record-breaking 07.50 South Lynn - Peterborough goods which took over eleven hours to cover the thirty-eight miles and arrived too late to be given a return working. The engine therefore stayed overnight at New England and returned the next day with the 11.45 Peterborough - South Lynn goods which, in contrast to the 07.50, flew back in seven and a quarter hours.

South Lynn may not have been the busiest station in Norfolk but from both the perspective of traffic and motive power, it was certainly one of the most interesting.

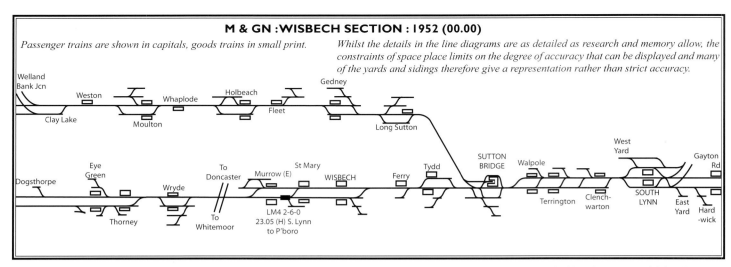

M & GN : WISBECH SECTION : 1952 (00.00)

Passenger trains are shown in capitals, goods trains in small print.

Whilst the details in the line diagrams are as detailed as research and memory allow, the constraints of space place limits on the degree of accuracy that can be displayed and many of the yards and sidings therefore give a representation rather than strict accuracy.

CONTROLLER'S LOG: It is surprising how busy the Midland & Great Northern can be although not, it has to be admitted, in the small hours of the morning when only one train can be seen running: the 23.05 South Lynn to Peterborough which takes traffic for the ex-LMS station via Crescent Yard, Peterborough. The engine is one of the ubiquitous LMS 4MT 2-6-0's which in recent times have dramatically updated the M&GN motive power picture and

was curious in that it invoked the reverse of the usual conservatism reserved for foreign engines, being generally better-liked on ex-LNER routes than on LMS metals where they got off to a poor start thanks to their original drafting and double-chimneys which made them very poor steamers. Once the latter problems had been ironed out, the class had the potential for doing some good work; the problem being that very little class 4 work remained to be covered on the ex-LMS.

2-6-0's probably the most widely dispersed engines on record.

Whatever the London Midland may have thought of them, the 2-6-0's were a Godsend to the M&GN, partly because their power was well in excess of most M&GN demands but also because of their cab-fitted tenders which put an end to the perennial complaints about tender-first running in one of the coldest regions of Britain. (The sages of Cambridgeshire would

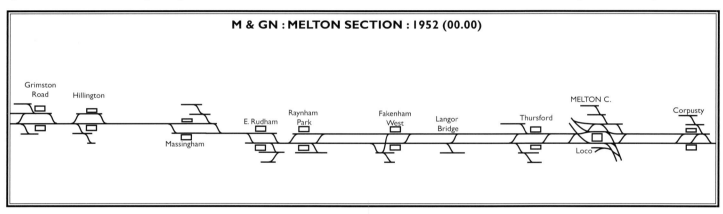

M & GN : MELTON SECTION : 1952 (00.00)

brought the system from being something of a museum piece to the most standardised line in the country. That is not to say that the 2-6-0's have a total monopoly - there are still plenty of GNR and GE classes providing an interesting array of variety - but they can be seen in far greater numbers than in any other part of the country.

First introduced in 1947, the 4MT 2-6-0's were optimistically intended to replace the seven hundred 4F 0-6-0's that worked much of the LM's mineral service but in fact construction ceased at 162 examples with few, if any, 4F engines being displaced. The class

How they would have fared under normal circumstances is a matter for debate but, as luck would have it, their construction coincided with the isthmus between nationalisation and the BR Standard design committee and in the interim it was decided that the 2-6-0's would be suitable for parts of the North Eastern and for the Midland & Great Northern which by 1950 was experiencing considerable difficulties with its motive power fleet.

The upshot was that by early 1952 about a third of the class was at work on the M&GN, the balance of the class being distributed amongst no less than twenty-seven sheds making the

delight in explaining how the cold winter winds were generated over the Russian Steppes and then blew, unchecked for hundreds of miles, until they hit the first obstruction in their path - Whitemoor down hump! South Lynn was no better protected and, as the writers can affirm, anyone who has spent a couple of winters in East Anglia will never feel cold again).

There was an unconscious irony in having so many LMS engines running around North Norfolk since in 1937 the LMS had washed its hands of the M&GN and handed the system over to the LNER who, from 1950 onwards, operated it almost entirely with LMS power.

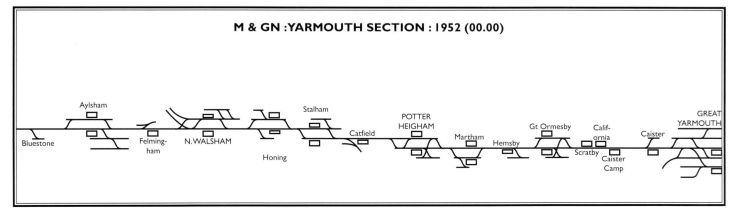

M & GN : YARMOUTH SECTION : 1952 (00.00)

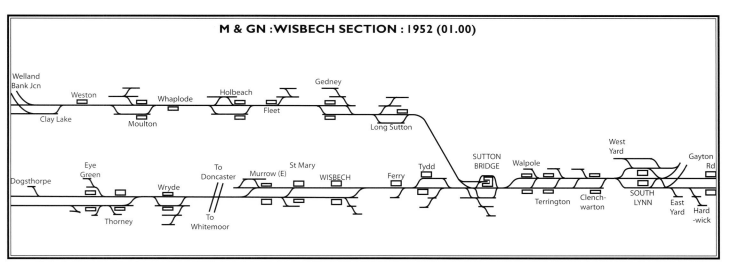

M & GN : WISBECH SECTION : 1952 (01.00)

CONTROLLER'S LOG: The 23.05 South Lynn goods disappears over Rhubarb bridge which takes the M&GN over the Great Northern and Midland lines and into the busy Peterborough complex. Its passage marks the end of main line movements for the next couple of hours and in fact the only engines at work on the system are the two J67 0-6-0T's which shunt the East and West yards at South Lynn and are presently involved in putting together

and still, thirty years after the grouping, gives the impression of being the principal route between London and Yarmouth. Since the 187 mile journey takes about six and a half hours (as opposed to about three and a half from Liverpool Street), few are fooled. However those with a bent for railways and time on their hands, the trek across North Norfolk is full of interest as the train threads its way through the many single track sections and pauses to change

whilst at the east, the Norwich line diverges.

One might have thought that the M&GN would have done better to run its principal trains to Norwich rather than Yarmouth but, fearing perhaps to compete head-on with the Great Eastern, Melton to Yarmouth has always been the main line with passengers having to change for Norwich.

The LMS 2-6-0's are fairly well established in the Peterborough - Yarmouth turns although

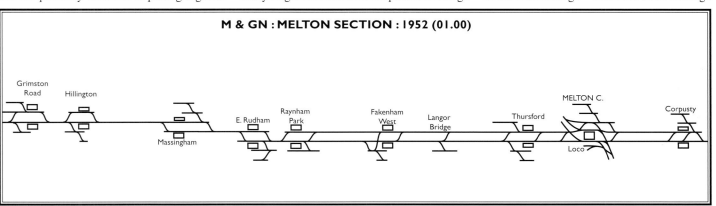

M & GN : MELTON SECTION : 1952 (01.00)

the twelve trains that leave South Lynn between 03.20 and mid-day.

The gap in trains gives time to reflect upon the nature of the M&GN and its workings. The main line runs east-west from Peterborough to Great Yarmouth with important junctions at Sutton Bridge, where the main line from the East Midlands joins, South Lynn (for King's Lynn) and Melton Constable for Cromer and Norwich. Although Yarmouth is the terminus of the line, it is also served by a branch which runs ten miles further south to Lowestoft.

The centrepiece of the passenger timetable is the Peterborough - Yarmouth service which connects with services from King's Cross

engines at least once. The stop at South Lynn is usually enlivened by the arrival of the push and pull connection from King's Lynn: a Great Eastern train worked by a Great Northern 4-4-2 tank and a pair of coaches that previously did service between Marylebone and Ruislip.

Of the passengers who board at Peterborough, 40% alight at Wisbech whilst a similar number leave at South Lynn; very few continuing beyond Fakenham. It is an unfortunate traveller who does not have a compartment to himself for the greater part of the journey.

At Melton Constable the branch from Cromer merges at the west end of the station

not exclusively so and it is still quite possible to make the journey behind another class. The 10.33 Peterborough - Yarmouth, for example, is worked from South Lynn by a B12 4-6-0 whilst the 15.40 Peterborough - Yarmouth which makes a detour via King's Lynn is worked throughout (apart from the South Lynn - King's Lynn element) by Melton Constable D16 4-4-0's. As an alternative, one can alight from the 15.40 at South Lynn and pick up the 13.45 Birmingham New Street - Lowestoft and continue east behind a B12 4-6-0.

The pre-grouping experience does not have to end at Yarmouth since the leg to Lowestoft is booked for an F6 2-4-2T!

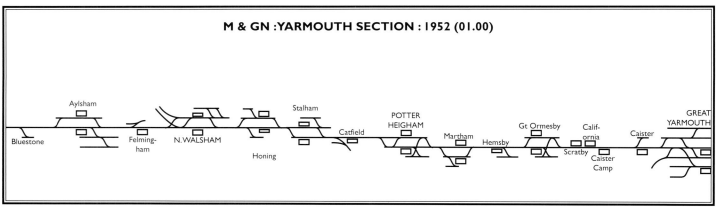

M & GN : YARMOUTH SECTION : 1952 (01.00)

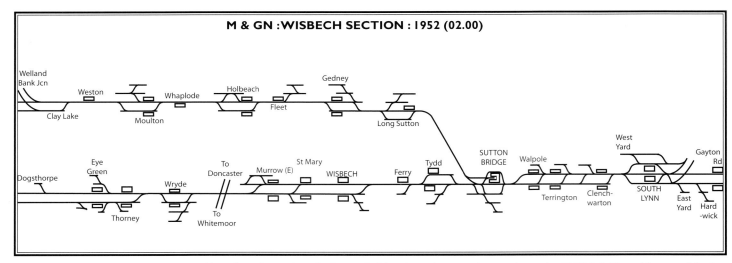

M & GN : WISBECH SECTION : 1952 (02.00)

CONTROLLER'S LOG: Although Peterborough - Yarmouth is the backbone of the system, the importance of the other lines should not be overlooked and the most important of these is the line that branches off at Sutton Bridge and runs to Saxby on the Midland Railway's Nottingham - St Pancras main line. Strictly speaking the M&GN finishes at Little Bytham Junction, eleven miles east of Saxby, where it makes an end-on Junction with the Midland. Because of this the working of trains in the border region is a little confused with the

that arrives in Sutton Bridge from the west is introduced to the system at Spalding which is a junction on the Peterborough - Grimsby and March - Doncaster main lines. Both these routes supply enough goods traffic for four services to the M&GN in addition to a pair of through trains from Colwick (Nottingham) which bring coal for most of the M&GN yards and stations. These Colwick workings are of interest since the engines used alternate between South Lynn and Colwick sheds and the latter will quite often substitute a J39 0-6-0 for

eschews the LMS 2-6-0's and is one of the last express services to be regularly worked by ex-Great Eastern B12 4-6-0's.

Although the M&GN was something of a junior partner at Spalding, it nevertheless dominated local motive power matters by having as many as eight engines allocated to the shed: five LMS 4MT 2-6-0's and three GNR J6 0-6-0's, all of which are engaged in M&GN service, working as far as Nottingham in one direction but no further than King's Lynn in the other.

M & GN : MELTON SECTION : 1952 (02.00)

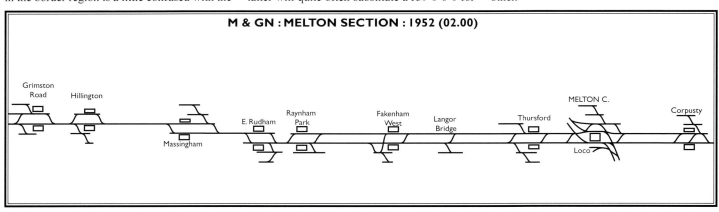

M&GN working some trains through to Saxby whilst others are handed over to the Midland at Bourne. Since most passenger trains run via Spalding, where a reversal is required, some interesting engine workings can be found: one such being the afternoon train from Nottingham which has a Midland 2-6-0 to Bourne, a Bourne 2-6-0 from Bourne to Spalding and a South Lynn D16 4-4-0 from Spalding to King's Lynn.

The level of traffic over the westernmost section is not heavy - Bourne produces only two goods trains a day - and the bulk of the tonnage

the booked K2 2-6-0.

Given the sparsity of population, the passenger service between Sutton Bridge and Saxby is quite lively and consists of a relatively frequent service of stopping trains. A few go beyond the boundary to terminate in Nottingham whilst the route is also used by the M&GN's best-known train; the daily Lowestoft - Birmingham service: the only regular passenger train on the system to both sport a restaurant car and avoid Spalding. The prestige of the service is further enhanced by the fact that it

With relatively large motive power depots only twenty miles apart at South Lynn and Spalding, the M&GN's North-West Frontier seems well provided for yet, as though the two mentioned were not enough, there is a third motive power establishment at Bourne - less than ten miles from Spalding - where two class 4 2-6-0's are based.

Like the Spalding engines, the Bourne 2-6-0's are found only in their home waters and are confined by their diagrams to the section of line between Spalding and Saxby.

M & GN : YARMOUTH SECTION : 1952 (02.00)

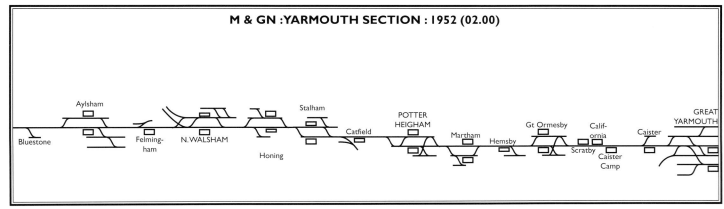

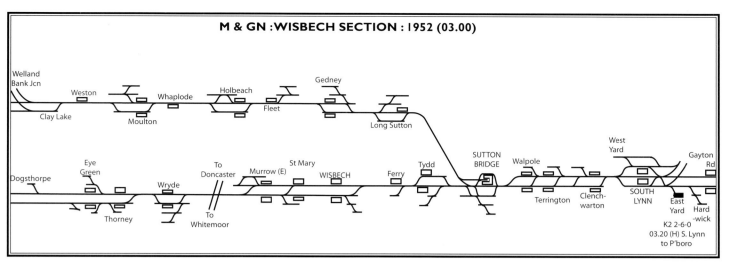

CONTROLLER'S LOG: The first sign of a new day is the departure of a K2 'Ragtimer' 2-6-0 from South Lynn loco to the East Yard to work the first train of the day: the 03.20 goods to Peterborough; quite a fast train which calls only at Horse Shoe Lane, Wisbech, to set down and pick up traffic. The half dozen Great Northern K2 2-6-0's allocated to the system in 1947 came - in some M&GN eyes - as something of a mixed blessing and whilst they gave South Lynn a reasonable rugged and powerful batch of engines at a time when the rest of the fleet was

the Great Eastern which will form the 04.00 trip to King's Lynn. Its opposite number in the East Yard will also be shunting out Great Eastern traffic and will work a transfer trip to the West Yard as soon as the Peterborough train is out of the way. This will be the final task for the 0-6-0T which is booked to finish at 04.00. Any remaining shunting in the East Yard has to be covered by the West Yard pilot until midday when the East Yard engine resumes work. Until recently the East Yard shunt was a continuous duty and this alteration with the loss of a shift

rarely the same since goods trains tend to be liberally timed) and the whereabouts of trains in the opposite direction. Not infrequently special goods trains - which have no timings whatsoever - have to be run and their progress is very much dependant on much careful navigation by Signalmen and Controllers.

The fact that the longest continuous length of double track runs over the relatively quiet Corpusty to Raynham Park section whilst the much busier South Lynn to Peterborough line has several stretches of single track often

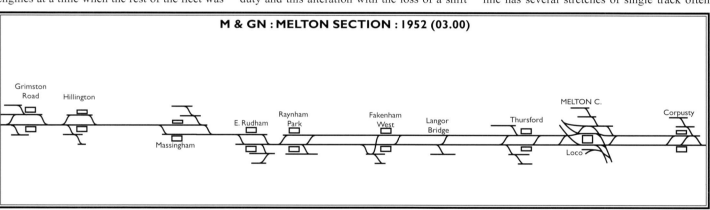

in questionable condition, they were neither in the peak of condition nor comfortable to work on and it took no little effort by the South Lynn Motive Power Management to knock them into some sort of shape. No other M&GN sheds received an allocation of K2's; Melton and Yarmouth struggling on with D16 4-4-0's and J17 0-6-0's until the LMS 2-6-0's started to appear in 1951.

This stirring of activity on the East Yard is matched by some energetic shunting in the West Yard as the J67 pilot shunts out traffic for

has caused some resentment locally.

As can be seen from the track diagram, much of the M&GN is single tracked and the problems that this can cause are not difficult to appreciate. Single-line sections are all very well on passenger railways since passenger trains are generally reliable in their timekeeping; freight trains, however, are anything but predictable and their presence on the main line tends to be accompanied by a good many mental calculations involving booked running times, probable running times (the two are

attracts rather wry comments on past priorities.

Regulation of traffic is not the only problem and to ensure that trains maintain a reasonable average speed, the line is equipped with automatic tablet exchanging devices which allows trains to exchange single line tokens at relatively high speeds. From time to time trains appear with foreign engines that lack the exchange apparatus and have to slow to 10 mph at every token point with the result that quite an accumulation of late running builds up very quickly.

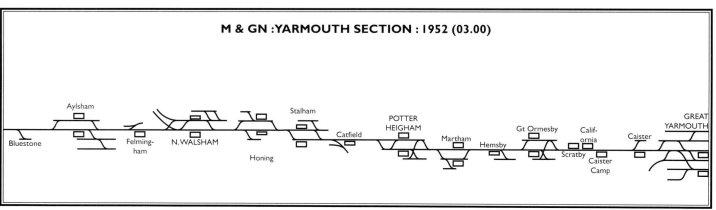

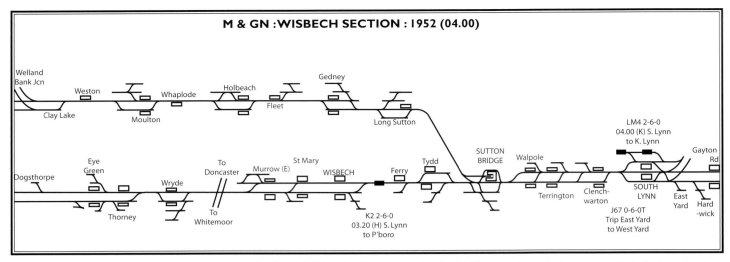

CONTROLLER'S LOG: The 03.20 from South Lynn train passes Tydd and Ferry stations and a few quick sentences are directed to Horse Shoe Lane advising the time the train will arrive and discussing the traffic to be put off and taken up. Thirty-seven minutes are allowed for the operation which is on the generous side since the wagons do not have to be marshalled in any specific order.

This is unusual since Peterborough is a maze of separate marshalling yards and most

for the M&GN and will go on to take the 06.30 Cromer goods as far as Melton Constable where it will be relieved by a D16 4-4-0.

At 04.45 Horse Shoe Lane announces that the 03.20 is ready to leave and gives the amended load which is passed on to the GN Controller at Knebworth, the point from which all movements on the GN main line between King's Cross and Barkeston are controlled. The Midland Controller at Peterborough is also advised, more as a matter of protocol

gentlemen's hours since their first service does not appear until around eight o'clock.

Mention has been made of the small shed at Bourne and its pair of 2-6-0's, yet this is not the only depot of its type on the M&GN and similar establishments exist at Norwich City and Cromer Beach. The former houses a pair of D16 4-4-0's and a J69 0-6-0T pilot whilst the latter has two F6 2-4-2T's which make a couple of appearances on Cromer - Melton Constable workings but otherwise stick to the Cromer -

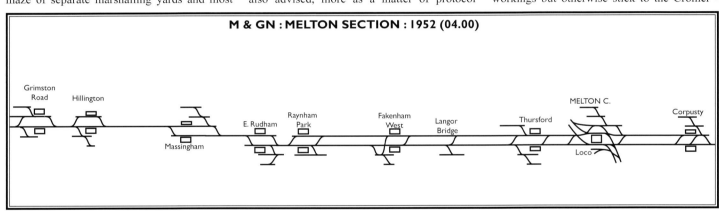

trains from the M&GN call at both Wisbech Sidings and Westwood Yard before terminating in New England. In the case of most trains, care has to be taken to ensure that the wagons are marshalled to reflect this but since the 03.20 runs straight to New England, its load can be in any order. Most of the traffic in the train will either be for the Great Northern termini in the King's Cross area or for the Southern via Ferme Park and the widened lines.

An LMS 4MT 2-6-0 leaves South Lynn for King's Lynn with a train of Great Eastern exchange goods. On reaching King's Lynn, the engine will be coupled up to a return load

than anything else since the train is only in his section for a few moments. This procedure is known as 'wiring on' and is done for every train that crosses a control boundary. Details given are the engine number, the time that the crew took duty, the number of wagons and their equivalence in weight and length.

In contrast to the slight signs of life west of Lynn, the line to the east continues to sleep and will remain dormant until the boxes start to open, like stars coming out at night, a quarter of an hour ahead of the 05.32 South Lynn - Norwich. Some of the boxes in the Far East - Hemsby and Potter Heigham, for example - almost keep

Mundesley - North Walsham branch.

The two Norwich engines are even less adventurous than their Cromer neighbours and their workings confine them solely to passenger services between Norwich City and Melton Constable. In spite of this, the Norwich branch offers quite a good range of motive variety: its nine daily departures calling for the services of no less than six different engines.

The J69 - usually 68623 - only leaves Norwich when called in by Melton Constable for attention and otherwise spends its days shunting the yard and station between 07.00 and 21.15.

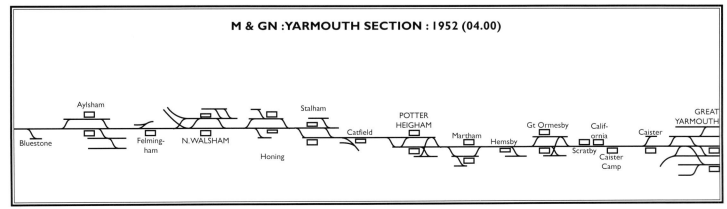

46

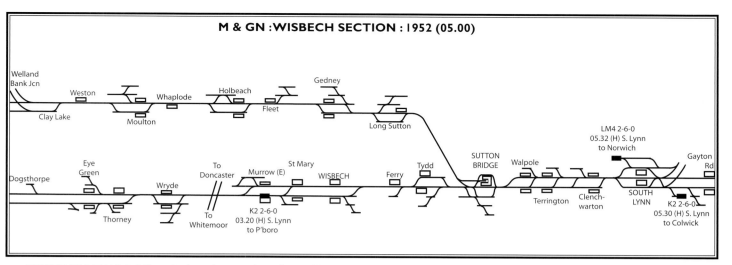

M & GN : WISBECH SECTION : 1952 (05.00)

CONTROLLER'S LOG: At long last, there are signs of life to the east of South Lynn as a 4MT 2-6-0 comes off Melton Constable loco and makes its way across to the yard for the 05.40 goods to South Lynn. On most days of the week this train conveys traffic of a general nature plus a load (sic) of empties for Gayton Road, the only intermediate call. On Tuesdays however, the working is altered since King's Lynn market is held and the train has to call at any intermediate station to attach wagons of

class rings off South Lynn loco and runs light to the East Yard, ready to take the 05.30 mineral empties to Colwick. This is a curious working because instead of the engine working to Colwick and back in the same day - hardly the most onerous of expectations - the K2 retires to Colwick shed after arriving in the yard at 10.30 and remains there until returning south with the 06.40 Colwick - South Lynn the following day. To balance matters, a Colwick engine - in theory a K2 2-6-0 but in practice often a

crews of the Colwick trains do not work through but changeover en route, usually at Sleaford although the exact location is dependent upon the running of the trains and is arranged by the Lincoln Controller . The engine of the inward working sings a little harder for its supper than its mate since it goes on to work an afternoon goods from South Lynn to Peterborough.

As soon as the K2 for the Colwick has disappeared into the East Yard, a 4MT 2-6-0 comes off South Lynn shed to work the 05.32

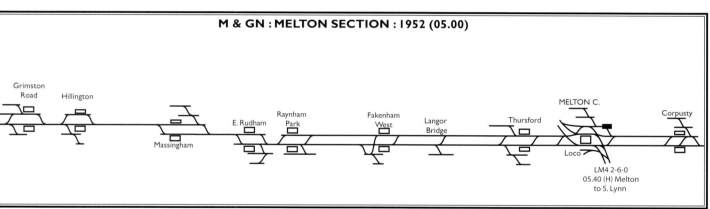

M & GN : MELTON SECTION : 1952 (05.00)

cattle. An extra brakevan is marshalled next to the engine so that by the time the train reaches South Lynn, the ordinary traffic is on the rear of the train and can be removed at a single stroke, allowing a spare engine to back onto the cattle and work them without delay to King's Lynn. Advance notice of cattle to be picked up is given to the Controller by the night before so that he is able to regulate matters accordingly. It is an illustration of how flexible the M&GN is towards the carriage of irregular traffic.

As one K2 2-6-0 heads past Murrow on its way to Peterborough, another member of the

J39 or J6 0-6-0 - works the 06.40 up and the 05.30 on alternate days. With the loads of each arrival from Colwick having to be distributed amongst something like fifty stations, some of which have more than one coal merchant and may receive several wagons, it is a serious matter when the booked type of engine is not provided. As a concession a K2 is allowed a class 5F load and can bring 54 loaded wagons into South Lynn but if a J6 has to be substituted, then the train has to be lightened by no less than fourteen wagons - enough to have several coal merchants warming up the telephone lines. The

goods from West Yard to Norwich; a class E express service which runs non-stop, apart from odd pauses to allow other trains to pass on the single line, and reaches Norwich just after 08.00. The engine spends much of the day on the Norwich branch and will not return to South Lynn until 21.00.

So far only goods workings have stirred but just over the horizon an LM4 2-6-0 of New England is preparing to leave Peterborough with the 05.10 to King's Lynn; the M&GN connection with the 01.00 King's Cross - Edinburgh passenger and newspaper express.

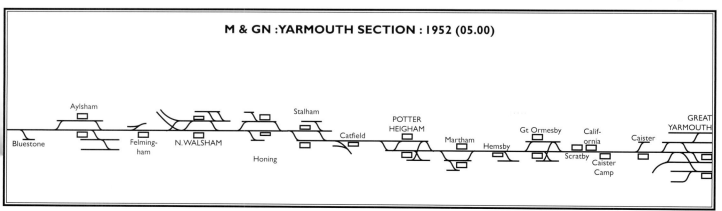

M & GN : YARMOUTH SECTION : 1952 (05.00)

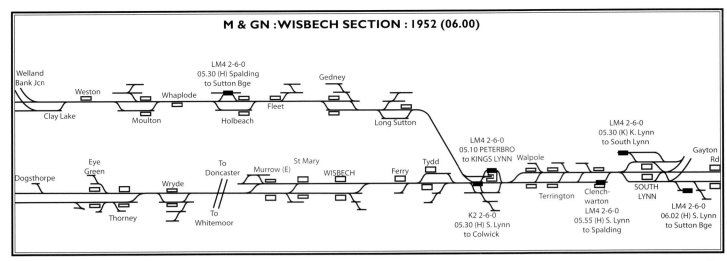

M & GN : WISBECH SECTION : 1952 (06.00)

LM4 2-6-0
05.30 (H) Spalding
to Sutton Bge

LM4 2-6-0
05.30 (K) K. Lynn
to South Lynn

LM4 2-6-0
05.10 PETERBRO
to KINGS LYNN

K2 2-6-0
05.30 (H) S. Lynn
to Colwick

LM4 2-6-0
05.55 (H) S. Lynn
to Spalding

LM4 2-6-0
06.02 (H) S. Lynn
to Sutton Bge

Welland Bank Jcn, Weston, Whaplode, Gedney, Clay Lake, Moulton, Holbeach, Fleet, Long Sutton, Dogsthorpe, Eye Green, Wryde, To Doncaster, Murrow (E), St Mary, WISBECH, Ferry, Tydd, Walpole, Gayton Rd, Thorney, To Whitemoor, Terrington, Clench-warton, SOUTH LYNN

CONTROLLER'S LOG: Now we begin to see the real M&GN - and one that bears no relationship to the rather feeble impression given by the public timetable. The last half an hour has seen an array of up trains leaving South Lynn with the Colwick empties leading the field, closely followed by 05.55 to Spalding and the 06.02 for Sutton Bridge. Slotted between them is the 05.30 trip from King's Lynn which in addition to rough goods brings in traffic from Bishopsgate and Whitemoor for the east part of the M&GN. The 05.55 Spalding is quite a marathon and although it only travels twenty-five miles, it will not reach its destination until lunchtime. It will spend over an hour shunting the dock at Sutton Bridge before serving the stations on the Spalding line. It also conveys London Midland traffic to be taken forward by the afternoon goods from Spalding to Bourne. The 06.02 from South Lynn is a train of recent origin, introduced to work Sutton Bridge traffic left behind by the preceding Spalding train. It is a train that has to be worked quite smartly since the next working of the engine is the 08.00 Sutton Bridge - Spalding passenger

train - a piece of diagramming that generates its fair share of moans against the timetabling section at Liverpool Street. Since the running of goods trains can be unpredictable at times, it is considered a very bad practice to diagram an engine to work a passenger train immediately after a freight.

Swimming against the tide at Sutton Bridge is the 05.10 Peterborough - King's Lynn which brings newspapers (and the odd passenger) from London. Calling only at Murrow, Wisbech, Sutton Bridge and Terrington, it is actually (apart from the time of day) quite a good service and is one of the few M&GN trains to be formally described as an Express Passenger. On reaching King's Lynn, the engine runs-round the train and draws it back to South Lynn to form the 07.08 to Peterborough.

On the Midland & Eastern section, the 05.30 Spalding - Sutton Bridge goods has arrived at Holbeach and will shunt there for half an hour before going forward to work the intermediate station to Sutton Bridge. Care has to be taken to remember to provide this train with a second brakevan which is left at Long

Sutton for the 16.45 Long Sutton - Spalding goods this afternoon.

In the eastern quarter, the down Norwich goods is making good progress as it approaches Massingham and seems to have every chance of making the double-line section at Raynham Park before either of the Melton - South Lynn trains arrive.

It may seem strange to have two Lynn trains leaving Melton within a few minutes of each other but the difference is that the first

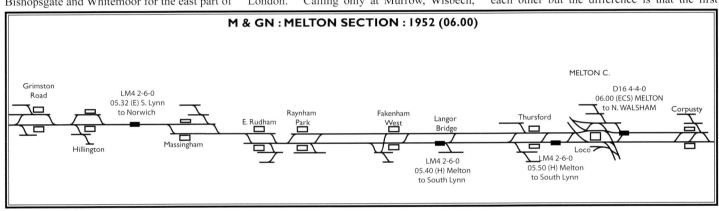

M & GN : MELTON SECTION : 1952 (06.00)

LM4 2-6-0
05.32 (E) S. Lynn
to Norwich

MELTON C.

D16 4-4-0
06.00 (ECS) MELTON
to N. WALSHAM

Grimston Road, Hillington, Massingham, E. Rudham, Raynham Park, Fakenham West, Langor Bridge, Thursford, Loco, Corpusty

LM4 2-6-0
05.40 (H) Melton
to South Lynn

LM4 2-6-0
05.50 (H) Melton
to South Lynn

the M&GN. The 05.55 Spalding is quite a marathon and although it only travels twenty-five miles, it will not reach its destination until lunchtime. It will spend over an hour shunting the dock at Sutton Bridge before serving the stations on the Spalding line. It also conveys London Midland traffic to be taken forward by the afternoon goods from Spalding to Bourne. The 06.02 from South Lynn is a train of recent origin, introduced to work Sutton Bridge traffic left behind by the preceding Spalding train. It is a train that has to be worked quite smartly since the next working of the engine is the 08.00 Sutton Bridge - Spalding passenger

Sutton Bridge and Terrington, it is actually (apart from the time of day) quite a good service and is one of the few M&GN trains to be formally described as an Express Passenger. On reaching King's Lynn, the engine runs-round the train and draws it back to South Lynn to form the 07.08 to Peterborough.

On the Midland & Eastern section, the 05.30 Spalding - Sutton Bridge goods has arrived at Holbeach and will shunt there for half an hour before going forward to work the intermediate station to Sutton Bridge. Care has to be taken to remember to provide this train with a second brakevan which is left at Long

runs direct whilst the other serves many of the intermediate stations and will not reach South Lynn until almost eleven o'clock.

One can see that whilst the LM4 revolution has been particularly thorough, it has not been total as a pair of D16 4-4-0's join the fray. One of these comes off Yarmouth loco for a seemingly unlikely duty: the goods trip to White Swan yard which is a short distance up the Lowestoft branch. The other D16 is leaving Melton Constable with a train of empty stock to form the 06.40 North Walsham to Yarmouth passenger. This engine will next work the 09.00 Birmingham express as far as Melton.

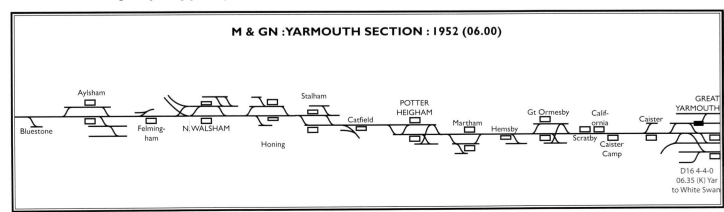

M & GN : YARMOUTH SECTION : 1952 (06.00)

GREAT YARMOUTH

Aylsham, Bluestone, Felming-ham, N. WALSHAM, Honing, Stalham, Catfield, POTTER HEIGHAM, Martham, Hemsby, Gt Ormesby, California, Scratby, Caister Camp, Caister

D16 4-4-0
06.35 (K) Yar
to White Swan

48

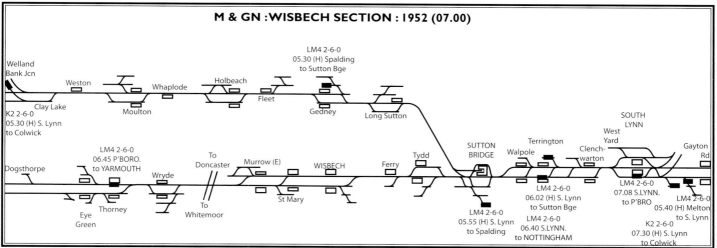

CONTROLLER'S LOG: The system is well and truly alive with more trains on it than most would believe. Who says the M&GN is some creaking backwater! Chief amongst the up trains are the four passenger services, three for Peterborough North and one for Nottingham. The last-mentioned, the 06.40 from South Lynn, sounds as though it has the makings of an express but in fact it is a three coach LMS set that stops at every nook and cranny and is about as slow as it is possible for a train to be. Its motive power is modern, however, and the train to Peterborough is standing in the up platform at South Lynn but has no engine because the New England LM 2-6-0 that brought the empty stock in from King's Lynn did so tender first - it had just arrived with the 05.10 from Peterborough - has gone to the shed to turn and its place is about to be taken by a South Lynn 2-6-0.

The permissive signalling at Melton Constable - actually an application of Rule 96 in the case of the up platform - is being used to advantage with the 07.05 to Liverpool Street standing at the West end of the station with the by a New England LM4 2-6-0. The 4-6-0 will spend a couple of hours on South Lynn loco before taking over the 10.33 Peterborough - Yarmouth.

In the down direction, the 06.45 Peterborough - Yarmouth - now at Thorney - will swap its New England LM4 2-6-0 for a South Lynn example.

One hopes that the D16 'Claud' 4-4-0 on the 06.40 Walsham - Yarmouth is in the peak of condition because it is covering what is probably the most arduous working on the system. On

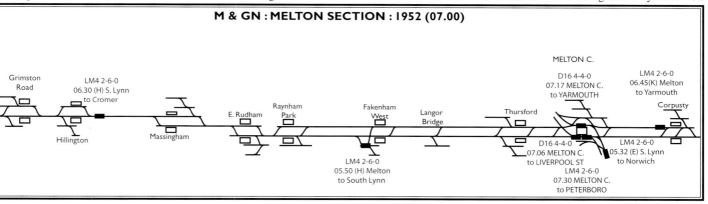

is worked to Saxby by 4MT 2-6-0's; the South Lynn engine giving way to one of the Bourne allocation during the reversal at Spalding. At Saxby the Bourne engine is replaced by a Nottingham 4MT 2-6-4T, the 2-6-0 working back to Spalding with the 09.55 Saxby - King's Lynn.

A notable feature of M&GN passenger operations is the engine changing that takes place at either Melton Constable or South Lynn - more often the latter - and in fact there is only one instance of a train running from Yarmouth to Peterborough without changing the engine. The stock of the 07.08 South Lynn

07.30 Melton Constable to Peterborough at the East. The platform can hold the equivalent of ten coaches.

The 07.30 will change engines at South Lynn, its Melton 2-6-0 giving way to the New England 2-6-0 that is now turning at South Lynn. The displaced engine will return to Melton Constable with the 09.40 goods from the East Yard.

Further back, the early Yarmouth - Peterborough passenger is approaching Great Ormesby; its engine being one of Yarmouth's trio of B12 4-6-0's. The engine works only as far as South Lynn where it will be relieved

reaching Yarmouth, it will be turned and placed on the 08.15 Lowestoft - Birmingham express which it will work as far as South Lynn. Its stay in the latter is, to say the least, brief and within twelve minutes it is once again working westward, having been hurriedly transferred to the 11.13 King's Lynn - Peterborough. Since this diagram is at times proving rather too much for the 4-4-0 - or rather its coal capacity - the working is about to be changed to allow the Birmingham train to have a B12 4-6-0 as far as South Lynn; the D16 working instead the 10.05 Yarmouth to Peterborough as far as Melton Constable.

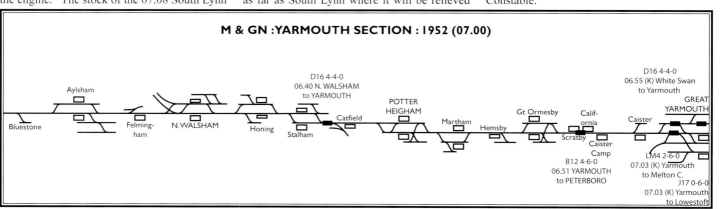

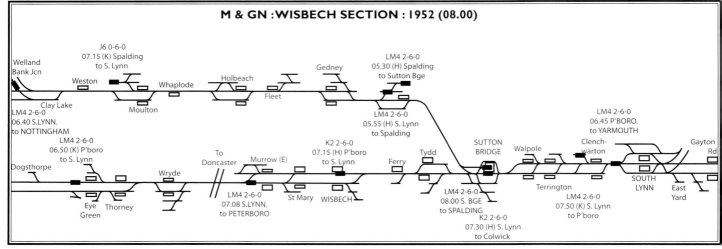

M & GN : WISBECH SECTION : 1952 (08.00)

CONTROLLER'S LOG: For the next few minutes South Lynn has to be on its toes as the 06.45 Peterborough - Yarmouth approaches. An LM4 2-6-0 rings off shed and crosses over to the down side to wait for the arrival of the 06.45, the New England engine of which is quickly uncoupled to run light to the shed for its next working, the 06.51 Yarmouth - Peterborough. The relieving engine backs down onto the train and as it is being coupled up, the 08.00 push and pull from King's Lynn

makes another appearance from King's Lynn, returning at 08.45, exactly as the Peterborough train pulls away. There are times when South Lynn can seem (and indeed be) very busy.

At Sutton Bridge, the 08.00 Spalding passenger pulls out and is followed by the 07.30 South Lynn - Colwick mineral empties. As with the earlier service, this is a turn that is split between South Lynn and Colwick with the crews changing over at Spalding. The engine working it on 'Colwick' days will be something

shunting at Aylsham - is in a similar category and taking over eight hours to cover the 42 miles, its engine has to remain overnight in Yarmouth before returning with the 07.02 Yarmouth - Melton goods.

Returning to the passenger front, the 06.51 Yarmouth - Peterborough is approaching Aylsham, its B12 4-6-0 will work to South Lynn where it will give way to a New England LM4 2-6-0. Twenty miles behind it the 07.45 Yarmouth - Aylsham works its way through

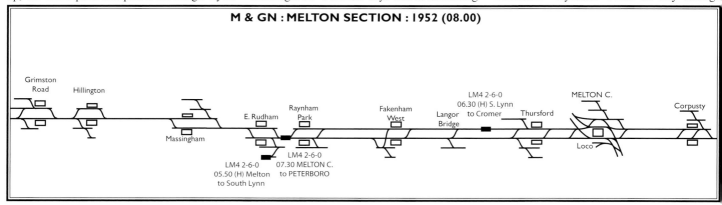

M & GN : MELTON SECTION : 1952 (08.00)

arrives in the centre road. Sixteen minutes is allowed for the engine-change and in that time the push and pull reverses and returns to King's Lynn.

Hardly has the dust settled when the New England 2-6-0 that brought in the 05.10 from Peterborough comes off shed and is positioned ready to take over the 07.30 Melton Constable to Peterborough which it runs in at 08.35. The incoming engine is another LM4 2-6-0 and runs to the shed to turn before taking the 09.40 goods from the East Yard to Melton Constable. As the replacement engine backs onto the Peterborough train, the push and pull

of a lottery. A short distance to the north east, Long Sutton receives the attention of two goods trains as the 05.30 from Spalding and the 05.55 ex South Lynn arrive in the yard.

Railways have long been the butt of jokes about 'things that crawl upon the face of the earth' and the originator of the jest may well have been the 07.50 South Lynn - Peterborough which will not reach its destination until seven o'clock this evening and too late for a return working the same night. The engine therefore alternates with a New England 2-6-0 and the 11.45 Westwood - South Lynn.

The 06.45 Melton to Yarmouth goods - now

the coastal stations, testifying as it does to the motive power variety that can still be found in the nether regions of the railway. The 06.51 from Yarmouth has a B12 4-6-0 to work its four coaches whilst the 07.45 - exactly the same weight and timings but with a few more passengers - is booked to nothing larger than an F6 2-4-2T!

From the traditionalists viewpoint, it is pleasing to note that most of the day's passenger departures from Yarmouth remain in the hands of pre-grouping motive power and it is not until 18.15 that a passenger service departs behind one of the LM4 2-6-0's.

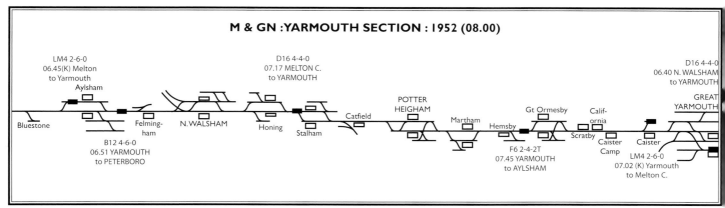

M & GN : YARMOUTH SECTION : 1952 (08.00)

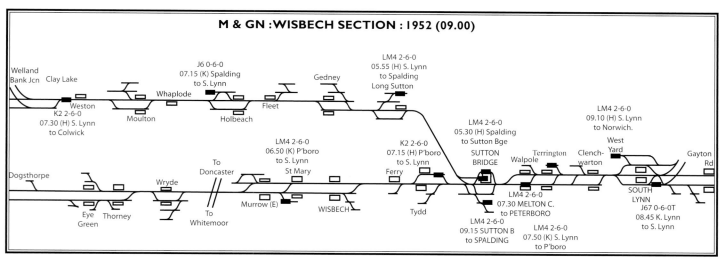

M & GN : WISBECH SECTION : 1952 (09.00)

CONTROLLER'S LOG: Whilst it has been established that there are many more M&GN trains than many people imagined, it has to be conceded that express services do not make a significant contribution to the numbers. This paucity therefore lends the through Lowestoft - Birmingham express an extra air of exclusivity although the promise of the timetable is not exactly reflected in reality since the service - which is now getting the right

on Saturdays.

The 07.17 from Melton has arrived in Yarmouth and the engine is being turned before working the 10.30 Yarmouth - Melton goods: another instance of a 4-4-0 on freight work. The stock of the 07.17 will form the 10.05 Yarmouth - Peterborough.

Elsewhere on the Eastern Section there are a number of matters to be monitored. One is the 07.45 Yarmouth - Aylsham passenger

the 05.50 Melton - South Lynn goods is keeping its head down in the yard at Massingham until the up train has cleared the section. At Melton itself, the South Lynn - Cromer goods has reduced its load to thirty wagons, reversed its brakevan and changed direction, the 2-6-0 that brought the train from South Lynn being replaced by a D16 4-4-0: not, in many eyes, the ideal engine for a goods train.

Sutton Bridge is a location that deserves

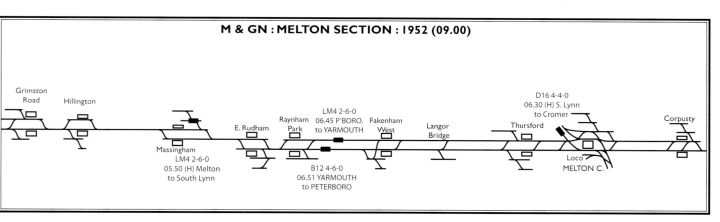

M & GN : MELTON SECTION : 1952 (09.00)

away from Yarmouth - consists of no more than two LMS corridor coaches which have arrived from Lowestoft behind an F6 2-4-2T and are about to leave behind a D16 4-4-0 which will hand over to a B12 4-6-0 at South Lynn. As it proceeds, the service grows in size and at Melton Constable three more coaches are added (one from Norwich and two from Cromer) to make a total of five. A sixth vehicle - a dining car which goes as far as Leicester - will be added at South Lynn and although six vehicles does not seem much of a train, during the Summer it loads to eight vehicles on weekdays and eleven

which is approaching its destination and has only fifteen minutes to turn round and form the 09.16 back to Yarmouth. The other concerns the 06.45 Melton - Yarmouth and 07.02 Melton - Yarmouth goods trains which are closing on each other and have, at some point, to exchange crews. With luck the changeover should be made at Stalham but a close watch has to be kept on their running so that an adjustment can be made if necessary.

Matters are relatively quiet on the Melton section. A pair of passenger trains have just passed each other near Raynham Park whilst

more attention than it gets and at the moment is of some interest given the number of trains hovering around. In the bay, the coaches of the 09.15 to Spalding which connects with the 07.30 Melton Constable - Peterborough wait for their engine; the LM4 2-6-0 which only arrived twenty minutes ago with the 05.30 goods from Spalding. Meanwhile in the down platform, the 07.40 Bourne - King's Lynn makes a brief stop before crossing the single-line bridge. Since the 42' turn-table at Sutton Bridge is too small for the 2-6-0's, the benefits of tender cabs are immediately apparent.

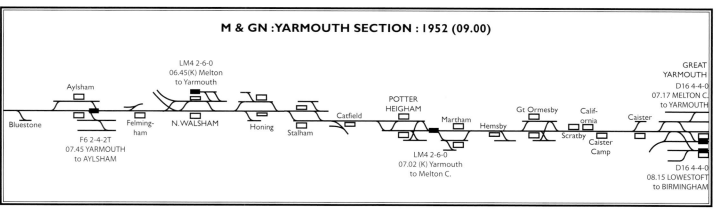

M & GN : YARMOUTH SECTION : 1952 (09.00)

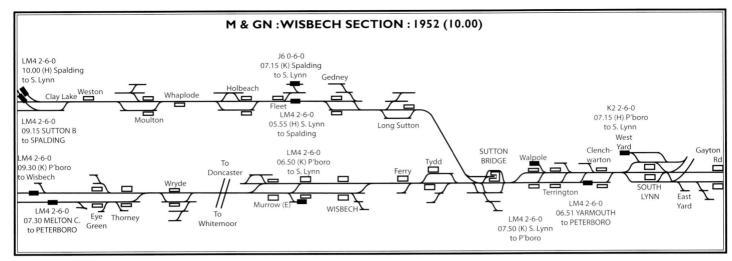

CONTROLLER'S LOG: Having kept us company for two and a half hours, the 07.30 Melton to Peterborough finally leaves M&GN territory and rumbles over Rhubarb Bridge which takes it over the GN main line and the parallel Midland tracks to join the maze of lines that form the very complex approach to Peterborough. Due to arrive in Peterborough North at 10.21, the chances of a significantly early arrival are excellent since no less than thirty-one minutes are allowed for

time to be whipped twenty minutes early into the excursion platform at Peterborough North without blemishing the sanctity of the East Coast Main Line. The next working of the engine is the 12.45 Peterborough - Yarmouth as far as South Lynn whilst the stock remains in the Nene Sidings ('The Wharf') to form the 22.45 to King's Lynn.

A glance is made into the Norwich and Cromer quarters to ensure that their connections with the 'Leicester' are running to time. The

the 16.25 Corpusty school train and the engine to the loco to be turned for the 13.32 back to Norwich. At 10.20 the D16 4-4-0 with its two coaches from Lowestoft and Yarmouth runs into the up platform, the Cromer engine backs its three coaches down and at 10.28 the express resumes its journey towards South Lynn where the 4-4-0 will be replaced by a B12 4-6-0 and a dining car will be added.

The importance of Wisbech - which also has a GE station on the March - King's Lynn line

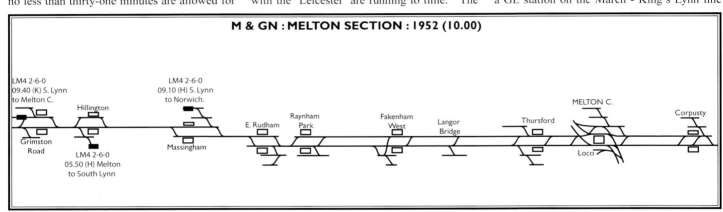

the eight and a half miles between Thorney to Peterborough. This is because the 07.20 Leeds - King's Cross and its occasional relief happen to pass Peterborough at the time the Melton Constable train would otherwise arrive and the GN - which are not held in the highest regard east of the Nene - are quite happy to have an M&GN train blowing off steam at Westwood for a quarter of an hour rather than risk one of its expresses catching sight of a distant. (There is an oft-told story that whenever an up express leaves Grantham, everything else for fifty miles is consigned to the goods lines......). In practice the M&GN train usually gets to Westwood in

main train has passed Aylsham and will be in Melton by 10.20 where the two sections have to be attached. The Norwich connection consisting of five coaches, the rearmost of which goes through to Birmingham, arrives in the up platform at 10.14 whilst the Cromer section - two coaches, both of which go to Birmingham - arrives two minutes later in the down platform. The Cromer train shunts across into the down main, picks up the rear coach of the Norwich train and then draws forward to wait the arrival of the Lowestoft coaches. In the meantime the Norwich engine and its four vehicles vacate the up main platform; the coaches to be berthed for

- is emphasised by the fact that two trains are approaching it from Peterborough. The first is the 06.50 from Westwood which brings empties to Eye Green and the two Wisbech stations. At present it is shunting out the yard at St Mary before moving on to Horseshoe Lane Junction, the quaintly named sidings for Wisbech North.

The second train - the 09.30 from Crescent Yard - serves all stations from Dogsthorpe to Horse Shoe Lane, much of its traffic consisting of empty wagons for tomorrow's traffic. The real importance of the stations west of Wisbech will be seen later in the day when an impressive number of trains are needed to serve them.

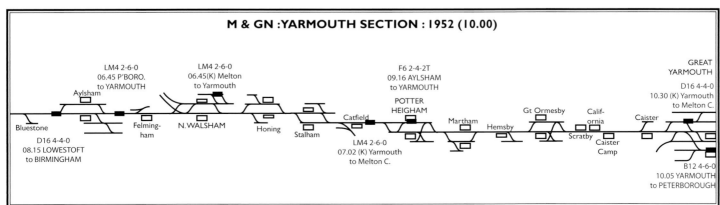

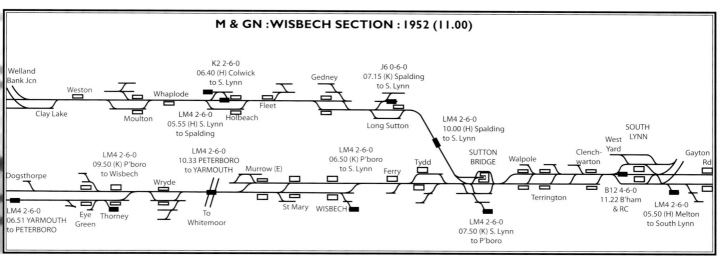

CONTROLLER'S LOG: The Midland & Eastern has some interesting movements taking place. The 10.00 Spalding - South Lynn with its load of variegated goods from the Joint and East Lincs lines is getting close to Sutton Bridge where it will spend three quarters of an hour, setting down and taking up Peterborough road traffic. Not far behind it is the 06.40 from Colwick with 54 wagons of coal - quite possibly one wagon for each station on the system - and a K2 2-6-0. It is to be hoped that the engine

in a train of empty stock and is now standing with its B12 4-6-0, ready to back onto the front of the express as soon as its D16 has been released. All eyes are on the B12 although it is the 4-4-0 that deserves the plaudits because of the extremely lengthy day it is working. Having started with a Melton Constable to Yarmouth service, it has now worked the Leicester up to South Lynn where, instead of returning to its home station, it will take over the 11.13 King's Lynn to Peterborough. Later in the afternoon it

train raises the eyebrows, it is the result of Melton Constable's relatively large allocation. As time goes by, these duties are gradually being taken over by LM4 2-6-0's.

On the passenger front the 06.45 from Peterborough is about to finish its lengthy pilgrimage whilst the 10.05 Yarmouth to Peterborough - another B12 duty - approaches North Walsham.

Where speed is concerned, few trains can compete with the 07.50 South Lynn to

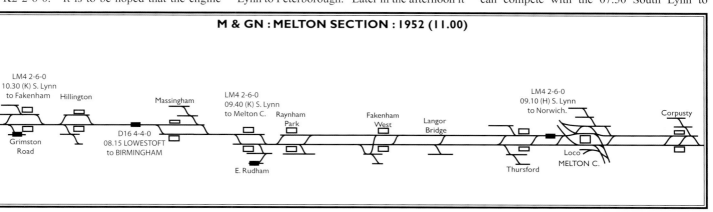

- some of which are showing signs of age - is in reasonable shape since after turning and coaling on South Lynn Loco, it is required to work the 15.58 express goods to Peterborough. This is the first of two trains from Colwick; the second will appear in about two hours time. The K2 and the J6 0-6-0 on the 07.15 Spalding - South Lynn local goods make an interesting, if momentary, balance to the GE motive power seen elsewhere on the M&GN.

Preparations are well in hand at South Lynn for the reception of the Lowestoft - Birmingham express which is approaching Hillington. The dining car has been worked in from King's Lynn

will work the 15.40 Peterborough to South Lynn and the 18.01 South Lynn to Melton Constable. The total of 222 miles (plus some ECS and light engine running) is possibly a post-war record for a 4-4-0. The length of the diagram is proving rather too much at times and it is proposed to alter the working in the near future.

The state of play in the Yarmouth section shows a healthy volume of goods traffic on the move. A pair of local goods trains are about to cross each other at Stalham whilst another local makes its way towards Hemsby. The last-mentioned is worked by a 'Claud' 4-4-0 and whilst the sight of such an engine on a goods

Peterborough goods which, in just over three hours, has only managed to cover the nine miles to Sutton Bridge! At first glance, it appears to be the stuff on which music hall jokes are based but on closer examination it bears testimony to the volume of trade done by the stations between Lynn and Peterborough.

The South Lynn men working the 07.50 are booked to be relieved at Horse Shoe Lane by a set of New England men who travel out passenger in the 12.45 ex Peterborough. The engine works through to Peterborough and remains overnight, working back the next day with the 11.45 Westwood to South Lynn.

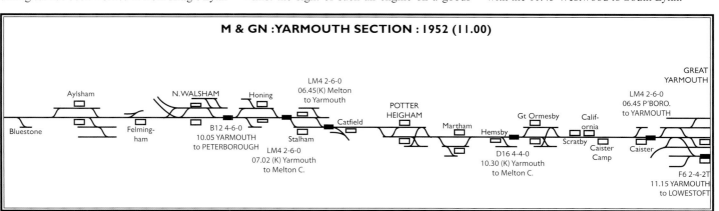

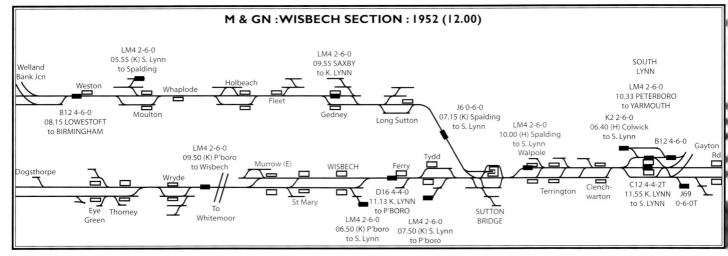

M & GN : WISBECH SECTION : 1952 (12.00)

CONTROLLER'S LOG: Our overworked D16 4-4-0 has handed over the 08.15 Lowestoft - Birmingham to a B12 4-6-0 which will work it to Leicester and is now approaching Wisbech with the 11.13 King's Lynn to Peterborough. The latter is a three coach service which returns as the 17.55 Peterborough to King's Lynn and was brought into South Lynn by the LM4 2-6-0 which had previously worked the 08.15 Spalding - South Lynn. If South Lynn were stripped of all else, it would still be busy on account of the engine-changing that takes place.

compensate a three-coach connecting train is run at 11.45 from Spalding to Bourne which, on reaching Bourne shunts clear to allow the Leicester to go by before proceeding westwards as a connection out of the express. Since the Leicester calls at Saxby one wonders if demand for Castle Bytham and South Witham really justifies such an arrangement, especially as the train changes one LM4 2-6-0 for another during the time it is at Bourne. An additional item of interest at Bourne in the early afternoon is the arrival of the goods from Sleaford via the

and although a pleasing sight to the spectator, the fireman probably has a harsher opinion since the distance between the firebox and tender is much greater than on most engines. Ask most Great Eastern men to suggest the best express engine and most will nominate a 'Claud'. The B12 will return to Yarmouth with the 'Leicester'.

A glance at the locomotive allocation table reveals that, to date, Yarmouth has been given one of the new LM4 2-6-0's: an unusual matter since engines are rarely allocated singly. The

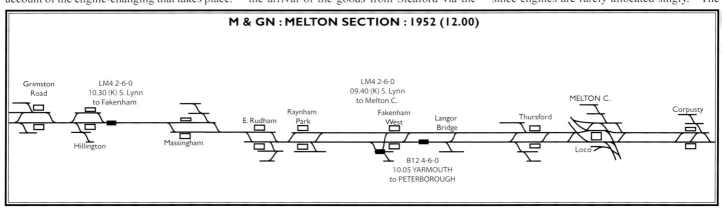

M & GN : MELTON SECTION : 1952 (12.00)

As we speak, more of the same is taking place as the 10.33 Peterborough - Yarmouth has its 4MT 2-6-0 exchanged for a B12 4-6-0, during which the King's Lynn push and pull arrives and departs. In the background a K2 2-6-0 arrives with 06.40 coal from Colwick whilst a J69 0-6-0T comes off shed and runs to the East Yard to cover the afternoon pilot.

There is rather an interesting passenger movement taking place 'off screen' in the North-West section of the system. The 'Leicester' avoids Spalding by running direct from Welland Bank to Cuckoo Junction and to

Aswarby branch. The branch lost its passenger service as long ago as September 1930 but maintains a hold on life by virtue of the daily goods working and its J6 0-6-0.

Things have quietened down a little in the east. The 09.40 Lynn to Melton goods is being held at Fakenham for the 10.05 Yarmouth - Peterborough passenger while the 10.30 Lynn - Fakenham makes a run for cover at Massingham and should make it without hurting the passenger. The B12 4-6-0 on the 10.05 is a consequence of the large numbers of B1 4-6-0's that have been allocated to the Great Eastern

reason for this is that the engine of the 06.45 Melton - Yarmouth goods, now at Martham, has no return working and therefore remains overnight at Yarmouth before working the 07.02 Yarmouth - Melton which at present is at Felmingham.

In order to provide the same type of engine for both trains, Yarmouth loco was given 43145 with which to balance the Melton engine of the same class and it is condemned therefore to a somewhat humdrum life - at least until some more of the class are sent to Yarmouth - of running to Melton one day and back the next.

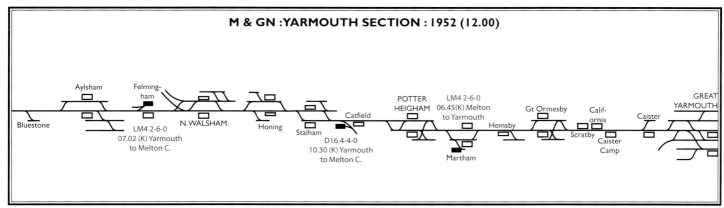

M & GN : YARMOUTH SECTION : 1952 (12.00)

Although Cromer High was the Great Eastern station in Cromer, there were times when the M&GN Cromer Beach station could present quite a Great Eastern face and such was the case on Wednesday 30th August 1950 when D16 4-4-0 62578 (Melton Constable) prepared to depart with the 16.45 to Melton Constable and F6 2-4-2T 67228 (Cromer Beach) waits to leave with the 16.33 Norfolk & Suffolk Joint service to North Walsham via Overstrand. 62578 remained at Melton Constable until being taken out of traffic in October 1957 whilst 67228 was transferred to Stratford for work on the Braintree branch after the closure of the North Walsham line and was withdrawn from Southend, where it had spent five months in store, in April 1958. A set of eleven LMS coaches for the Saturday 08.40 to Birmingham New Street stands in the carriage sidings. (V. R. Webster / Kidderminster Railway Museum).

D16 62578 pauses at Sheringham with a Melton Constable to Cromer service on Tuesday 22nd August 1950. Although an M&GN station, the principal trains from Sheringham were Great Eastern workings which ran to Liverpool Street via Cromer High and Norwich Thorpe. Apart from the daily service to Birmingham New Street, M&GN services at Cromer consisted of stopping trains between Melton Constable and Cromer. (V. R. Webster / Kidderminster Railway Museum).

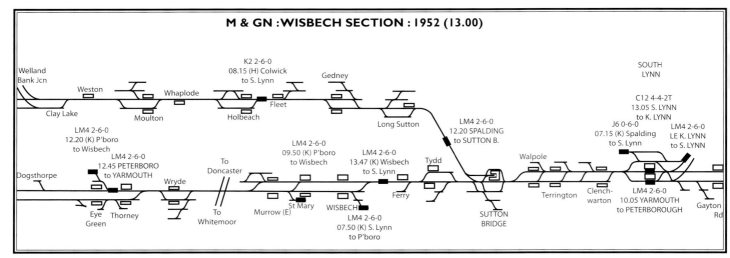

M & GN : WISBECH SECTION : 1952 (13.00)

CONTROLLER'S LOG: In spite of the fact that it is only lunchtime, the last train of the day from Yarmouth to Peterborough (and, therefore, London) is already on its way! The passenger who turns up at Yarmouth Beach any later than 12.42 *might* be told that other trains *may* go from South Town and Vauxhall but the information is likely to be vague and stems from the fact that nationalisation, far from unifying the system in the minds of its staff, has had the effect of strengthening the historical insularity of pre-grouping times. Railwaymen now wave their company flags far more enthusiastically than at any time in the past. Human nature can be a very strange thing!

Operationally the 12.42 Yarmouth - Peterborough is something of an odd-man-out since instead of changing engines at South Lynn, it exchanges its D16 4-4-0 for another at Melton Constable; the latter running through to Peterborough and becoming the second Melton engine of the day to visit the city.

Not far behind is the 12.55 Yarmouth - Peterborough parcels which is the first train of the day to leave Yarmouth Beach behind an LM4 2-6-0. Made up of of three bogie brakes and six vanfits, the train consists of two portions; one for Peterborough and the other for Spalding which is removed at Sutton Bridge and taken formed by the 13.25 parcels from Yarmouth (Vauxhall), a joint GE/M&GN working which runs via Acle, Norwich, Wymondham, Dereham, Swaffham and King's Lynn. At Spalding the M&GN vehicles (a van each for Newcastle, Doncaster, Bradford Exchange, Liverpool Central and Manchester Central) are worked forward by the 18.30 Whitemoor - York parcels. The Peterborough section comprises vans for Peterborough, King's Cross, Birmingham and Leicester respectively, the last two being worked forward by the 20.18 Peterborough East - Leicester passenger. The engine working the train does not go through but is replaced at South Lynn by another of the same class.

South Lynn is as busy as ever with the B12 4-6-0 of the 10.05 ex Yarmouth giving way to an LM4 2-6-0, an operation that, as usual, runs simultaneously with the arrival and departure of the King's Lynn Motor Train and its C12. Adding to matters is a Spalding LM4 2-6-0 which arrives tender-first from King's Lynn, this being the engine that worked the 09.55 passenger from Saxby. It will go onto the Loco to turn before leaving with the 13.50 goods to Long Sutton.

The second train from Colwick has just passed Holbeach and completes the day's quota of coal - a little more than one hundred wagons in total - from the Nottingham coalfield. On arrival at South Lynn the engine will go on shed until coming out for the 07.30 empties to Colwick in the morning.

The 12.45 Peterborough - Yarmouth is approaching Thorney and is a relatively well-used service since it connects with the 10.18 King's Cross - Leeds. It will connect at Sutton Bridge with the 12.20 passenger from Spalding which, in turn, is a connection out of the 09.07 Doncaster - Peterborough via Lincoln and Spalding. The 12.45 will change engines at South Lynn in the usual manner but, its New England LM4 2-6-0 being replaced by another of the same class at South Lynn, there is a lack of pre-grouping flavour.

M & GN : MELTON SECTION : 1952 (13.00)

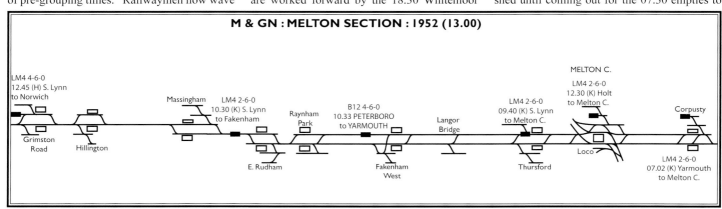

M & GN : YARMOUTH SECTION : 1952 (13.00)

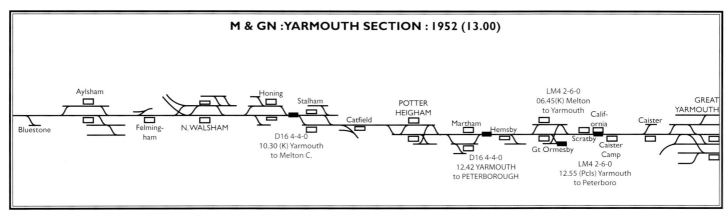

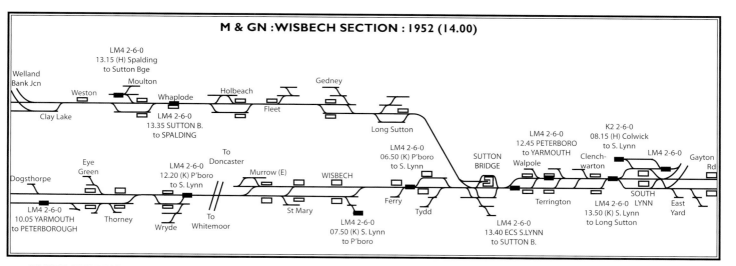

M & GN : WISBECH SECTION : 1952 (14.00)

CONTROLLER'S LOG: As the 10.05 Yarmouth to Peterborough, which runs as an express from South Lynn, passes over to the Great Northern, an LM4 2-6-0 comes off South Lynn loco and is positioned ready to take over from the New England engine that is working in with the 12.45 ex Peterborough. Both engines have already considerable mileages, the incoming engine being the same that worked the 05.10 Peterborough - King's Lynn

engine will turn and return to Yarmouth with a series of local trains whilst the fresh engine will work through to Peterborough and return with the 20.10 Peterborough - Melton passenger.

One cannot help but be struck at the level of goods work in the Wisbech and Sutton Bridge areas. After spending some time shunting Horse Shoe Lane, the 06.50 Peterborough - South Lynn has been relieved by a set of South Lynn men and is now about to shunt the yards

also to be monitored carefully since it collects, amongst other matter, vegetable traffic for London which has to connect with the 20.05 trip from South Lynn to King's Lynn and the 21.20 King's Lynn to Spitalfields. The man who allowed the 07.50 to be delayed so that the connection was broken would put himself at risk of being broken. A spectator watching the 12.20 shunt at one of the yards might conclude that it was a very unimportant service: how

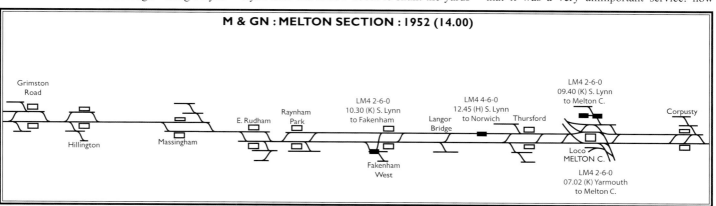

M & GN : MELTON SECTION : 1952 (14.00)

whilst the relieving engine arrived with the 10.33 from Peterborough and will therefore cover the entire M&GN main line before the day is out. In this connection it is interesting to note that none of the New England engines employed on the M&GN venture east of South Lynn, a feature mirrored by Yarmouth engines which under normal circumstances do not work west of South Lynn. Only Melton and South Lynn engines can be seen at the extremities of the line.

Similar arrangements are being made at Melton Constable where a D16 4-4-0 is about to ring off shed into order to take over the 12.42 Yarmouth - Peterborough. The incoming

at Tydd and Sutton Bridge before getting to South Lynn at 15.15. The progress of this train will have to be watched carefully since the engine's next working is the 12.55 Yarmouth - Peterborough parcels and the margin of time to turn the engine round is by no means generous.

The 07.50 South Lynn - Peterborough has been relieved and will be pulling out of Horse Shoe Lane at any moment although it still has another five hours to go before it will get to Peterborough. In the opposite direction the 12.20 Peterborough to Wisbech - the engine for tomorrow's 07.50 South Lynn to Peterborough - is leaving Wryde and also has a long way to go before its journey finishes. Its progress has

wrong he would be since the value of the goods moved was high and the time taken the result of the number of stations between Peterborough and South Lynn.

The 12.45 ex- South Lynn is in section between Langor Bridge and Thursford and is another example of the M&GN's importance, this being the third service of the day to run through from South Lynn to Norwich. The engines will be changed at Melton Constable, the inward engine being used to re-engine the 14.35 South Lynn to Yarmouth goods - an interesting cyclic working - whilst the replacement engine will be the South Lynn engine that came down with the 05.32 South Lynn - Norwich goods.

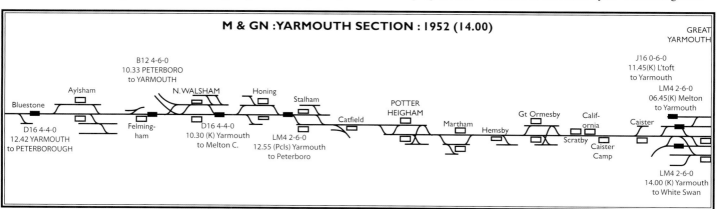

M & GN : YARMOUTH SECTION : 1952 (14.00)

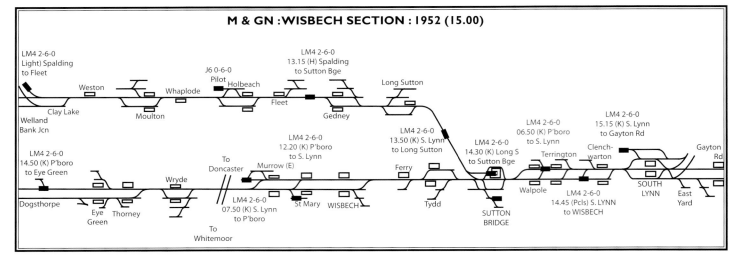

CONTROLLER'S LOG: The Sutton Bridge - Spalding section is starting its evening rush hour which consists not of season ticket holders but of agricultural produce, some of which is moved as passenger-rated traffic in the 15.30 Long Sutton - Moulton parcels train; the rest being loaded into wagons and moved by goods train. To assist in the process two engines, a J6 0-6-0 and a LM4 2-6-0, are despatched from Spalding loco to Holbeach

Passenger traffic is rather quiet at the moment: the 10.33 ex Peterborough is just arriving in Yarmouth which the two lunchtime services have just passed each other at East Rudham. Passengers on the up train will be spared the usual lengthy stop at South Lynn since the engine, a D16 4-4-0, works through from Melton Constable and the stop at Lynn is simply to connect with the King's Lynn Push & Pull. (The stop could actually be pared a

paper clash with the 08.35 Glasgow to King's Cross - which itself has eighteen (!) minutes recovery time between Doncaster and London - at Peterborough. With these lavish amounts of recovery - without which the railway would be better off - the chances of the two trains coming within five minutes of each other are remote and the D16 and its train usually arrives in Peterborough North the best part of a quarter of an hour before time.

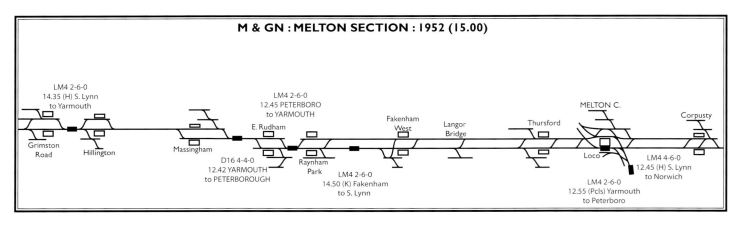

and Fleet to shunt as needed, the 2-6-0 going on to shunt Gedney and Long Sutton later in the afternoon. A considerable tonnage of traffic is required to persuade Liverpool Street to part with two engines thus! The morning traffic is being taken to Sutton Bridge by the 13.15 ex Spalding, which is on its way from Holbeach to Long Sutton whilst in the opposite direction, the 13.50 goods from South Lynn is approaching Long Sutton where its train will recess until 16.45 and therefore be in a position to pick up westbound traffic from the intermediate stations between Gedney and Spalding.

little were it not for the fact that the King's Lynn connection arrives after the Yarmouth - Peterborough train has arrived. The reason for this is that the Push & Pull connects at King's Lynn with the 14.45 Hunstanton - Liverpool Street and cannot therefore leave until 15.25. Such is the intensity of service deep in the fen).

Should, however, something go awry with these arrangements, some comfort may be derived from the fact that the 12.42 can leave South Lynn no less than thirteen minutes late yet reach Peterborough on time because of a

The local goods trains continue to ply their trade between South Lynn and Peterborough and have been joined by a newcomer, the 14.50 Westwood to Eye Green; a unique working since it has a Spital Bridge engine rather than one from New England which is the Peterborough shed upon which all other M&GN turns are based. Observers, however, should not take this as an omen that something like an 8F 2-8-0 or G2a 0-8-0 is likely to turn up at Eye Green since 4MT 2-6-0 43064 has been allocated to Spital Bridge in order to ensure that its M&GN turn has an engine that is suited to the line.

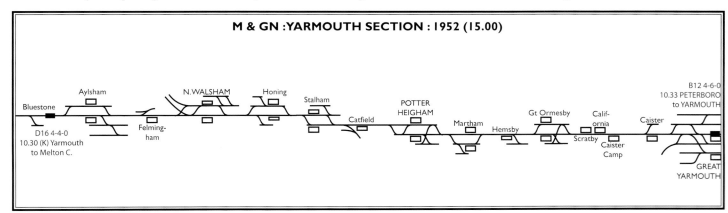

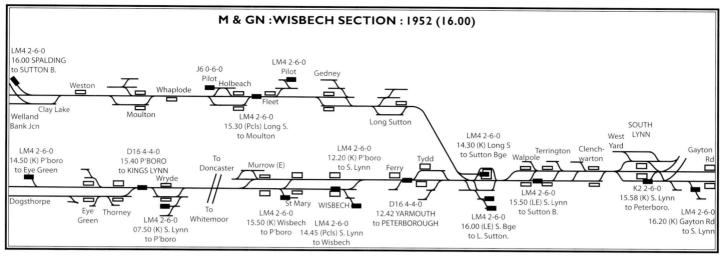

M & GN : WISBECH SECTION : 1952 (16.00)

CONTROLLER'S LOG: Although the process of M&GN motive power standardisation still has some way to run, one realises how much progress has been made by looking at the fourteen trains to the west of South Lynn and noting that no less than twelve are worked by LMS 4MT 2-6-0's. How many years have passed since the system was last able to boast that 86% of its trains were handled by engines that were less than five years old? The exceptions are the 12.42 Yarmouth - Peterborough which is

Although the principal yards in the area are those of South Lynn, the role of Sutton Bridge should not be overlooked since it deals with much of the traffic to and from local stations on both the Spalding and Peterborough lines and takes, thus, a considerable weight from the shoulders of South Lynn. Sutton Bridge Yard deals with thirteen arrivals and fourteen departures a day - more than one train an hour on average - yet even this is not enough and some marshalling has to be done at Long Sutton

the 15.30 van train from Long Sutton which merges at Moulton to become the 18.00 goods to Spalding. Goods rated traffic from Long Sutton for the North is conveyed in the 16.45 goods to Spalding whilst traffic for the south has already been cleared by the 13.15 Spalding - Sutton Bridge.

Things are quieter in the east although Melton is doing a brisk trade in school trains; a tender-first Yarmouth D16 4-4-0 working the six-coach 15.55 to Fakenham to form the

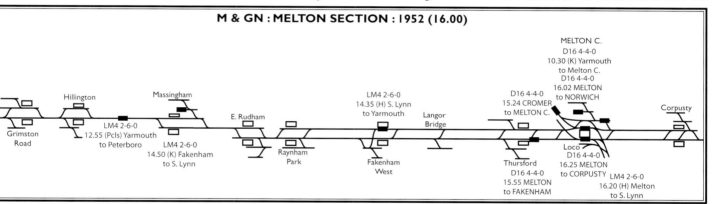

M & GN : MELTON SECTION : 1952 (16.00)

worked by a Melton D16 4-4-0 and the Spalding J6 0-6-0 on the Holbeach pilot.

While many of the fourteen trains mentioned are occupied with the clearing of agricultural and general traffic, the 14.50 ex Peterborough is an exception since its principal traffic is made up of bricks from Dogsthorpe sidings and Eye Green. The engine will clear all traffic from Dogsthorpe and will marshal the wagons into up and down trains at Eye Green; the up road traffic forming the return working to Peterborough at 20.52. Down road wagons will be taken to South Lynn for remarshalling by the 18.10 Peterborough - South Lynn.

which sees several evening departures for the North including one service that runs through to Saxby.

A considerable proportion of agricultural traffic is classified as passenger-rated and are catered for by a wide variety of parcels trains. Traffic for the Peterborough road is taken by the 14.45 South Lynn - Wisbech parcels train which, despite its designation, is actually a train of passenger stock (which goes on to form the 16.25 Wisbech to Peterborough) whilst, later in the evening, the 12.55 Yarmouth - Peterborough parcels clears any lingering traffic. Passenger rated traffic on the Spalding line is taken by

17.02 to North Walsham and Yarmouth whilst another tender-first D16 prepares to leave with the 16.25 for Corpusty. With the paucity of turntables in this neck of the woods, one can understand the popularity of the LMS 2-6-0's with their tender-cabs.

Business is very slack on the Yarmouth section where the only train in motion is the 12.45 from Peterborough which, in spite of having been running for over three hours, still has another hour and a quarter to go.

Quiet as it is, Yarmouth still has a few trains to despatch, one of them being something of a unique working.

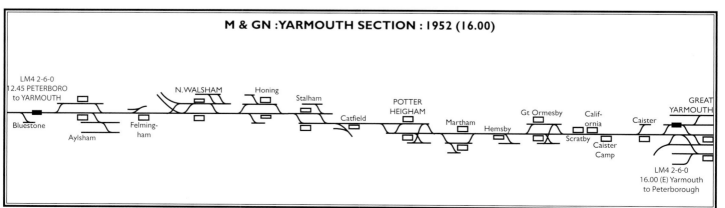

M & GN :YARMOUTH SECTION : 1952 (16.00)

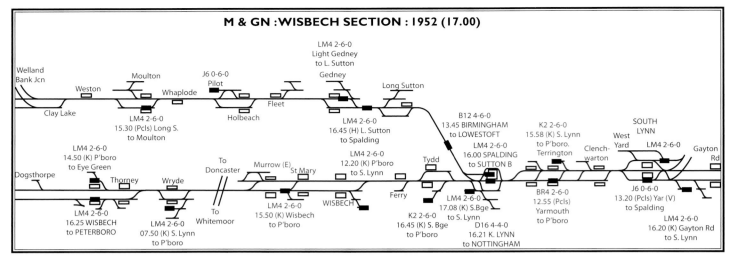

M & GN : WISBECH SECTION : 1952 (17.00)

Welland Bank Jcn — Weston — Moulton — Whaplode — Holbeach — Fleet — Gedney — Long Sutton — Clay Lake

LM4 2-6-0 / Light Gedney to L. Sutton
J6 0-6-0 Pilot
LM4 2-6-0 / 15.30 (Pcls) Long S. to Moulton
LM4 2-6-0 / 16.45 (H) L. Sutton to Spalding

Dogsthorpe — Thorney — Wryde — To Doncaster — Murrow (E) — St Mary — WISBECH — Ferry — Tydd — To Whitemoor — To

LM4 2-6-0 / 14.50 (K) P'boro to Eye Green
LM4 2-6-0 / 16.25 WISBECH to PETERBORO
LM4 2-6-0 / 07.50 (K) S. Lynn to P'boro
LM4 2-6-0 / 15.50 (K) Wisbech to P'boro
LM4 2-6-0 / 12.20 (K) P'boro to S. Lynn
K2 2-6-0 / 16.45 (K) S. Bge to P'boro

B12 4-6-0 / 13.45 BIRMINGHAM to LOWESTOFT
LM4 2-6-0 / 16.00 SPALDING to SUTTON B
LM4 2-6-0 / 17.08 (K) S.Bge to S. Lynn
D16 4-4-0 / 16.21 K. LYNN to NOTTINGHAM

SOUTH LYNN — West Yard — Clench-warton — Gayton Rd

K2 2-6-0 / 15.58 (K) S. Lynn to P'boro. Terrington
BR4 4-6-0 / 12.55 (Pcls) Yarmouth to P'boro
J6 0-6-0 / 13.20 (Pcls) Yar (V) to Spalding
LM4 2-6-0 / 16.20 (K) Gayton Rd to S. Lynn
LM4 2-6-0

CONTROLLER'S LOG: The unique train referred to in the preceding page is the 16.00 express goods from Yarmouth to Peterborough which is the only train to be worked over the entire 112 miles by the same engine. One or two engines do see both Yarmouth and Peterborough in the same shift but never, except in the case of the 16.00, on the same train. It would be an exaggeration to say that the engine - a South Lynn LM4 2-6-0 - was especially groomed for the job but the

to Moulton making a train for every two route miles which is a extraordinarily high figure. On a single-line system to boot! Most of the trains are goods services but their number includes one or two celebrities, the chief of which is the returning Leicester - the 13.45 Birmingham to Lowestoft - with the same B12 4-6-0 and dining car that accompanied the outward train this morning. As usual, engines will be changed at South Lynn; the relieving engine being the B12 that brought up the 10.05 Yarmouth -

reasonably good trains from Norwich to the West Midlands via Peterborough, one wonders why the M&GN took no advantage of its Spalding - Bourne line to run a similar service to the East Midlands. Were the 16.21 King's Lynn - Nottingham to start back at Norwich and called only at the principal stations, it would doubtless attract as much traffic as the cross-country trains on the Great Eastern but as it is, it seems designed to deter rather than the opposite since it makes no less than twenty-one calls to Melton

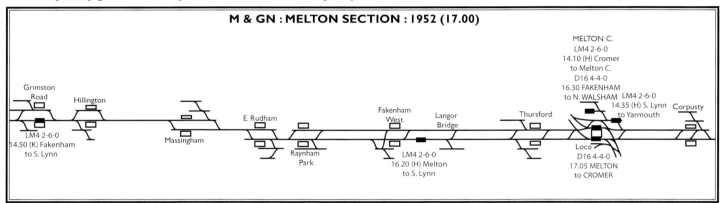

M & GN : MELTON SECTION : 1952 (17.00)

Grimston Road — Hillington — Massingham — E. Rudham — Raynham Park — Fakenham West — Langor Bridge — Thursford — MELTON C. — Corpusty — Loco

LM4 2-6-0 / 14.50 (K) Fakenham to S. Lynn
LM4 2-6-0 / 16.20 (H) Melton to S. Lynn

MELTON C.
LM4 2-6-0 / 14.10 (H) Cromer to Melton C.
D16 4-4-0 / 16.30 FAKENHAM to N. WALSHAM
LM4 2-6-0 / 14.35 (H) S. Lynn to Yarmouth
D16 4-4-0 / 17.05 MELTON to CROMER

only work it has done since arriving last night with the 14.35 from South Lynn is the afternoon trip to the White Swan. In fact the engine for tomorrow's 16.00 can be seen getting ready to leave Melton Constable where the South Lynn 2-6-0 has just relieved a Melton engine of the same class. (Nothing in the world of M&GN diagrams is straightforward!)

Was there ever a single-line system that could boast such a concentration of trains as can be seen at the West end of the system? Such is the demand for farm produce that there are now no less than twenty trains between South Lynn and Eye Green and from Sutton Bridge

Peterborough. Preceding the Leicester is the 15.40 Peterborough to King's Lynn which will also change engines, the D16 4-4-0 giving way to an LM4 2-6-0. The D16 does not disappear but merely waits for the 15.40 to reappear as the 17.55 King's Lynn - Yarmouth and proceeds to work it forward as far as Melton Constable.

On the up road, the 16.25 Wisbech - Peterborough (an extension of the 14.45 parcels from South Lynn) is at Eye Green whilst the 16.21 King's Lynn - Nottingham and its D16 4-4-0 waits at Sutton Bridge for the 13.45 Birmingham to clear the single line. Given that the Great Eastern ran a regular service of

Mowbray before - finally - donning the mantle of an express and running non-stop over the remaining eighteen miles to Nottingham. Three hours and thirty-nine minutes to cover seventy-four miles is not much of an advertisement and the only admirers the train possesses are the enthusiasts who marvel at the fact it requires as many as three engines. The first is a South Lynn D16 4-4-0 which goes as far as Spalding where it is relieved by a LM4 2-6-0 which takes the train the 10 miles to Bourne. At the latter point the Nottingham 2-6-4T that brought in the 16.20 Nottingham - King's Lynn takes over and completes the journey.

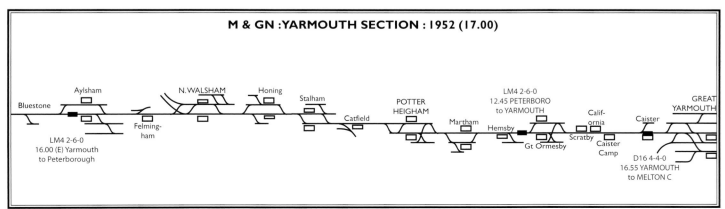

M & GN : YARMOUTH SECTION : 1952 (17.00)

Bluestone — Aylsham — Felming-ham — N. WALSHAM — Honing — Stalham — Catfield — POTTER HEIGHAM — Martham — Hemsby — Gt Ormesby — Scratby — Caister Camp — California — Caister — GREAT YARMOUTH

LM4 2-6-0 / 16.00 (E) Yarmouth to Peterborough
LM4 2-6-0 / 12.45 PETERBORO to YARMOUTH
D16 4-4-0 / 16.55 YARMOUTH to MELTON C

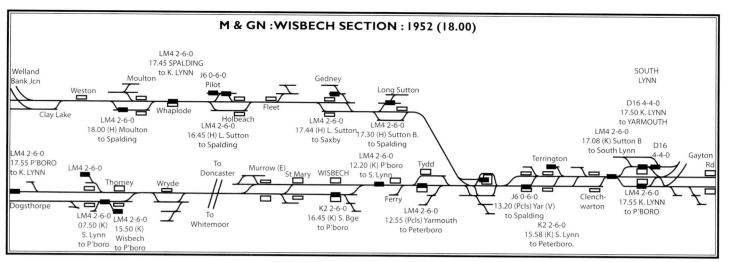

M & GN : WISBECH SECTION : 1952 (18.00)

CONTROLLER'S LOG: The number of trains west of Lynn is still at record numbers whilst some have been around for some time: the record being held by the 07.50 from South Lynn which has been on the run for over ten hours but has not yet got to Eye Green! One train of especial importance is the 17.44 from Long Sutton which is the only M&GN goods train to run through to Saxby and conveys through traffic for the Midland. The service actually started back at South Lynn at 13.50 but recessed at Long Sutton in order to leave at a

the Melton D16 4-4-0 that earlier worked the Leicester between Yarmouth and South Lynn and arrived in South Lynn a short while ago with the 15.40 Peterborough - King's Lynn. The train does rather well for 4-4-0's since it will have a third D16 for the Melton Constable - Yarmouth stage.

It is interesting to see the two parcels trains from Yarmouth - one at Tydd and the other at Walpole - both of which started at about the same time yet have reached South Lynn by very different routes. The 12.55, which has just

services that have just passed each other at North Walsham. The up train, the 16.55 from Yarmouth, is notable since it conveys six coaches rather than the standard set of four; the two additional vehicles being the balance of the 06.43 North Walsham - Yarmouth. The down train, which is waiting for the right-away, is a continuation of the 16.30 Fakenham West which consists of only two coaches although, earlier in its journey it conveyed six vehicles between Fakenham and Melton Constable.

At Yarmouth, the six-coach 18.15 to

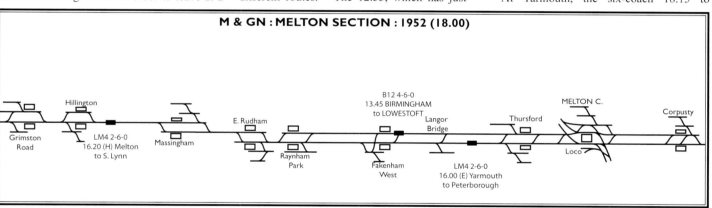

M & GN : MELTON SECTION : 1952 (18.00)

time convenient for picking up afternoon traffic from the intermediate stations.

South Lynn, as ever, is busy with passenger trains and has received two services in quick succession from King's Lynn. The first is the 17.50 to Yarmouth which reversed at South Lynn whilst the second is the 17.55 to Peterborough. The Yarmouth train is notable since it produces one of the few Great Eastern engines to be seen at South Lynn; the service being worked in by a King's Lynn D16 4-4-0 which returns light shortly after the train has departed. The train engine, which backs onto the trailing end, is

been re-engined at South Lynn, has followed the M&GN main line whilst the other, the 13.20 from Yarmouth Vauxhall, has come via the Great Eastern to join the M&GN at South Lynn after reversing at King's Lynn. As befits a train with such a peculiar routing, it is booked to a suitably distinctive class of engine and is worked by the J6 0-6-0 that worked down with the 07.15 Spalding - South Lynn goods.

Although goods trains are rather thin on the ground east of Melton, there are a number of interesting passenger trains in the offing, not the least of which are the two D16-worked

Cromer is preparing to depart behind an LM4 2-6-0 and one wonders how many passengers, if any, have booked through to Cromer and how many of them know that for the sake of a few minutes, their journey could be three quarters of an hour faster since the 18.15 reaches North Walsham only three minutes after the departure of a train to Cromer via Mundesley. Why this should be is a mystery although it is doubtful if it is an attempt to deliberately make the line unprofitable if only because the volume of traffic between Yarmouth and Cromer is scarcely worth a conspiracy.

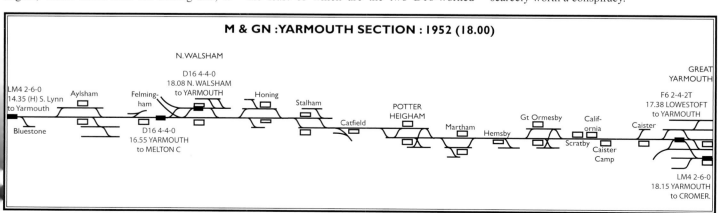

M & GN : YARMOUTH SECTION : 1952 (18.00)

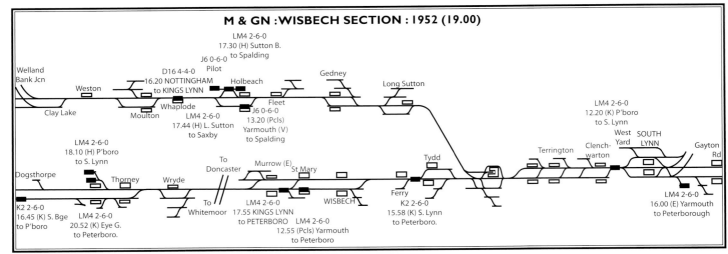

M & GN : WISBECH SECTION : 1952 (19.00)

LM4 2-6-0
17.30 (H) Sutton B.
to Spalding

J6 0-6-0
Pilot

D16 4-4-0
16.20 NOTTINGHAM
to KINGS LYNN
Holbeach

Gedney

Long Sutton

Welland
Bank Jcn

Weston

Whaplode

Clay Lake

Moulton

Fleet
J6 0-6-0
13.20 (Pcls)
Yarmouth (V)
to Spalding

LM4 2-6-0
17.44 (H) L. Sutton
to Saxby

LM4 2-6-0
12.20 (K) P'boro
to S. Lynn

West
Yard

SOUTH
LYNN

Terrington

Clench-
warton

Gayton
Rd

LM4 2-6-0
18.10 (H) P'boro
to S. Lynn

Dogsthorpe

Thorney

Wryde

To
Doncaster

Murrow (E)

St Mary

Tydd

LM4 2-6-0
16.00 (E) Yarmouth
to Peterborough

K2 2-6-0
16.45 (K) S. Bge
to P'boro

LM4 2-6-0
20.52 (K) Eye G.
to Peterboro.

To
Whitemoor

WISBECH

Ferry

K2 2-6-0
15.58 (K) S. Lynn
to Peterboro.

LM4 2-6-0
17.55 KINGS LYNN
to PETERBORO

LM4 2-6-0
12.55 (Pcls) Yarmouth
to Peterboro

CONTROLLER'S LOG: The number of trains west of Lynn has diminished noticeably although there remains quite a collection at Holbeach where goods trains for Saxby and Spalding sort themselves out in the yard - assisted by the J6 pilot - whilst the Yarmouth Vauxhall parcels is dealt with in up platform and waits for the afternoon train from Nottingham to clear the section from Whaplode. (The position at Holbeach is being reviewed and the Sutton Bridge - Spalding train is to be retimed to run a little later than at present). On the Peterborough

The M&GN's principal goods train, the 16.00 Yarmouth - Peterborough has arrived at South Lynn and is allowed thirty-five minutes to attach traffic and to remove a Great Eastern section which will be taken to King's Lynn, along with the vehicles off the 12.20 ex Peterborough, by the 20.05 trip.

The Yarmouth train consists of four sections - Peterborough fitted, South Lynn GE transfers, Peterborough Midland and New England. The third section consists largely of traffic for Liverpool and Manchester and is detached at

Whaplode, the 17.50 King's Lynn - Yarmouth approaching Melton where one D16 will be replaced by another, and the 18.08 ex North Walsham which is just outside Yarmouth. To crown matters, the Leicester, which is passing the 18.15 Yarmouth - Cromer at Stalham, has a B12 4-6-0 at its head. The remainder have the all-encroaching LMS 2-6-0's as their engines.

Quite a number of M&GN trains have run through to King's Lynn lately and a visitor might well wonder why, when it is not so long ago that the push and pull service was introduced.

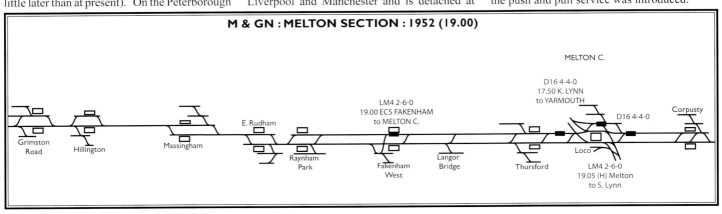

M & GN : MELTON SECTION : 1952 (19.00)

MELTON C.

D16 4-4-0
17.50 K. LYNN
to YARMOUTH

D16 4-4-0

Corpusty

LM4 2-6-0
19.00 ECS FAKENHAM
to MELTON C.

E. Rudham

Grimston
Road

Hillington

Massingham

Raynham
Park

Fakenham
West

Langor
Bridge

Thursford

Loco

LM4 2-6-0
19.05 (H) Melton
to S. Lynn

line, a through goods has called at Eye Green to collect Dogsthorpe traffic from the Eye Green shunt whilst, in the opposite direction, the 15.58 Lynn to Peterborough goods has, apart from a brief halt at Wisbech North, finished the list of stations it has to serve and is right-away to Westwood Yard from Tydd.

The 12.20 goods from Peterborough has almost completed its journey and is approaching South Lynn with a full load, much of which consists of vegetable traffic for the Great Eastern. This will be hurriedly shunted out and made ready for the 20.05 trip to King's Lynn.

Wisbech Sidings, Peterborough to be tripped to Peterborough East in time to connect with the 00.40 Peterborough to Derby goods.

Despite the time spent at South Lynn, the engine - a South Lynn LM4 2-6-0 - works through and the train is the only service to be worked from Yarmouth to Peterborough without a change of engine. Much of the traffic conveyed by the service consists of Potato Crisps, frozen food and bottles of lemonade.

In passenger circles, pre-grouping engines seem to be in temporary vogue with D16 4-4-0's on the 16.20 Nottingham - King's Lynn at

The answer is that the Push and Pull is not an M&GN working but is allocated to the Great Eastern who - possession being nine points of the law - abstract it for the 17.43 King's Lynn to Dereham and the 19.11 return which results in the set being away from South Lynn for about four hours. Equally, the through trains concerned are of sufficient importance to warrant being extended to King's Lynn and thus they take the part of the shuttle which will next appear in South Lynn with the 21.30 from King's Lynn: the connection for the 20.10 Peterborough to Melton Constable.

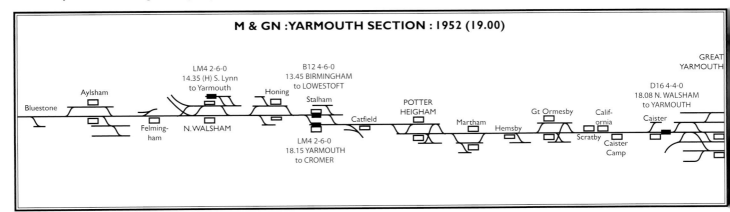

M & GN : YARMOUTH SECTION : 1952 (19.00)

GREAT
YARMOUTH

LM4 2-6-0
14.35 (H) S. Lynn
to Yarmouth

B12 4-6-0
13.45 BIRMINGHAM
to LOWESTOFT

Honing

D16 4-4-0
18.08 N. WALSHAM
to YARMOUTH

Bluestone

Aylsham

Felming-
ham

N. WALSHAM

Stalham

Catfield

POTTER
HEIGHAM

Martham

Hemsby

Gt Ormesby

Calif-
ornia

Caister

LM4 2-6-0
18.15 YARMOUTH
to CROMER

Scratby

Caister
Camp

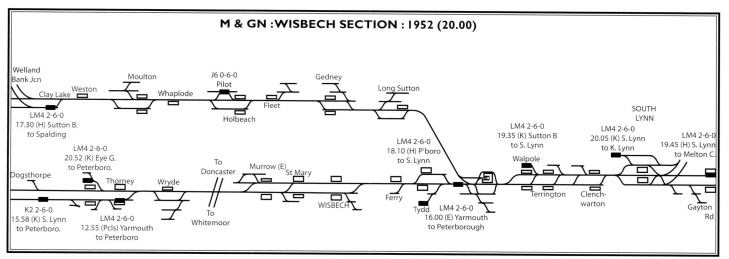

CONTROLLER'S LOG: The 17.44 ex Long Sutton and the 17.30 from Sutton Bridge have at last cleared Holbeach and Moulton yards and are on their way; the first passing North Drove on its way to Bourne and Saxby and the other at Clay Lake, about to take the road for Spalding. All that remains of several hours hearty activity is the J6 0-6-0 pilot at Holbeach which will spend the next hour clearing up the mess. There is still some activity on the Peterborough road, especially at the far end where the 15.58 ex South Lynn runs the gauntlet ahead of the Yarmouth Parcels.

The planning people could not have made this seemingly simple operation more complicated had they tried since not only are the engines changed - an LM4 2-6-0 for a D16 4-4-0 - but the leading four coaches have to be detached leaving only the trailing pair to go forward to Cromer. The 2-6-0 therefore draws the train well down the platform and after a brief pause, shunts the leading portion over to the down platform onto the rear of the newly arrived 19.25 from Cromer. A D16 4-4-0 backs onto the two Cromer coaches in the down platform the rear half of which is suddenly occupied by

twenty-four miles between North Walsham and Yarmouth: quite a distance for an M&GN goods. A lowly class H service, in many respects it is the complement to the 16.00 Yarmouth - Peterborough and although nothing like as fast, its schedule of 63 minutes from North Walsham to Yarmouth is about the same as most stopping trains.

In common with most M&GN trains, it undergoes a change of engines, the 2-6-0 working into Yarmouth having taken over at Melton after bringing down the 12.45 goods from South Lynn. Although the engine is

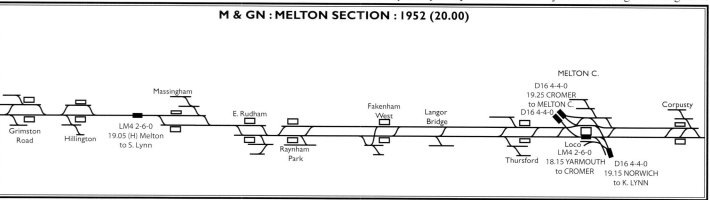

The express goods from Yarmouth has left South Lynn for a non-stop run to Wisbech Sidings, Peterborough and is now approaching Tydd. When it reaches Peterborough, the engine will spend a couple of hours on Spital Bridge Loco before returning to the M&GN with the 23.45 Crescent - South Lynn goods.

The number of passenger trains has also diminished and most of those that remain seem to be heading for Melton Constable whose staff are in for a lively few minutes as the 18.15 Yarmouth - Cromer runs into the up platform.

the 19.15 Norwich - King's Lynn passenger. The D16 4-4-0 that has arrived with the latter is uncoupled as the Cromer train pulls out and is released to the Loco via the intermediate crossover in the down platform. Finally the 2-6-0 which brought in the 18.15 from Yarmouth backs onto the Norwich train and works it away to South Lynn. All this has to be accomplished in no more than ten minutes!

The down goods that has just passed Martham is something of a celebrity in East Norfolk circles since it runs non-stop over the

based at South Lynn, when the train reaches Yarmouth, it will stable for nearly eighteen hours; its next task being the 16.00 express goods to Peterborough. This is one of several cyclic workings on the M&GN although this one is strange since South Lynn 2-6-0's work both parts. It is more usual to divide the work between two depots.

Approaching Stalham is the 17.50 passenger from King's Lynn which is a disguised extension of the 15.40 Peterborough - King's Lynn. The stock is the return of the 10.05 ex Yarmouth.

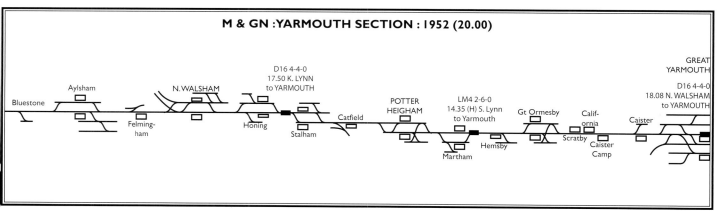

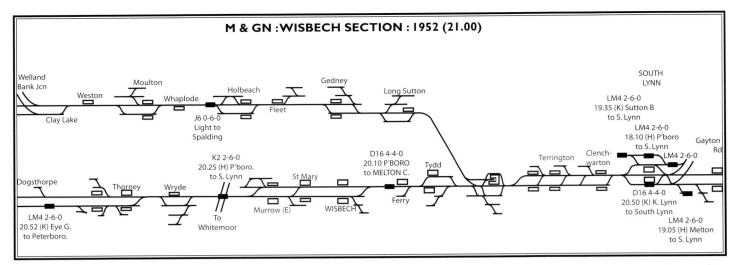

M & GN : WISBECH SECTION : 1952 (21.00)

Welland Bank Jcn · Weston · Clay Lake · Moulton · Whaplode · J6 0-6-0 Light to Spalding · Holbeach · Fleet · Gedney · Long Sutton · Tydd · Ferry · D16 4-4-0 20.10 P'BORO to MELTON C. · Terrington · Clenchwarton · SOUTH LYNN · LM4 2-6-0 19.35 (K) Sutton B to S. Lynn · LM4 2-6-0 18.10 (H) P'boro to S. Lynn · LM4 2-6-0 · Gayton Rd

Dogsthorpe · LM4 2-6-0 20.52 (K) Eye G. to Peterboro. · Thorney · Wryde · K2 2-6-0 20.25 (H) P'boro. to S. Lynn · To Whitemoor · Murrow (E) · St Mary · WISBECH · D16 4-4-0 20.50 (K) K. Lynn to South Lynn · LM4 2-6-0 19.05 (H) Melton to S. Lynn

CONTROLLER'S LOG: Night is falling and so is the number of trains and although there is a fair bit of activity at South Lynn, the general state of play contrasts starkly with affairs of only two hours ago. Jokes by uninformed outsiders about running trains by the calendar are too stale to be amusing yet at Yarmouth there are occasions when it is almost true. Normally the last departure is the 18.15 to Cromer but on Wednesdays (and Saturdays) Yarmouth market is held and an additional train is run at 21.00 for all stations to North Walsham in the rather touching belief that farmers still

of protest audible from Gorleston to Gedney. The operation of the train is quite interesting since the four corridor coaches are those of the previous day's 17.55 King's Lynn - Yarmouth which have a layover for cleaning before leaving with the 07.45 to Aylsham. On the cleaning day, the set works the 13.20 Yarmouth - Potter Heigham on Wednesdays (early closing day) or the 21.00 North Walsham on Thursdays and Saturdays. On the other days the set simply sits spare at Yarmouth. The engine used for the 21.00 is one of Yarmouth's F6 2-4-2 tanks.

The 19.15 Norwich (City) to King's Lynn

then the 2-6-0 working the train in from Melton will have to run-round and continue forward to King's Lynn.

The goods trips to and from King's Lynn are as important as any train on the system, especially as they are the conduit by which traffic for the M&GN is funnelled in from the huge yard at Whitemoor. There are seven a day booked to run from King's Lynn - slightly less in the opposite direction - and are powered by a variety of main line engines except for a pair of trips which are worked by the West Yard pilot. Most trains are booked to LM4 2-6-0's but one

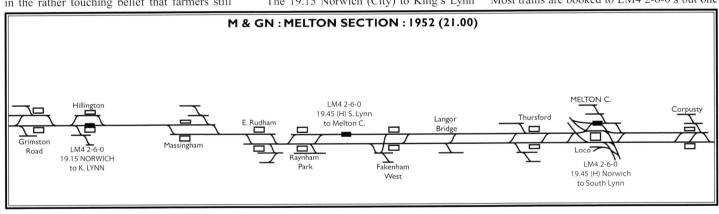

M & GN : MELTON SECTION : 1952 (21.00)

Grimston Road · Hillington · LM4 2-6-0 19.15 NORWICH to K. LYNN · Massingham · E. Rudham · Raynham Park · LM4 2-6-0 19.45 (H) S. Lynn to Melton C. · Fakenham West · Langor Bridge · Thursford · MELTON C. · Loco · LM4 2-6-0 19.45 (H) Norwich to South Lynn · Corpusty

rely on public transport. In fact, thanks to recent subsidies of one sort and another, farmers are the postwar *nouveaux riche* - many have not seen the inside of a train for ten years - and East Anglian farmers are amongst the wealthiest of the lot with a high car ownership to boot. Thus the 21.00 on Wednesdays carries but a handful of passengers out of Yarmouth and even less on the way back. Liverpool Street do not seem to be fully abreast of the changing times but, of course, if anyone was to propose withdrawing the 21.00, there would be a howl

- surprisingly the only through train between the two points - is at Hillingdon and a check must be made to ensure that the engine to work it forward from South Lynn is standing by. The check is more than usually necessary since the engine was last seen working the 17.55 Peterborough - King's Lynn and remains with the Great Eastern until reappearing on the M&GN with the 20.30 trip from Harbour Junction. Goods trips can be unpredictable in their movements and therefore it pays to keep one's finger on the pulse - if the trip is delayed

- the 20.50 from King's Lynn (Exton Road) - is booked to a D16 4-4-0 which, since the Claud's have a freight classification three wagons less than a C12 4-4-2T, is not always helpful.

The 20.10 Peterborough to Melton is approaching Ferry and is notable for being one of the few trains not to be booked to change engines at South Lynn. This is because the D16 4-4-0 working the train is one of the two Melton duties to run to Peterborough and the engine is on its way home. Its inward working was with the 12.42 Yarmouth - Peterborough.

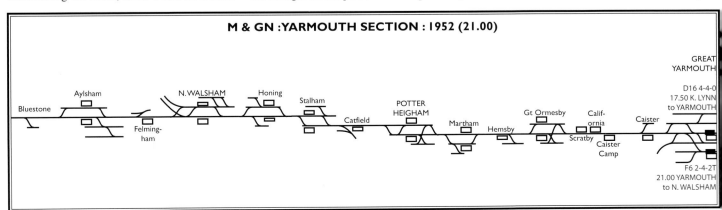

M & GN : YARMOUTH SECTION : 1952 (21.00)

Bluestone · Aylsham · Felmingham · N. WALSHAM · Honing · Stalham · Catfield · POTTER HEIGHAM · Martham · Hemsby · Gt Ormesby · Scratby · California · Caister Camp · Caister · GREAT YARMOUTH · D16 4-4-0 17.50 K. LYNN to YARMOUTH · F6 2-4-2T 21.00 YARMOUTH to N. WALSHAM

M & GN : WISBECH SECTION : 1952 (22.00)

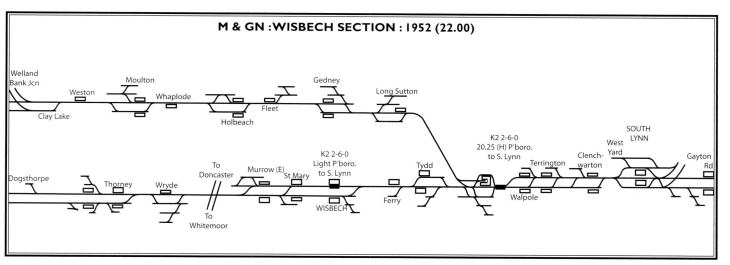

CONTROLLER'S LOG: The night shift takes over and takes stock of what remains of the train service. The Bourne line has switched out as far as Little Bytham Junction and even the Peterborough line, normally so busy, can only field a K2 2-6-0 en route from New England Loco to South Lynn, returning light after working the 15.58 South Lynn to Westwood goods. Technically the engine is 'as required' when it reaches Peterborough and although this is intended to mean that it may work any special

for the 05.30 South Lynn - Colwick in the morning.

When the tables are turned and South Lynn finds itself with an unbalanced New England engine and uses it on a special to Colwick, the reaction is apocalyptic with threatening letters being generated on a wide scale........

Ahead of the light engine, another K2 makes its way over the Nene at Sutton Bridge with the 20.25 from Crescent Yard, this being the return of the 16.45 Sutton Bridge - Peterborough

the running of the 20.10 from Peterborough is closely watched and if it leaves South Lynn more than a few minutes later, it will have to be held at either Hillington or Grimston Road to keep the up goods on time.

The 19.45 was remarshalled before leaving Melton (the order being: engine, LMR goods, South Lynn roughs and New England transfers) and on reaching South Lynn the first and last sections are shunted onto the 23.05 departure whilst the centre section is hurriedly shunted

M & GN : MELTON SECTION : 1952 (22.00)

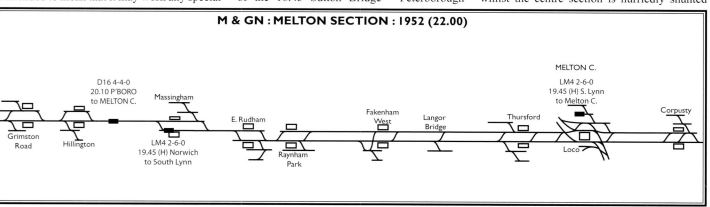

trains New England may have for the M&GN, the GN Controller at Knebworth is quite likely to have his own interpretation of the working with the result that the engine might be used for a Peterborough - Doncaster special.

Knebworth has a reputation for being somewhat high-handed where other people's engines are concerned and will almost certainly not volunteer the fact that the engine has been taken to work an urgent (all GN trains seem to be urgent) special of vans to Doncaster, tempers often become frayed. To make matters worse the engine is one of those involved in the joint South Lynn/Colwick working and is required

goods. This particular engine has had a long day and started work at 03.20 this morning.

If the 16.00 Yarmouth - Peterborough is the most important goods service on the system, then the second is the 19.45 Norwich City to South Lynn which at the moment is waiting at Massingham for the 20.10 Peterborough - Melton passenger to clear the section.

Worked throughout by a South Lynn LM4 2-6-0, the Norwich goods has something of a race against time since it is due into South Lynn at 22.45 yet has to have much of its traffic transferred to the 23.05 and 23.25 Peterborough and King's Lynn services. Because of this,

in order to extricate all wagons that have to connect with the trip to King's Lynn.

The 19.45 Melton - South Lynn and the 19.45 South Lynn - Melton Constable are the trains that signal the end of goods activities on the Eastern Section for the day and whilst South Lynn has to deal with a handful of trains during the night, all that remains to be done at Melton Constable is the berthing of the 20.10 Peterborough passenger after it arrives at 22.45.

In the meantime the J67 0-6-0T pilot will shunt out the wagons of the 19.45 from South Lynn before finishing at 23.00.

M & GN : YARMOUTH SECTION : 1952 (22.00)

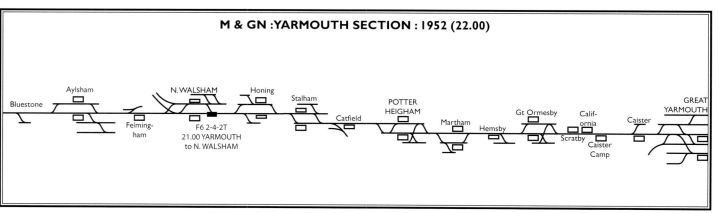

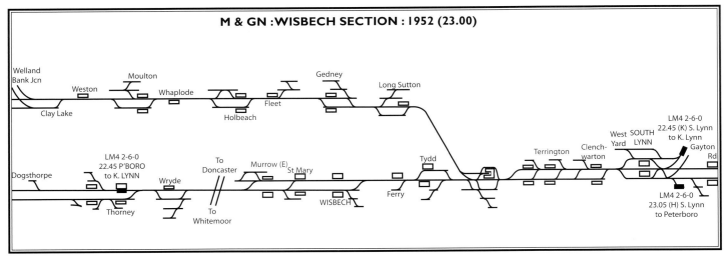

M & GN : WISBECH SECTION : 1952 (23.00)

CONTROLLER'S LOG: It is pleasing to find an instance where the M&GN does not play second-fiddle to the Great Eastern and one such concerns the final service of the day between London and King's Lynn which starts from King's Cross; the last service from Liverpool Street being the 19.20 Liverpool Street to Norwich with a change at Ely, reaching King's Lynn at 22.20. The M&GN is able to plug the gap by running a train in connection with the 20.20 King's Cross - Edinburgh, reaching

is the same 2-6-0 that went up with the 17.55 from King's Lynn and although the diagram is a relatively short one, starting at five in the evening, the engine may well have been in traffic for much longer since fourteen engines for thirteen diagrams cuts things rather fine and in times of famine the engine of the 12.55 Yarmouth - Peterborough which is spare at South Lynn from 16.30 is hurriedly coaled and used to double up.

As the passenger train makes its way east,

minutes away from terminating in Yarmouth. It is strange that the train should return from North Walsham as a booked passenger train since most services of this type usually return as empty stock.

So, with the railway all but closed for the night, it is time to scrutinise the traffic sheets to see what each yard has on hand for the morning trains and what requirements there are for empty wagons. Details of traffic moved, trains cancelled and specials run are written up in the

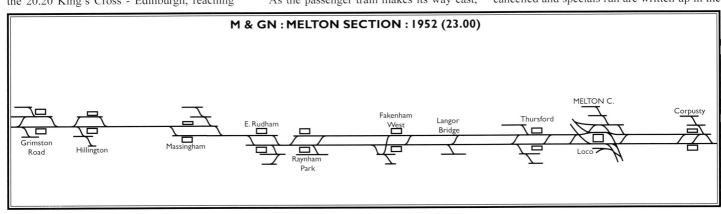

M & GN : MELTON SECTION : 1952 (23.00)

King's Lynn at 23.59; an hour of the overall time being accounted for by almost an hour's wait at Peterborough during which mails are sorted and loaded. The journey is certainly value for money with an A4 Pacific to Peterborough followed by the best M&GN timing of the day - 67 minutes from Peterborough to South Lynn with stops at both Wisbech stations, Sutton Bridge and Terrington only. As for the hour's wait, if anyone can tire of an hour at a busy railway station like Peterborough North then, like Johnson's Londoner, they must indeed be tired of life...........

The engine of the 22.45 ex Peterborough

at South Lynn a trio of 4MT 2-6-0's fuss about the East Yard, one having arrived with the 19.45 goods from Norwich whilst another stands by to back down on the 23.05 goods to Crescent Yard, Peterborough. A third pulls away with the 22.45 trip to King's Lynn and will return with the 23.25 goods. The Peterborough train works forward traffic brought in by the Norwich service and the activity on the yard is considerable.

East of Lynn, the railway sleeps unless it happens to be one of the nights when the late Yarmouth - North Walsham train runs in which case the F6 and its four coaches will be a few

Controller's log together with recommendations for altered permanent workings, changes to engine diagram and similar cri des coeur intended to improve the method of working but which - as the writer in his heart of hearts knows full well - may draw a smile of amusement in the long cold corridors of Liverpool Street but not much else.

So concludes this tour of a typical day in the life of the M&GN which, the authors hope, will have dispelled the notion that the system was some sort of ramshackle system from the world of Emmett. It should be remembered for being the busy and hard-worked system that it was.

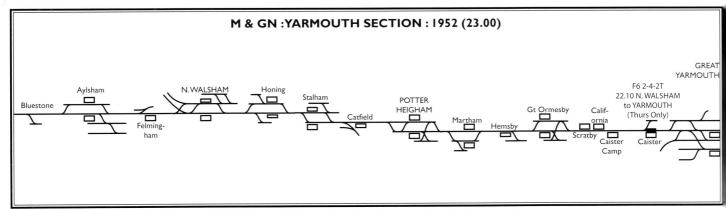

M & GN : YARMOUTH SECTION : 1952 (23.00)

Five miles from the western extremity of the Midland & Great Northern, LMS 4MT 2-6-0 43110 (South Lynn) leaves Bourne with the eleven-coach 08.40 Cromer Beach to Birmingham New Street on Saturday 4th August 1954. The 2-6-0 worked the train as far as Leicester where it was relieved by Compound 4-4-0 41059 of Derby. (V. R. Webster / Kidderminster Railway Museum)

4F 0-6-0 44414 (Nottingham) runs into Bourne on the 7th August 1954 with the nine-coach 08.50 Chesterfield to Yarmouth Beach which it worked as far as South Lynn. 4F 0-6-0's were classified by the ex-LNER as RA 5 engines but were given a dispensation to work over the RA 4 line between Sutton Bridge and South Lynn which allowed them to play a significant role in M&GN Summer Saturday workings. Another advantage enjoyed by the 4F's was that, being a goods engine, they were allowed to haul 10% more than a 4P or 4MT locomotive. Thus where a B12 4-6-0 or LMS 2-6-0 was limited to nine coaches (on standard running times) between Saxby and Bourne, a 4F could take ten. A further point of interest concerns the two coaches next to the engine which appear to be GWR non-corridor vehicles. Prior to entering service the train had been stabled in Unstone Colliery Sidings next to the vehicles that had formed the 09.15 Weston-super-Mare to Sheffield and were unbalanced. Two of the latter were GWR coaches with no return working and appear to have been commandeered for a trip to East Anglia. 44414 returned from South Lynn with the 11.30 Yarmouth Beach - Mansfield which it worked as far as Nottingham where it was relieved by 4F 0-6-0 44470 (Kirkby) (V. R. Webster / Kidderminster Railway Museum)

W hilst the M&GN proclaimed the names of both the Midland and the Great Northern, there is no doubt that links with the latter were far stronger than with the former, even though the system had direct access to both. A glance at the timetables of the early 1950's - not that things changed much - indicated that of the ten principal trains in the down direction, eight came from the Great Northern station at Peterborough whilst services from the Midland amounted to no more than one train from Birmingham via Leicester and an appalling slow service from Nottingham to King's Lynn. However, it has to be conceded that the through train from Birmingham was the only dining car express the M&GN possessed even though the facility was limited to a buffet car that accompanied the train only between Leicester and South Lynn.

Leaving the main line at Sutton Bridge, the Midland line - for want of a better description - ran in a roughly north-westerly direction for 30 miles to make an end-on connection with the Midland proper at Little Bytham Junction, thirteen miles east of Saxby on the Kettering - Nottingham main line. The thirty M&GN miles were largely single line with passing loops at most stations although one had to take care when arranging passenger train paths since only goods trains could pass each other at Long Sutton and Fleet. Whilst freight - especially agricultural - traffic could be heavy, the area was a wilderness for passengers and the only point of importance was Spalding which through trains could only reach via a diversion and a reversal. This posed a dilemma for train planners who had to weigh up the respective merits of running direct from Welland Bank to Cuckoo Junctions (three minutes) or going via Spalding which took six minutes running time plus (at least) as many to reverse and change engines.

Faced with such a poser, timetable compilers preferred to avoid the issue by regarding Spalding as the starting point for most passenger trains which had the depressing effect on passengers from Bourne to Holbeach - admittedly not a numerous ensemble - of extending their journey times out of all proportion to the distance travelled. Spalding, however, was an important market town and a major railway junction and almost certainly contributed more to the M&GN passenger coffers than most M&GN stations. In BR days, Spalding's importance was such that only two trains a day used the avoiding line, one being an evening goods from Long Sutton to Saxby and the other being the express from Lowestoft to Birmingham. (By June 1956 the search for passengers reached such heights that the express - the *Leicester* as it was widely known - was rerouted to call at Spalding at the cost of an extra sixteen minutes running time).

The avoiding line was useful on Summer Saturdays when a number of through trains between the Midlands and the Norfolk coast entered the M&GN at Little Bytham but such matters were an aberration - they did not contribute a post-war penny to the M&GN's costs - and have been given a disproportionate amount of credit. In fact the additional trains

BOURNE STATION WORKING - 1952						
Train	Arrive	Loco	Shed	Stock	Depart	Destination
		LM4 2-6-0	BN1	25/3	07.40	King's Lynn
06.40 King's Lynn	08.51	LM4 2-6-0	BN1	29/3	08.53	Nottingham
09.55 Saxby	10.36	LM4 2-6-0	BN1	30/3	10.39	King's Lynn
11.45 Spalding	12.06	LM4 2-6-0	BN1	21/3		
08.15 Lowestoft	12.22	B12 4-6-0	SL14	36/6	12.27	Birmingham
		LM4 2-6-0	BN2	21/3	12.38	Saxby
13.45 Saxby	14.22	LM4 2-6-0	BN2	21/3	14.26	Spalding
13.45 Birmingham	16.20	B12 4-6-0	SL14	37/6	16.25	Lowestoft
16.08 Spalding	16.29	2 x LM4 2-6-0	BN1/SP8	21,31/6	(16.31)	Detach pilot/carriage set
Detach pilot/carriage set	(16.29)	LM4 2-6-0	SP8	31/3	16.31	Nottingham
		LM4 2-6-0	BN2	21/3	16.35	Spalding
16.20 Nottingham	17.53	4MT 2-6-4T	NM1	29/3	(18.10)	(Change engines)
(Change engines)	(17.53)	LM4 2-6-0	BN1	29.3	18.10	King's Lynn
16.21 King's Lynn	18.29	LM4 2-6-0	BN2	30/3	(18.40)	(Change engines)
(Change engines)	(18.29)	4MT 2-6-4T	NM1	30/3	18.40	Nottingham
20.36 Spalding	20.57	LM4 2-6-0	BN1	25/3		(Stable for 07.40)
19.42 Nottingham	21.04	LM4 2-6-0	SP8	21/3	21.07	Spalding

numbered only seven in each direction and were as nothing compared to the value of the workaday goods traffic that the M&GN dealt with other days of the year.

In the motive power sense, the Bourne branch was remarkably self-contained and, indeed, was remarkably well equipped since not only was there a relatively large establishment at Spalding, responsible for supplying eight M&GN engines each day, but there was another at Bourne which had an allocation of two modern LMS 4MT 2-6-0's and which, from the perspective of the train-spotting community, must have been some of the least-seen engines in Britain since the duties of both engines were bounded by Saxby in the West and Spalding in the South. The three sets of men at Bourne followed similarly unadventurous lives and in theory one could spend one's life at Sutton Bridge and never see a Bourne engine or driver. In reality the engines were shuffled around by Spalding which, in turn, received its allocation from New England so that an engine working from Bourne in one week might be seen at Yarmouth the next. Similarly gaps in Bourne's driving and firing links were patched up by Spalding.

One exercise in which the Bourne line excelled was the changing of engines and the Leicester was the only passenger train to reach Saxby with the same engine with which it had left Sutton Bridge. Naturally, most of the engine changes were because of the reversal at Spalding but Bourne, which was a rather unremarkable through station, also had its moments. Opening its doors at half-past seven each morning, it survived until lunch time on two engines: the Leicester B12 and one of its own 2-6-0's which spent the day shuttling between Saxby and Spalding. In the evening matters became more interesting, the show starting with the arrival of the through afternoon train from Spalding to Nottingham, the train running in with no less than six coaches - the same as the Leicester on an ordinary day - and a pair of LMS moguls.

Although double-heading was not expressly forbidden on the M&GN (East Anglia generally had more prohibitions on double-heading than

most parts of the country), it was barred over the Ouse Bridge, just West of South Lynn and as a result double-heading was unusual. It need hardly be added that the weight of M&GN services were such that two engines were rarely a consideration

The fact, then, that one should stumble across it at the distant outpost of Bourne made it all the more strange. The fanciful side of the observer's nature suggested that since a train going from the M&GN to industrial Nottingham was an event of moment, the second engine and the extra coaches might have been attached as some sort of a mark of respect: East Anglia doffing its cap to the mighty Midland. The reality, however, was that the double-heading was a balancing move since the second engine was needed to re-engine the 16.20 Nottingham to King's Lynn whilst the rear three coaches were uncoupled for immediate return to Spalding as the 16.35 local.

Variety was hardly the watchword of motive power affairs at Bourne but the flame of interest brightened each day with the approach of the 16.20 Nottingham to King's Lynn which was booked to a Nottingham class 4, either a 4MT 2-6-4T or a 4MT 2-6-0 although it tended to take whatever Nottingham happened to have available at that time of day. Bourne was as far as the stranger was allowed to get and it was replaced by an M&GN 2-6-0; the Nottingham engine returning home with the 16.21 King's Lynn to Nottingham.

Foreign engines were a rarity on the M&GN for the very good reason that they were not equipped with automatic token exchanging apparatus and therefore had to reduce speed to ten mph every time a token had to be exchanged. In the event of a train being worked by an unequipped engine, it had to be signalled in a particular way (the 'is line clear' signal was given a suffix of four beats on the bell) so that the signalmen on the line of route had time to position themselves.

As with the rest of the M&GN, passenger traffic was largely of secondary consequence and the real business of the railway was the movement of goods traffic and amongst the most active locations in this sense were the

WORKING TIMETABLE : 1951/2

Train	05.30	05.05	05.20	05.20	05.30	05.15	05.30	05.30	07.15	07.40	07.40	08.30	08.30	07.15	07.15	10.00	10.00	07.15	06.40	07.15	09.55
From	Spalding	Saxby	Saxby	Saxby	Spalding	Toton	Spalding	Spalding	Spalding	Bourne	Bourne	Bourne	Bourne	Spalding	Spalding	Spalding	Spalding	Spalding	Colwick	Spalding	Saxby
Class	Goods	Goods	Goods	Goods	Goods	EBV	Goods	Goods	Goods	Pass	Pass	Goods	Goods	Goods	Goods	Goods	Goods	Goods	Goods	Goods	Pass
Engine	SP 1	LTR 315	NM234	NM234	SP 1	TOT515	SP 1	SP 1	SP 3	BN 1	SL 7	SP 2	SP 2	SP 3	SP 3	SL 6	SL 6	SP 3	CC 1	SP 3	BN 1
Class	LM 4	4F	4F	4F	LM 4	8F	LM 4	LM 4	J6	LM 4	LM 4	LM 4	LM 4	J6	J6	LM 4	LM 4	J6	K2	J6	LM 4
Carriage Wkg/Vehicles										25/3	25/3										30/3
SAXBY		05.05	05.20		07.03																09.55
Edmondthorpe		05/18	05/34		07/13																10.02
Pains Sdgs					07.20																
Buckminster			05.45	05.55																	
South Witham		05/32		06.00																	10.13
Castle Bytham																					10.22
Little Bytham Junction		05/51																			10/27
BOURNE			06.10																		10.36
BOURNE										07.40		08.30									10.39
Twenty										07.47		08.45	08.54								10.46
Counter Drain										07.51											10.50
North Drove										07.55											10.54
Cuckoo Jcn										07/57					09.08						10/56
SPALDING										08.00					09.14				10.32		10.59
SPALDING	05.30								07.15	(08.15)	08.15					10.00		10.45			(11.31)
Welland Bank Jcn	05/33								07/18		08/18					10/05		10/47			
Clay Lake	05/35										08/19					10/07		10/49			
Weston											08.24										
Moulton									07.29		08.27										
Moulton	05/42								08.05		08.28					10/14		10/54			
Whaplode											08.31										
HOLBEACH	05.52								08.18		08.35			(08.18)		10.24					
HOLBEACH	06.26								(09.23)		08.37			09.23		10.29		11.00			
Fleet	06.36			06.51							08.42			09.33		10.25	10/37	11.04			
Gedney				07.00		07.23					08.46					10.34	10/41	10.50	11/07		
Long Sutton						07.31	08.24				08.50					10.46	10.51	10.58	11/09	11.47	
Dock Junction							08.36				08.56						11/02		11/16	11/58	
SUTTON BRIDGE							08.42				08.58						11.07		11/23	12.03	
Destination											K. Lynn						S. Lynn		S. Lynn	S. Lynn	

Train		06.15	06.40		05.30	06.40		06.40	06.40	06.40	06.40	05.55		07.30		05.55	05.55		11.45		05.55
From		Holwell	Bourne		Lynn	Bourne		Bourne	Bourne	K. Lynn	K. Lynn	Lynn		Lynn		Lynn	Lynn		Spalding		Lynn
Class	Goods	Goods	Goods	Goods	Goods	Goods	Goods	Goods	Goods	Pass	Pass	Goods	Pass	Goods	Pass	Goods	Goods	Goods	Pass	Goods	Goods
Engine	NM234	NM234	LTR 315	SP 2	SL 4	LTR 315	TOT515	LTR 315	LTR 315	SL 7	BN 1	SL 5	SL 6	SL 9	SP 1	SL 5	SL 5	NM234	BN 1	TOT73	SL 5
Class	4F	4F	4F	LM 4	K2	4F	8F	4F	4F	LM 4	LM 4	LM 4	LM 4	K2	LM 4	LM 4	LM 4	4F	LM 4	Garratt	LM 4
Carriage Wkg/Vehicles										29/3	29/3		22/3							21/3	
SUTTON BRIDGE				06/00						07.14		07.30	08.00	08.03	09.15						
Dock Junction				06/04						07/16		07/35	08/02	08/07	09/17						
Long Sutton				06/13						07.22		07.45	08.08	08.15	09.23	09.34					
Gedney				06/18						07.25			08.11	08/18	09.26	09.40	09.55				
Fleet				06/24						07.29			08.15	08.22	09.30		10.02				
HOLBEACH										07.33			08.19	08.29	09.34						10.35
HOLBEACH				06/31						07.35			08.20	08.44	09.36						11.12
Whaplode										07.40			08.25		09.41						
Moulton										07.42			08.27		09.43						11.25
Moulton				06/41						07.43			08.30	08/54	09.44						(12.27)
Weston										07.47			08.34		09.48						
Clay Lake				06/50						07/51			08/38	09/01	09/52						
Welland Bank Jcn				06/51						07/52			08/39	09/03	09/53						
SPALDING				06.56						07.56		(07.56)	08.41	09.08	09.58						
SPALDING			06.27	06.58							(08.30)				09.30				11.45		
Cuckoo Jcn			06/34								08/33								11.47		
North Drove											08.36								11.51		
Counter Drain											08.40								11.55		
Twenty			06/43								08.44								11.59		
BOURNE			06.55								08.51								12.06		
BOURNE						06.40					08.53								(12.38)		
Little Bytham Junction						07/00					09/05										
Castle Bytham						07.08	07.30				09.11										
South Witham	06.15						07.50	08.15			09.22										
Buckminster	06.20	06.40														11.20					
Pains Sdgs								07.55												12.25	
Edmondthorpe		06/52				08.05		08.41	08.55		09.31					11/32				12/35	
SAXBY		07.02						08.15	09.05		09.36					11.43				12.45	
Destination		Holwell	Colwick				Toton				Notts				Colwick				Holwell	Frod	

stations between Sutton Bridge and Spalding where extraordinary amounts of farm produce were loaded each evening.

The first goods train of the night was the 16.45 Long Sutton to Spalding which called at Gedney, Fleet, Holbeach and Moulton, taking traffic for London and the North of England. The latter had to be worked on the engine and were taken forward from Spalding by the 22.00 Whitemoor - Doncaster. The greater part of the traffic was for London and was worked from Spalding at 21.10 by the 15.57 Boston - Ferme Park express goods.

The 16.45 was followed an hour later by the 17.30 from Long Sutton which took the recessed load of the 13.50 from King's Lynn, adding to it at Gedney, Fleet, Holbeach and Moulton with traffic for stations other than London or the North of England.

Not all the traffic presenting itself was goods rated and for the passenger rated traffic, something of a hybrid service preceded the two goods trains from Long Sutton, running from Long Sutton to Moulton as a parcels trains and onward to Spalding as an express goods service.

The three services described were Great Northern in terms of destination and to cater for Midland traffic, a through service for Saxby departed from Sutton Bridge at 17.30. There was also a service from Spalding to Bourne with LM transfer traffic at 15.05.

Whilst the service appeared adequate on paper - and often was - much of the traffic fluctuated with the seasons and it was often difficult to plan ahead with any degree of accuracy. The solution was to develop a highly flexible approach and nowhere was this better demonstrated than by the arrangements for

Table 1

	09.55	09.48	07.30	07.30		08.15	12.10	12.10	12.10		13.15		13.45	13.45			13.15			13.45	
Train From	Saxby	Holwell	Toton	Toton		Colwick	Holwell	Holwell	Holwell		Spalding		Saxby	Saxby			Spalding			B'ham	
Class	Pass	Goods	Goods	Goods	Pass	Goods	Goods	Goods	Goods	Goods	Goods	Light	Pass	Pass	Light	Goods	Goods	Light	Pass	XP	Light
Engine	SP 4	NM234	TOT73	TOT73	SP 1	CC 2	TOT 84	TOT 84	TOT 84	SL 7	SP 5	SP 6	BN 2	BN 1	SP 2	SFD1	SP 5	SP 2	SP 1	SL 14	SP 2
Class	LM 4	4F	Garratt	Garratt	LM 4	K2	4F	4F	4F	LM 4	LM 4	J6	LM 4	LM 4	LM 4	J6	LM 4	LM 4	LM 4	B12	LM 4
Carriage Wkg/Vehicles	30/3				31/3								21/3	21/3						22/3	37/6
SAXBY		10/32	11.10			12/45							13.45							15.48	
Edmondthorpe		10/44	11.20	11.33		12.55	13.15						13/51							15/54	
Pains Sdgs				11.45																	
Buckminster			10.52					13.30	13.43												
South Witham									13.48				14.00							16.02	
Castle Bytham													14.09								
Little Bytham Junction													14/13							16/11	
BOURNE													14.22	(14.22)						16.20	
BOURNE													(14.26)	14.26			15.15			16.25	
Twenty														14.33		(To				16/31	
Counter Drain														14.37		Sleaford)					
North Drove														14.41							
Cuckoo Jcn														14.43						16/37	
SPALDING		(10.59)				11.39								14.46						A	
SPALDING		11.31			12.20	12.42				13.15	14.15						15.00		16.00	L	
Welland Bank Jcn		11/32			12/22	12/44				13/18	14/18						15/03		16/02	16/40	
Clay Lake		11/33			12/23	12/46				13/20	14/20						15/05		16/03	16/41	
Weston		11.38			12.28														16.08		
Moulton		11.41			12.31					13.29	14.27								16.11		
Moulton		11.42			12.32	12/51				14.05	14.30						15/12		16.12	16/46	
Whaplode		11.45			12.35														16.15		
HOLBEACH		11.49			12.39					14.18	14.38								16.20		
HOLBEACH		11.52			12.40	12/57				14.50	(pilot)						15/20		16.21	16/51	
Fleet		11.57			12.45	13/01											15.25	16.10	16.26	16/54	
Gedney		12.01			12.49	13/04											(pilot)	16.13	16.30	16/56	
Long Sutton		12.04			12.52	13/06					15.15					15.35		(pilot)	16.33	16/58	17.00
Dock Junction		12.09			13/01	13/13				14.30							15/45		16/38	17/02	
SUTTON BRIDGE		12.11			13.05	13/16				14.35							15.48		16.40	17/03	
Destination		K. Lynn				S. Lynn														Yar	

Table 2

	08.15	11.45	05.55	10.55			13.50		15.05	15.30	15.05	16.08	16.08	15.30		15.30		15.30			15.05
Train From	L'toft	Spalding	S. Lynn	Sleaford			S. Lynn		Spalding	Long S	Spalding	Spalding	Spalding	Long S		Long S		Long S			Spalding
Class	XP	Pass	Goods	Goods	Pass	Goods		Goods	Goods	Pcls	Goods	Pcls	Goods	Pass	Pass	Pcls	Light	Pcls	Goods		Goods
Engine	SL 14	BN 2	SL 5	SFD1	SP 1	SL 7	TOT 84	TOT 84	SP 4	SP 7	SP 4	SP 7	SP 4	SP 7	SP8/BN1	SP 8	SP 4	SP 5	SP 4	SP 5	SP 7
Class	B12	LM 4	LM 4	J6	LM 4	LM 4	4F	4F	LM 4	J6	LM 4	J6	LM 4	J6	2 x LM4	LM 4	LM 4	LM 4	LM 4	LM 4	J6
Carriage Wkg/Vehicles	37/6	21/3			31/3										31,31/6	31/3					
SUTTON BRIDGE	11.35				13.35	14.15			14.50								16.00				
Dock Junction	11.36				13/37	14.20			14/53								16/02				
Long Sutton	11.40				13.43				15.05		15.30						16.10			16.45	
Gedney	11.43				13.46				(stabled		15.33		15.43							16.50	
Fleet	11.45				13.50				to 17.44)				15.46				15.56				
HOLBEACH					13.54												16.02				
HOLBEACH	11.50				13.55												16.20				
Whaplode					14.00												16.24			16.41	
Moulton				(11.25)	14.02															16.43	
Moulton	11.56			12.27	14.10																
Weston																					
Clay Lake	12/01			12/37	14/16																
Welland Bank Jcn	12/02			12/39	14/17																
SPALDING	A			12.42	14.20																
SPALDING	L								15.05				16.08								
Cuckoo Jcn	12/06								15/12				16/11								
North Drove									15.16		15.40		16.14								
Counter Drain											15.50	16.00	16.18								
Twenty	12/13											16.09	16.22								17.15
BOURNE	12.22	(12.06)		13.40									16.29	(16.29)							17.30
BOURNE	12.27	12.38											(16.31)	16.31							
Little Bytham Junction	12/37	12/50												16/41							
Castle Bytham		12.55												16.47							
South Witham	12/49	13.05				14.25								16.57							
Buckminster						14.31		14.41													
Pains Sdgs																					
Edmondthorpe	12/56	13/13						14/53						17.06							
SAXBY	13.01	13.18						15/03						17.11							
Destination	B'ham							Holwell						Notts							

stations on the Saxby side of Moulton at times when the booked service was unlikely to have room to attach traffic at North Drove, Counter Drain and Twenty. In this event a special train was run in advance of the 17.30 ex Sutton Bridge from Spalding to Saxby. The notice required? An hour and a half.

A measure of the volume of traffic despatched between Sutton Bridge and Spalding can be gauged by the fact that Spalding Loco had to send a J6 0-6-0 to shunt at Holbeach for six and a half hours and a 2-6-0 to assist with the shunting at Fleet, Gedney and Long Sutton.

Most of the exchange traffic with the Midland or the GN was allowed to filter in at either Spalding or Saxby but an exception was made for coal which came from the ex-Great Northern's Nottingham district via Sleaford and Spalding and was worked in train loads from Colwick to South Lynn. The number of trains a day varied from two to three, depending on the time of year, and additional services were run when needed. With every house and factory dependant upon coal for heating, the Colwick trains were of especial importance to the M&GN. They also provided one of the few instances in which foreign engines could be regularly seen on M&GN metals since the workings were shared between South Lynn and Colwick; each shed providing an engine on alternate days. M&GN train crews worked as far as Sleaford.

For legal and technical purposes the M&GN ended at Little Bytham Junction but in geographical terms many people considered Saxby to be the boundary *de facto* since this was the point at which traffic from the M&GN joined the Midland system proper and there were no obvious signs that one was leaving one railway and joining another.

If this territorial elasticity can be accepted for the moment, then there were some very

WORKING TIMETABLE : 1951/2

			16.20	16.20	16.20	18.45	18.45	18.30	18.30	18.30	19.42	19.42
Train			Notts	Notts	Notts	Bourne	Bourne	Saxby	Saxby	Saxby	Nott'm	Nott'm
From / Class	Pass	Pass	Pass	Pass	Pass	Goods	Goods	Goods	Goods	Goods	Pass	Pass
Engine	BN 2	SL 5	NM	BN 1	SL 12	SP 7	SP 7	NM234	NM234	NM234	SP 8	SP 2/8
Class	LM 4	LM 4	LM4	LM 4	D16	J6	J6	4F	4F	4F	LM 4	2 X LM4
Carriage Wkg/Vehicles	21/3	21/3	29/3	29/3	29/3						31/3	31/3
SAXBY			17.15					18.30			20.27	
Edmondthorpe			17.22					18/40			20/33	20/33
Pains Sdgs												
Buckminster												
South Witham			17.32					18.57	19.07		20.43	
Castle Bytham			17.41						19.23	19.33	20.52	
Little Bytham Junction			17/45							19/41	20/56	
BOURNE			17.53	(17.53)						20.00	21.04	(21.04)
BOURNE	16.35			(18.10)	18.10	18.45					(21.07)	21.07
Twenty	16.42				18.20	18.59	19.42					21.14
Counter Drain	16.46				18.24							21.18
North Drove	16.50				18.28							21.22
Cuckoo Jcn	16/52				18/30		19/54					21/24
SPALDING	16.56				18.32	(18.32)	20.00					21.26
SPALDING		17.45			(18.47)	18.47						
Welland Bank Jcn		17/47				18/48						
Clay Lake		17/48				18/49						
Weston		17.53				18.54						
Moulton		17.56				18.57						
Moulton		17.57				18.58						
Whaplode		18.00				19.01						
HOLBEACH		18.04				19.05						
HOLBEACH		18.06				19.06						
Fleet		18.11				19.11						
Gedney		18.15				19.15						
Long Sutton		18.18				19.18						
Dock Junction		18/23				19/23						
SUTTON BRIDGE		18.25				19.25						
Destination						K. Lynn						

	16.21	16.45	16.21		16.21	16.45	17.44	17.30	17.44	17.30	17.44	17.30	13.20	17.44	17.30		17.44	
From	K. Lynn	Long S	K. Lynn		K. Lynn	Long S	Long S	Sutton B.	Long S	Sutton B.	Long S	Sutton B.	Yar	Long S	Sutton B.		Long S	
Class	Pass	Goods	Pass	Goods	Pass	Goods	Goods	Goods	Goods	Goods	Goods	Goods	Pcls	Goods	Goods	Pass	Goods	Light
Engine	SL 12	SP 5	BN 2	SP 4	NM	SP 5	SP 2	SP 1	SP 1	SP 1	SP 2	SP 1	SP 3	SP 2	SP 1	BN 1	NM234	SP 6
Class	D16	LM 4	LM 4	LM 4	LM4	LM 4	LM 4	LM 4	LM 4	LM 4	LM 4	LM 4	LM 4	LM 4	LM 4	LM 4	4F	J6
Carriage Wkg/Vehicles	30/3				30/3	30/3							14 Vans			25/3		
SUTTON BRIDGE	17.02							17.30					18.43					
Dock Junction	17/04							17/36					18/45					
Long Sutton	17.11						17.44	17.46		18.21			18/51					
Gedney	17.14	17.16						17.52	18.15	18.29		18.39	18/53					
Fleet	17.18	17.23			17.40				18.23		18.33	18/45	18/56					
HOLBEACH	17.23				17.50						18.42	18.53	19.01	(18.42)	(18.53)			
HOLBEACH	17.24				18.10						(19.19)	(19.28)	19.09	19.19	19.28			21.00
Whaplode	17.29																	
Moulton	17.31				18.23									19.30	19.39			
Moulton	17.39	18.00			18.35								19/14	19.42	19.49			21/08
Weston	17.43																	
Clay Lake	17/46	18/10			18/44								19/19	19/50	20/00			21/15
Welland Bank Jcn	17/47	18/12			18/46								19/20	19/51	20/05			21.16
SPALDING	17.50	18.15			18.51	(17.50)							19.23	A	20.10			21.20
SPALDING	18.05	(18.05)											L			20.36		
Cuckoo Jcn	18/08												19/56 (i/c			20/39		
North Drove	18.11												25 carr			20.42		
Counter Drain	18.15												set)			20.46		
Twenty	18.19													20/05		20.50		
BOURNE	18.29	(18.29)												20.16	(20.16)	20.57		
BOURNE	18.40	(18.40)												21.00	(21.00)			
Little Bytham Junction	18/51													21/22				
Castle Bytham	18.56																	
South Witham	19.07													21/43				
Buckminster																		
Pains Sdgs																		
Edmondthorpe	19/15													21/57				
SAXBY	19.19													22.06				
Destination	Notts																	

interesting pickings to be discovered in the thirteen-mile isthmus which spanned the iron ore workings to the South of Nottingham; picking that included the largest engines the London Midland had in their fleet.

Much of Britain's iron ore lay in an arc stretching from South Lincolnshire to Oxfordshire at a distance approximately 100 miles North of London and it was the M&GN's great misfortune that it finished only a stone's throw from the mines at South Witham. (Had history been able to allow the M&GN's forefathers to make an independent connection with the Midland main line, the line's history might have been very different. With iron ore mines at the western end of the line, who knows how many steelworks might have sprung up at places like Caister or Potter Heigham..........).

Three mines lay between Castle Bytham and Edmondthorpe and produced sufficient traffic for five trains of ore daily. The largest of the mines was that of the Stanton Ironworks at Pain's, Edmondthorpe, which despatched two trains a day, one to Toton and the other to Frodingham; the latter being distinctive since it was booked to one of the thirty Garratt 2-6-6-2 locomotives which worked the train as far as Mexborough. The Toton train was usually handled by an 8F 2-8-0 and such engines were necessary since ore was a heavy traffic whilst the full load of a train was no less than 75 wagons.

It was on workings such as this that the Garratt - equal to a 4F and a 3F 0-6-0 - came into its own and whereas an 8F 2-8-0 was limited to 60 wagons of ore, a Garratt could handle 76.

The mines at South Witham and Buckminster dealt less in block loads than in wagons for a variety of destinations which were worked on the trip basis by a pair of Toton 4F 0-6-0's that worked to a two-day cycle based at Holwell Sidings, Melton Mowbray.

One major difference between the M&GN and the Bourne - Saxby section was that of route availability and whereas the former contained engine restrictions and small print galore, the latter had only three restrictions - LMS Pacifics, unrebuilt Royal Scot 4-6-0's and 46170 - and there was very little chance of any of them appearing in the area. The only other limitations placed by the Midland concerned the Garratts, which were not allowed east of South Witham, and the fact that only one of the larger LMS engines was allowed on the M&GN bridge over the GN main line at a time.

It is surprising that Bourne at one end of the link should have a full-blown motive power establishment whilst Saxby, which could be quite busy at times, had not and had to rely on foreign sheds for its supply of engines. The early morning goods from Saxby to Bourne was booked to a 4F 0-6-0 from Leicester whilst the evening working that came back with the through goods from Sutton Bridge was worked by a Toton 4F.

Passenger traffic west of Bourne was not designed to inspire. The first train of the day from Saxby to Bourne and beyond did not start until 09.55 whilst the second did not leave until 13.45. Two of the five M&GN trains that arrived in Saxby terminated there and one wonders what it was that prevented the Midland from extending them the four miles to Melton Mowbray, a move that might have attracted

BOURNE YARD WORKING - 1952					
Train	Arrive	Loco	Shed	Depart	Destination
05.50 Saxby	06.10	4F 0-6-0	Leicester		
		4F 0-6-0	Leicester	06.40	Saxby
06.27 Spalding	06.55	LM4 2-6-0	Spalding 2		
		LM4 2-6-0	Spalding 2	08.30	Spalding
10.55 Sleaford	13.40	J6 0-6-0	Sleaford		
		J6 0-6-0	Sleaford	15.15	Sleaford
15.05 Spalding	17.30	J6 0-6-0	Spalding 7		
		J6 0-6-0	Spalding 7	18.45	Spalding
17.44 Long Sutton	20.16	LM4 2-6-0	Spalding 2		
18.30 Saxby	20.00	4F 0-6-0	Nottingham		
		4F 0-6-0	Nottingham	21.00	Saxby

some patronage.

There were odd glimpses of brightness. The westbound (up) *Leicester*, of which the M&GN men were so proud, ran non-stop from South Lynn to Bourne and in order to make sure as many passengers as possible were able to use it, preceded it with a connection from Spalding to Bourne that called at all stations, the same train then following the express from Bourne to Saxby for the benefit of passengers from Norfolk to Castle Bytham and South Witham. Such interlocking was worthy of the Southern Electric and had the added spice of variety since the stopping train, during its half-hour at Bourne, changed its 2-6-0 for another.

The working in the opposite direction was not quite so nicely arranged and although a connection was run from Bourne to Spalding, passengers returning from Castle Bytham or South Witham to Norfolk had a two-hour wait at Bourne.

One cannot talk of Bourne, Spalding or Saxby without making reference to Sutton Bridge which was the root of the 43-mile branch to the Midland main line.

Although the focal point for trains was South Lynn, many of the stations on the Bourne road had a healthy appetite for empties and it was generally convenient to station these vehicles at Sutton Bridge and leave South Lynn free for main line traffic. Congregating empties at Sutton Bridge also made them more accessible and if Holbeach suddenly called out for twenty vans, it was very much easier and faster to get an engine from Spalding loco to do the job than it was to put on a special from South Lynn.

The two principal trains from Sutton bridge were the 07.30 to Spalding (05.55 ex South Lynn) which collected empty wagons and distributed them as it proceeded up the line and the 17.40 to Spalding which took empties for the local stations, exchanging them en route for loaded traffic routed via Spalding. Not all the traffic collected by this train - much of which was perishable - was destined for the north of England and a considerable amount of London traffic was conveyed since it was easier and faster to work it via Spalding rather than taking it back to Sutton Bridge and transferring it to Peterborough or South Lynn services.

Apart from a 42' turntable -

SUTTON BRIDGE YARD (1952)					
Train	Arrive	Loco	Diagram	Depart	Destination
23.45 Peterborough	01.56	LM4 2-6-0	S. Lynn 15	02.20	South Lynn
05.55 South Lynn	06.24	LM4 2-6-0	S. Lynn 5	(07.30)	
		LM4 2-6-0	S. Lynn 5	07.30	Spalding
06.02 South Lynn	07.40	LM4 2-6-0	S. Lynn 6		
05.30 Spalding	08.42	LM4 2-6-0	Spalding 1		
07.50 South Lynn	10.40	LM4 2-6-0	S. Lynn 10	(11.19)	
10.00 Spalding	11.07	LM4 2-6-0	S. Lynn 6	(11.55)	
(10.40)		LM4 2-6-0	S. Lynn 10	11.19	Peterborough
(11.07)		LM4 2-6-0	S. Lynn 6	11.55	South Lynn
07.15 Spalding	12.03	J6 0-6-0	Spalding 3	12.25	South Lynn
		LM4 2-6-0	S. Lynn 7	14.15	Long Sutton
06.50 Peterborough	14.25	LM4 2-6-0	NWE 4	(14.45)	
14.30 Long Sutton	14.35	LM4 2-6-0	S. Lynn 7		
13.50 South Lynn	14.38	LM4 2-6-0	Spalding 4	(14.50)	
(14.45)		LM4 2-6-0	NWE 4	14.45	South Lynn
(14.38)		LM4 2-6-0	Spalding 4	14.50	Long Sutton
13.15 Spalding	15.48	LM4 2-6-0	Spalding 5		
		K2 2-6-0	S. Lynn 1	16.45	Peterborough
		LM4 2-6-0	S. Lynn 7	17.08	South Lynn
		LM4 2-6-0	Spalding 1	17.30	Spalding
12.20 Peterborough	18.10	LM4 2-6-0	NWE 6	(18.35)	
		LM4 2-6-0	NWE 6	18.35	South Lynn
		LM4 2-6-0	S. Lynn 5	19.35	South Lynn
20.25 Peterborough	21.48	K2 2-6-0	S. Lynn 1	22.00	South Lynn

LONG SUTTON YARD (1952)					
Train	Arrive	Loco	Diagram	Depart	Destination
05.30 Spalding	07.31	LM4 2-6-0	Spalding 1	(08.24)	
05.55 South Lynn	07.45	LM4 2-6-0	S. Lynn 5	(09.34)	
(07.31)		LM4 2-6-0	Spalding 1	08.24	Sutton Bridge
(07.45)		LM4 2-6-0	S. Lynn 5	09.34	Spalding
10.00 Spalding	10.46	LM4 2-6-0	S. Lynn 6	10.51	South Lynn
07.15 Spalding	10.58	J6/SP1	Spalding 3	11.47	South Lynn
13.50 South Lynn	15.05	LM4 2-6-0	Spalding 4	(15.30)	
13.15 Spalding	15.15	LM4 2-6-0	Spalding 5	(15.35)	
(15.05)		LM4 2-6-0	Spalding 4	15.30	Moulton (Vans)
(15.15)		LM4 2-6-0	Spalding 5	15.35	Sutton Bridge
		LM4 2-6-0	Spalding 5	16.45	Spalding
		LM4 2-6-0	Spalding 2	17.44	Saxby
17.30 Sutton Bridge	17.46	LM4 2-6-0	Spalding 1	18.21	Spalding

which was of rather limited use - and water columns, Sutton Bridge had no locomotive facilities and its trains were worked by no less than twelve different engines from South Lynn, Spalding and New England sheds; the majority being LMS 4MT 2-6-0's - thoughtfully provided with tender cabs since they were too long by five feet for the turntable - with a J6 0-6-0 and a K2 2-6-0 thrown on for good measure. (Visiting enthusiasts to the area were often nonplussed by the fact that so many engines working into Sutton Bridge from the North were allocated to Peterborough which lay in a completely different direction. Enlightenment came with the information that many of the working originated from Spalding shed which, having no formal allocation of its own, used New England engines for all its workings).

Sutton Bridge did not carry the weight of responsibility for the Saxby line unaided and a measure of respite was given by Long Sutton which not only received empties direct from South Lynn but had a number of afternoon starting services which reflected the considerable volume of originating traffic at stations in the area.

The busy period at Long Sutton started with the arrival of the 13.50 train from South Lynn which recessed until going forward to Saxby at 17.44. In the meantime the engine of the 13.50 worked a train of vans contained passenger rated goods to Moulton where it merged with more general traffic into a goods train for Spalding.

This was followed by a second Spalding service at 16.45 and an hour later the recessed 13.50 from South Lynn - its load much increased by traffic from Long Sutton - continued its journey to Saxby.

All these trains picked up traffic at the intermediate stations but to ensure that nothing was left behind a 'whipper-in' was run from Sutton Bridge to Spalding to clear the yards of any matter that the preceding trains may not have been able to accommodate.

The last two or three years of the Sutton Bridge - Saxby line was one of sad decline. In (or around) 1956 the Colwick services were withdrawn with the traffic being diverted via Whitemoor and the Great Eastern to be fed into the M&GN at either King's Lynn or Cromer. Also affected in this round of economies was the Yarmouth - Birmingham express which was diverted into Spalding at the cost of a quarter of an hour in time.

Quite where the economies were made is a rhetorical question but it is doubtful if the extra traffic - if any - generated by the call at Spalding compensated for the cost of the two additional sets of men needed to work the train after its diversion. (Nor was the quest for savings helped in the first week or so of operation when the engine B12 4-6-0 61545, to work the down service forward from Spalding to Yarmouth, started forward whilst the rear coach was still foul of the points and hit the restaurant car hard enough to derail it).

The next change came in September 1958 when the Spalding avoiding line - the Welland Bank Junction to Cuckoo Junction section - closed. The question, what was to happen to the 1959 summer Saturday service, was quickly answered. There wouldn't be one.

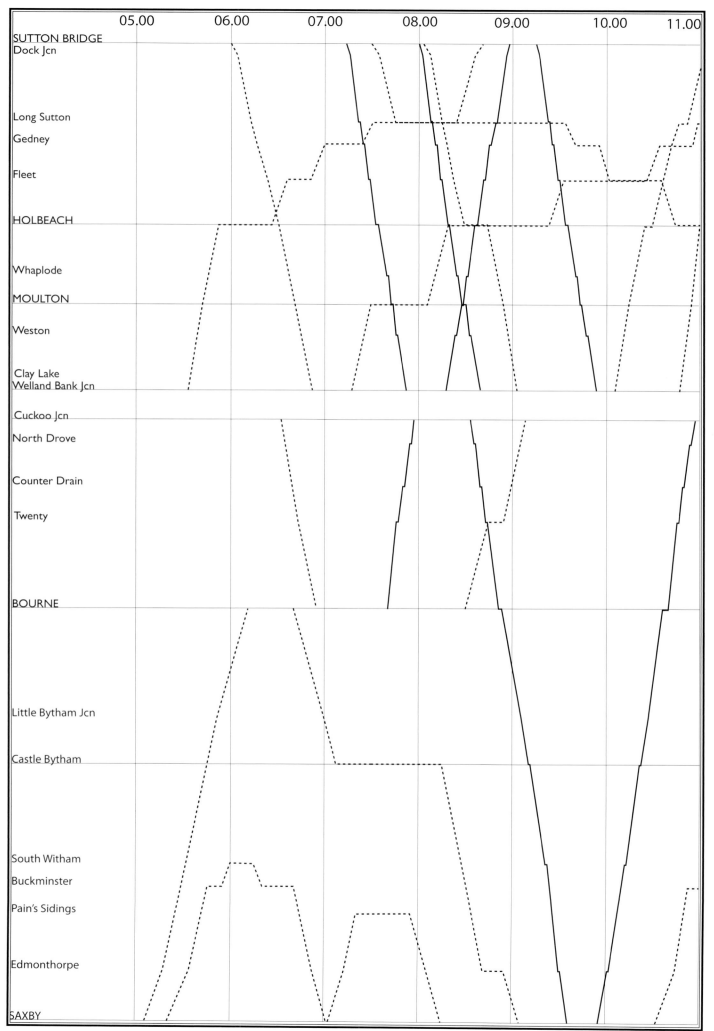

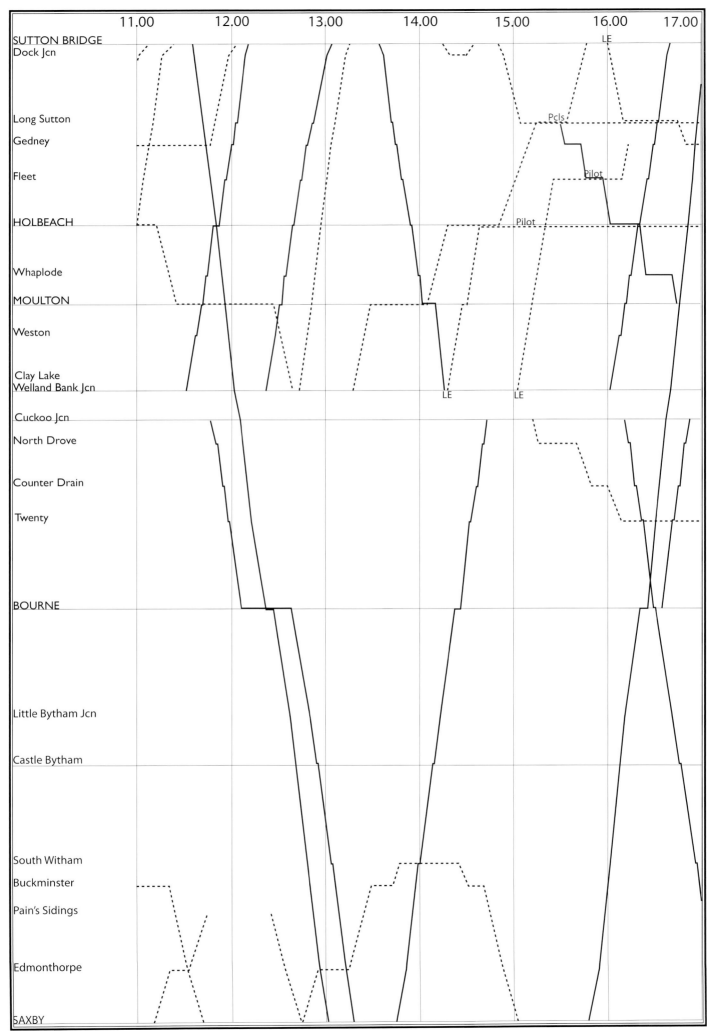

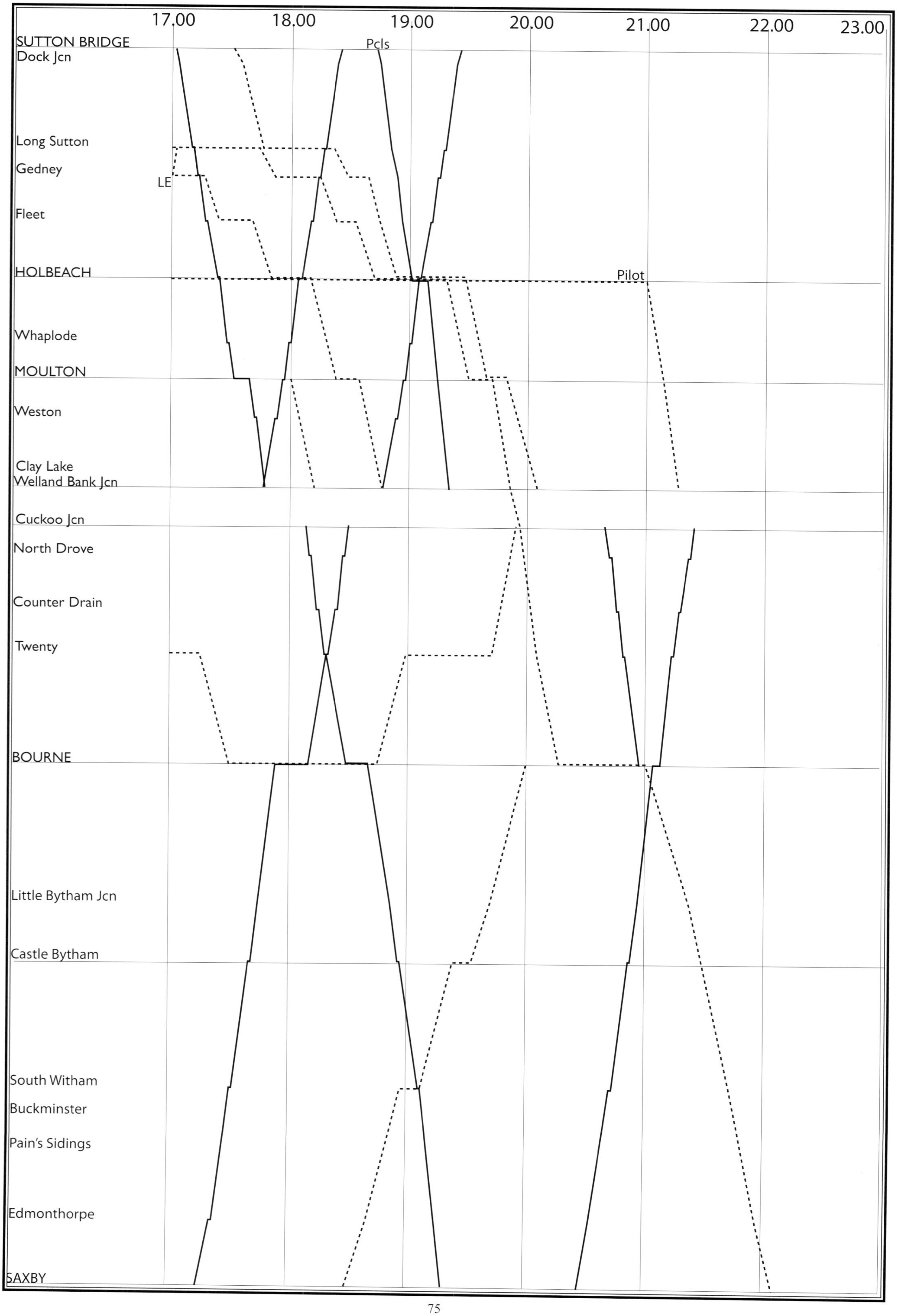

This is a railway train graph (time-distance diagram) showing services between Sutton Bridge and Saxby.

	17.00	18.00	19.00	20.00	21.00	22.00	23.00

SUTTON BRIDGE
Dock Jcn

Pcls

Long Sutton

Gedney

LE

Fleet

HOLBEACH

Pilot

Whaplode

MOULTON

Weston

Clay Lake
Welland Bank Jcn

Cuckoo Jcn

North Drove

Counter Drain

Twenty

BOURNE

Little Bytham Jcn

Castle Bytham

South Witham

Buckminster

Pain's Sidings

Edmonthorpe

SAXBY

75

MELTON CONSTABLE

A general view of Melton Constable looking towards Yarmouth and showing both the Loco and the Passenger Station. In the foreground LM4 2-6-0 43145 turns on the 70' turntable that was installed in 1953 whilst 43146 can be seen parked on the outer road next to the shed. The turntable had formerly served at Grantham and after the closure of the M&GN in 1959 was transferred to King's Cross. The passenger station consisted of no more than an island platform which could accommodate 12 coaches at each face. The up platform had an intermediate loco release crossover and was thus able to receive two trains at once. (Dr Ian C. Allen/Transport Treasury)

Because it was the location chosen for the M&GN's locomotive works, it is often assumed that Melton Constable was the focal point of the M&GN. In fact the works had next to nothing to do with the daily operations of the system and as a result Melton was simply a junction point on the main line roughly halfway between South Lynn and Yarmouth.

Most of its importance lay in the its two goods yards which sifted traffic to and from the Cromer and Norwich branches together with traffic for the outlying stations. (In this connection it should be noted that much through traffic for Cromer and Norwich was worked direct from South Lynn).

At the turn of the decade Melton did most of its work with seven J17 0-6-0 goods engines and eleven 4-4-0's for the main line passenger work. A handful of 2-4-2 tanks were retained for work between Cromer and North Walsham and were outbased at Cromer Beach.

In the Autumn of 1951 the first LMS 4MT 2-6-0 arrived at the shed and was quickly followed by a number of others until, by January 1952, the total stood at eleven.

Intended to be a replacement for the Midland 4F 0-6-0, the 2-6-0's were at first regarded in the light of a goods engine, working the diagrams indicated

in the accompanying table. It was not long, however, before they started to encroach on the 4-4-0 workings - principally those that called for a measure of tender-first running - and before many years had passed only an amended Diagram 2 remained in the hands of a 4-4-0.

As it was originally crafted, No.2 working asked a great deal of a D16 at a time when the effects of the war had not been wholly eradicated and the standard of engine maintenance could be questionable. The 4-4-0 worked to Yarmouth with an early morning passenger train and then returned with the 08.15 Lowestoft - Birmingham, working it through to South Lynn where it immediately took over the 11.13 King's Lynn to Peterborough. The second part of the diagram saw the engine working the 15.40 Peterborough to South Lynn and the 18.01 South Lynn to Melton Constable.

In 1952 the working was altered so that instead of working the Lowestoft - Birmingham from Yarmouth, the D16 worked the 10.05 Yarmouth - Peterborough to Melton Constable

and then, after a pause of nearly three hours, to Peterborough with the 12.45 from Yarmouth. The 4-4-0 returned to Melton Constable with the 20.10 from Peterborough.

Apart from giving the D16 a pause for breath during the first leg of the diagram, the alteration allowed the 08.15 Lowestoft - Birmingham to be worked by a B12 4-6-0 from Yarmouth to South Lynn; the engine that had previously worked the 10.05 Yarmouth - Peterborough and it was this diagram amendment that sparked off the association between the Leicester and the B12 4-6-0's.

Whilst the number of trains worked by D16's - the D15 4-4-0 did not long survive the coming of the 2-6-0's - declined, the number of engines at large assured local enthusiasts that no immediate pogrom was under consideration a circumstance that did not apply to the J17 0-6-0's which up to the end of 1950 had handled the lion's share of M&GN goods traffic all over the system. Melton had had an allocation of eight yet by Easter 1951 only one - 65557 - remained

Engine	Oct-50	Oct-51	Oct-52	Oct-53	Oct-54	Oct-55	Oct-56	Oct-57	Oct-58
LOCOMOTIVE SUMMARY : MELTON CONSTABLE									
5F: J39 0-6-0 (1926)									
4MT 2-6-0 (1947)		7	11	11	11		11	11	11
4F:J17 0-6-0 (1901)	7	8	1	1	2		4	3	1
3P:D16 4-4-0 (1923)	7	10	6	6	6		6	3	1
3P:D15 4-4-0 (1904)	4	2							
2F: J67 0-6-0T (1890)	1	1	1	2	2		3	2	
2F: J66 0-6-0T (1886)	1	1	1						
1P: F6 2-4-2T (1911)	2	2	4	3	3				
1P: F4 2-4-2T (1884)	2	1							
0F: Diesel 0-6-0									2
TOTAL	24	32	24	23	24		24	19	15

MELTON CONSTABLE 1

On Duty	04.30			
Prepare				MC1/LM4
Melton Loco	05.30	Light		MC1/LM4
05.35 Melton C	05.40	Goods		MC1/LM4
07.29 South Lynn	09.15	Goods		MC1/LM4
11.01 Melton C				MC1/LM4
Relieved				
12.39 Off duty				

MELTON CONSTABLE 2

On Duty	05.25			
Melton Loco	05.40	Light		MC2/LM4
05.45 Melton C	05.50	Goods		MC2/LM4
08.34 Massingham	08.46	Passenger		Travel
09.24 Melton	10.32	Goods		MC7/D16
10.48 Holt	12.30	Goods		MC7/D16
12.45 Melton C	12.50	Light		MC7/D16
12.55 Melton Loco				
13.25 Off Duty				

MELTON CONSTABLE 3

On Duty	04.50			
Prepare				MC3/D16
Melton Loco	05.50	Light		MC3/D16
Melton C	06.00	ECS		
06.35 N. Walsham	06.40	Passenger		
07.41 Yarmouth	09.00			
10.20 Melton C				
12.50 Off Duty				

MELTON CONSTABLE 4

On Duty	05.26			
Prepare				MC4/LM4
Melton Loco	06.26	Light		MC4/LM4
Melton C	06.36	Passenger		MC4/LM4
07.25 Norwich C	09.42	Goods		MC4/LM4
12.55 Melton C	13.05	Light		MC4/LM4
13.10 Melton Loco				
13.26 Off Duty				

MELTON CONSTABLE 5

On Duty	05.35			
Prepare				MC5/LM4
Melton Loco	06.35	Light		MC5/LM4
Melton C	06.45	Goods		MC5/LM4
10.40 Stalham	10.50	Goods		YAR1/LM4
13.28 Melton C	13.30	Light		YAR1/LM4
13.40 Melton Loco				
13.50 Off Duty				

MELTON CONSTABLE 6

On Duty	04.40			
Prepare				MC2/LM4
Prepare				MC7/D16
Melton Loco	06.55	Light		MC7/D16
Melton C	07.05	Passenger		MC7/D16
07.46 Cromer Jcn	07.47	Passenger		MC7/D16
07.49 Cromer High	08.02	Light		MC7/D16
08.14 Cromer Beach	09.40	Passenger		MC7/D16
10.16 Melton C				
12.40 Off Duty				

MELTON CONSTABLE 7

On Duty	06.20			
Prepare				MC9/LM4
Melton Loco	07.20	Light		MC9/LM4
Melton C	07.30	Passenger		MC9/LM4
08.35 South Lynn	08.37	Light		MC9/LM4
08.40 South Lynn Loco	09.30	Light		MC9/LM4
09.35 West Yard	09.40	Goods		MC9/LM4
13.16 Melton C	13.20			MC9/LM4
13.25 Melton Loco				
13.25 Off Duty				

MELTON CONSTABLE 8

On Duty	06.25			
Melton Loco	06.40	Light		MC6/D16
Melton Constable	06.50	Passenger		MC6/D16
06.59 Holt	07.35	Passenger		MC6/D16
07.44 Melton Constable	08.07	ECS		MC6/D16
08.16 Holt	09.05	Passenger		MC6/D16
09.14 Melton Constable	09.35	Passenger		MC6/D16
10.15 Cromer Beach	13.35	Passenger		MC6/D16
14.12 Melton Constable	14.15	Light		MC6/D16
14.20 Melton Loco				
14.30 Off Duty				

MELTON CONSTABLE 9

On Duty	06.52			
Melton Loco	07.07	Light		MC8/D16
Melton Constable	07.17	Passenger		MC8/D16
08.46 Yarmouth Beach	10.30	Goods		MC8/D16
15.24 Melton Constable				
15.34 Off Duty				

MELTON CONSTABLE 10

On Duty	09.15			
Melton Constable	09.35	Passenger		SL2/LM4
10.15 Cromer Beach	10.20	Light		SL2/LM4
10.25 Beach Loco	14.00	Light		SL2/LM4
14.05 Cromer Beach	14.10	Goods		SL2/LM4
16.40 Melton Constable	16.45	Light		SL2/LM4
16.50 Melton Loco				
17.15 Off Duty				

MELTON CONSTABLE 11

On Duty	10.08			
Melton Constable	10.28	08.15 Lowestoft	MC3/D16	
11.16 South Lynn	11.28	11.13 K. Lynn	MC3/D16	
12.46 Peterborough	13.00	ECS		MC3/D16
13.05 Nene Sdgs	13.10	Light		MC3/D16
13.15 Spital Bridge Loco	15.10	Light		MC3/D16
Nene Sidings	15.20	ECS		MC3/D16
15.25 Peterborough	15.40	Pass		MC3/D16
17.06 S. Lynn	17.24	Birmingham	Passenger	
18.12 Fakenham West				
18.22 Off Duty				

MELTON CONSTABLE 12

On Duty	11.05			
Melton Constable	11.25	Goods		MC1/LM4
13.51 Norwich City	15.26	Goods		MC1/LM4
16.39 Melton Constable	18.24	Passenger		MC1/LM4
18.42 Fakenham West	19.00	ECS		MC1/LM4
19.16 Melton Constable		Relieved		
19.26 Off Duty				

MELTON CONSTABLE 13

On Duty	13.15			
Prepare				MC11/D16
Melton Loco	14.15	Light		MC11/D16
Melton Constable	14.25	Passenger		MC11/D16
14.59 Cromer Beach	16.45	Passenger		MC11/D16
17.23 Melton Constable	18.25	Passenger		MC11/D16
19.02 Cromer Beach	20.30	Light		MC11/D16
20.03 Cromer Jcn	20.53	17.30 Lv St	MC11/D16	
21.32 Melton Constable		Relieved		
21.42 Off Duty				

MELTON CONSTABLE 14

On Duty	13.36			
Prepare				SL3/LM4
Melton Loco	14.36	Light		SL3/LM4
Melton Constable	14.46	Goods		SL3/LM4
16.08 Norwich City	19.45	Goods		SL3/LM4
20.53 Melton Constable				SL3/LM4
Relieved				SL3/LM4
21.36 Off Duty				

MELTON CONSTABLE 15

On Duty	14.00			
Melton Constable	14.20	12.42 ex Yar	MC10/D16	
16.40 Peterborough N	16.50	ECS		MC10/D16
16.55 Nene CS	17.05	Light		MC10/D16
17.10 Spital Bridge Loco	19.40	Light		MC10/D16
19.45 Nene CS	19.50	ECS		MC10/D16
19.55 Peterborough N	20.10	Pass		MC10/D16
22.45 Melton C				
22.50 Off Duty				

MELTON CONSTABLE 16

On Duty	15.10			
Prepare				MC9/LM4
Melton Loco	16.10	Light		MC9/LM4
Melton Constable	16.20	Goods		MC9/LM4
18.32 South Lynn	19.45	Goods		MC9/LM4
21.36 Melton Constable	21.40	Light		MC9/LM4
22.00 Loco				
23.10 Off Duty				

MELTON CONSTABLE 17

On Duty	15.10			
Prepare				MC6/D16
Melton Loco	16.10	Light		MC6/D16
16.20 Melton Constable	16.25	Pass		MC6/D16
16.33 Corpusty	16.42	ECS		MC6/D16
16.50 Melton Constable	17.05	Pass		MC6/D16
17.43 Cromer Beach	18.10	Pass		MC6/D16
18.46 Melton Constable	20.07	Pass		MC6/D16
20.42 Cromer Beach	21.10	Light		MC6/D16
21.41 Melton Loco				
23.10 Off Duty				

MELTON CONSTABLE 18

On Duty	15.35			
Prepare				MC7/D16
Melton Loco	16.35	Light		MC7/D16
Melton Constable	16.45	Pass		MC7/D16
17.33 Cromer Jcn	17.34	Pass		MC7/D16
17.37 Cromer High	18.00	Light		MC7/D16
18.03 Cromer Jcn	18.21	Pass		MC7/D16
18.34 Sheringham	18.42	Light		MC7/D16
18.52 Cromer Beach	19.25	Pass		MC7/D16
20.02 Melton Constable	20.05	Light		MC7/D16
20.15 Melton Loco				
23.35 Off Duty				

MELTON CONSTABLE 19

On Duty	15.55			
Prepare				MC8/D16
15.40 Melton Loco	16.55	Light		MC8/D16
17.00 Melton Constable	17.05	Pass		MC8/D16
17.52 Norwich	19.15	Pass		MC8/D16
20.04 Melton Constable	20.10	Light		MC8/D16
20.15 Melton Loco				MC8/D16
Melton Yard	20.45	Pilot		MC13/J67
Melton Yard	22.50	Light		MC13/J67
23.00 Melton Loco				
23.55 Off Duty				

MELTON CONSTABLE 22

On Duty	05.00			
Prepare				MC13/J67
Melton Loco	05.45	Light		MC13/J67
Yard Pilot		Shunt		MC13/J67
12.50 Relieved				
13.00 Off duty				

MELTON CONSTABLE 23

On Duty	12.45			
12.50 Yard Pilot		Shunt		MC13/J67
20.45 Relieved				
20.45 Off Duty				

MELTON CONSTABLE 24

On Duty	04.00			
Prepare				MC6/D16
Prepare				MC8/D16
As required				
12.00 Off duty				

MELTON CONSTABLE 25

On Duty	12.00			
Prepare				MC10/D16
Melton Loco	14.10	Light		MC10/D16
14.15 Melton Constable	15.24	Light		MC8/D16
15/30 Melton Loco				
As required				
20.00 Off duty				

MELTON CONSTABLE 26

On Duty	20.00			
Melton Constable	22.50	Light		MC10/D16
23.00 Melton Loco				
As required				
04.00 Off Duty				

the others having been summarily despatched to Norwich, Yarmouth GE and Stratford. 65557 was retained because the engine was equipped to carry a snow plough which could be a necessity during an East Anglian winter.

This exodus proved to be somewhat hasty since the new 2-6-0's 'postwar and jerry-built' seemed prone to mechanical failures and prolonged periods under repair. Why this should have been remains something of a mystery since the engines were simple in design with a degree of accessibility unknown in pre-grouping engines but there were times when the number of 2-6-0's out of action prompted the Running Office at Liverpool Street to draft in numbers of J3 and J39 0-6-0's to make good the deficit. The last-mentioned class had to be watched carefully since they were barred from the South Lynn - Sutton Bridge section (except in an emergency) and although Melton had no goods workings that went beyond South Lynn, their use on trains to the west always carried a latent risk. (What constituted an emergency was a matter for the District Controller at Cambridge but he was unlikely to declare one simply because a Melton - South Lynn train had been extended to Spalding and happened to have a J39 on the front).

MELTON CONSTABLE YARD

Train	Arrive	Loco	Depart	Destination
		LM4/MC1	05.40	South Lynn
		LM4/MC2	05.50	South Lynn
		LM4/MC5	06.45	Yarmouth
06.30 South Lynn	08.21	LM4/SL2	(08.45)	
	(08.21)	D16/MC6	08.45	Cromer
		D16/MC7	10.32	Holt
09.10 South Lynn	11.01	LM4/MC1	11.25	Norwich City
12.30 Holt	12.45	D16/MC7		
09.42 Norwich	12.55	LM4/MC4		
09.40 South Lynn	13.16	LM4/MC9		
07.02 Yarmouth	13.28	LM4/YAR1		
12.45 South Lynn	14.23	LM4/SL15A	(14.46)	
	(14.23)	LM4/SL3	14.46	Norwich City
10.30 Yarmouth	15.24	LM4/MC8		
		LM4/MC9	16.20	South Lynn
		D16/MC6	16.25	Corpusty
14.35 South Lynn	16.29	LM4/MC2	(17.34)	
15.26 Norwich	16.39	LM4/MC1		
16.32 Corpusty	16.50	D16/MC6		
	(16.29)	LM4/SL15A	17.34	Yarmouth
16.00 Yarmouth	17.21	LM4/SL15B	17.50	Peterborough
		LM4/SL2	19.05	South Lynn
19.45 Norwich	20.53	LM4/SL3	21.02	South Lynn
19.45 South Lynn	21.36	LM4/MC9		

Goods traffic at Melton Constable was dealt with in the up and down yards, devilishly arranged so that a shunt from one to the other could be performed by fly shunting of the most hair raising type. The J67 yard pilot would haul a string of transfer wagons from one yard and just as the engine was approaching the entrance points, one of the shunters would uncouple the first wagon, his colleague reversing the points the instant the engine had passed clear. Usually the movement worked but once in a blue moon the engine would stop too soon after passing over the points and be the object of an powerful

---

MELTON CONSTABLE LOCO DIAGRAMS : 1952

1: LMS 4MT 2-6-0

Melton Loco	05.30	Light
05.35 Melton Constable	05.40	Goods
07.29 South Lynn	09.10	Goods
10.55 Melton Constable	11.25	Goods
13.51 Norwich	15.26	Goods
16.51 Melton Constable	18.24	Pass
18.42 Fakenham W.	19.00	ECS
19.16 Melton Constable	19.20	Light
19.25 Melton Loco		

2: LMS 4MT 2-6-0

Melton Loco	05.40	Light
05.45 Melton Constable	05.50	Goods
10.58 S. Lynn	14.35	Goods
16.29 Melton Constable		
16.40 Melton Loco		

3: D16 4-4-0

Melton Loco	05.50	Light	
Melton Constable	06.00	ECS	
06.36 N. Walsham	06.40	Pass	
07.41 Yarmouth	09.00	XP	Birmingham
11.16 S. Lynn	11.28		11.13 ex K. Lynn
12.46 Peterborough	13.00	ECS	
13.05 Nene Sidings		Light	
Spital Bridge Loco	15.10	Light	
Nene Sidings	15.20	ECS	
15.25 Peterborough	15.40	Pass	K. Lynn
17.06 S. Lynn	18.01	Pass	17.55 ex K. Lynn
19.05 Melton Constable		Light	
19.15 Melton Loco			

4: LMS 4MT 2-6-0

Melton Loco	06.26	Light
Melton Constable	06.36	Pass
07.25 Norwich	09.42	Goods
12.55 Melton Constable	13.05	Light
13.15 Melton Loco		

5: LMS 4MT 2-6-0

Melton Loco	06.35	Light
Melton Constable	06.45	Goods
13.22 Yarmouth		Light
14.50 Beach Loco	(07.02)	

6: D16 4-4-0

Melton Loco	06.40	Light
Melton Constable	06.50	Pass
06.59 Holt	07.35	Pass
07.44 Melton Constable	08.45	Goods
10.39 Cromer	13.35	Pass
14.12 Melton Constable	14.15	Light
14.20 Melton Loco	16.10	Light
16.20 Melton Constable	16.25	Pass
16.33 Corpusty	16.42	ECS
16.50 Melton Constable	17.05	Pass
17.43 Cromer	18.10	Pass
18.46 Melton Constable	20.07	Pass
20.42 Cromer	21.10	Light
21.41 Melton Loco		

7: D16 4-4-0

Melton Loco	06.55	Light
Melton Constable	07.05	Pass
07.46 Cromer Jcn	07.47	Pass
07.49 Cromer High	08.02	Light
08.14 Cromer	09.40	Pass
10.16 Melton Constable	10.32	Goods
10.50 Holt	12.30	Goods
12.45 Melton Constable		
12.55 Melton Loco	16.35	Light
Melton Constable	16.45	Pass
17.33 Cromer Jcn	17.34	Pass
17.37 Cromer High	18.00	Light
18.03 Cromer Jcn	18.21	Pass
18.34 Sheringham	18.42	ECS
18.52 Cromer Beach	19.25	Pass
20.02 Melton Constable		
20.15 Melton Loco		

8: D16 4-4-0

Melton Loco	07.07	Light
Melton Constable	07.17	Pass
08.46 Yarmouth	10.30	Goods
15.24 Melton Constable	15.35	Light
15.40 Melton Loco	16.55	Light
17.00 Melton Constable	17.05	Pass
17.52 Norwich	19.15	Pass
20.04 Melton Constable		
20.15 Melton Loco		

9: LMS 4MT 2-6-0

Melton Loco	07.20	Light
Melton Constable	07.30	Pass
08.35 South Lynn	09.40	Goods
13.15 Melton Constable	16.20	Goods
18.32 South Lynn	19.45	Goods
21.36 Melton Constable		
22.00 Melton Loco		

10: D16 4-4-0

Melton Loco	14.10	Light	
Melton Constable	14.20	Pass	12.42 ex Yarmouth
16.40 Peterborough N	16.50	ECS	
16.55 Nene CS	17.05	Light	
17.10 Spital Bridge Loco	19.40	Light	
19.45 Nene CS	19.50	ECS	
19.55 Peterborough N	20.10	Pass	
22.45 Melton Constable			
22.55 Melton Loco			

11: D16 4-4-0

Melton Loco	14.15	Light
Melton Constable	14.25	Pass
14.59 Cromer	16.45	Pass
17.23 Melton Constable	18.25	Pass
19.02 Cromer	20.30	Light
20.36 Cromer Jcn	20.53	Pass
21.32 Melton Constable		
21.45 Melton Loco		

13: J67 0-6-0T

Melton Loco	05.35	Light
Pilot		
23.00 Melton Loco		

NORWICH LOCO DIAGRAMS : 1952
1: D16 4-4-0

Loco	06.18	Light
Norwich City	06.28	Passenger
07.19 Melton C.	07.49	Passenger
08.39 Norwich City	09.30	Passenger
10.14 Melton C.	10.20	Light
10.25 Melton Loco	13.20	Light
13.25 Melton C.	13.32	Passenger
14.21 Norwich City	14.25	Light
14.30 Loco	16.40	Light
16.45 Norwich City	16.50	Passenger
17.43 Melton C.	18.22	Passenger
19.00 Norwich City		
19.20 Loco		

2: D16 4-4-0

Loco	07.30	Light
Norwich City	07.40	Passenger
08.30 Melton C.	09.37	Passenger
10.27 Norwich City	10.35	Light
10.40 Loco	13.11	Light
13.16 Norwich City	13.21	Passenger
14.09 Melton C.	14.14	Light
14.20 Melton Loco	15.40	Light
15.45 Melton C.	16.02	Passenger
16.49 Norwich City	17.30	Passenger
18.21 Melton C.	19.25	Passenger
20.13 Norwich City		
20.30 Loco		

3: J67 0-6-0T

Loco	06.50	Light
07.00 Norwich Yard	21.15	Pilot
22.25 Loco		

example of the force of inertia.

With a score or more of small stations in its hinterland, each loading four or five wagons a day, both yards were kept busy with trains that, for the most part, were spread out so that as soon as one had been dealt with, another was on the doorstep. The average throughout the sixteen-hour day was an arrival or departure every half an hour which was not bad for a small station. Not all the trains were conveniently spread out and from four to five in the afternoon matters could get quite hectic.

The majority of departures were for South Lynn, conveying a mix of loaded traffic from stations on the east and empties for intermediate yards. The Norwich and Cromer lines had two trains each although one of the latter went no further than Holt or Weybourne. Yarmouth also had only two trains a day, the first a train that distributed empties all the way down the line and the second, an afternoon train that ran through from South Lynn but called at Melton to change engines and exchange traffic.

Paucity of trade the far side of North Walsham was an operational difficulty as well as a commercial problem; the diagrammers discovering that trains from Yarmouth were so few and far between that when the morning goods from Melton arrived at lunch-time, there was nothing for the engine to work back with. The upshot was that the engine had to remain in Yarmouth until the following morning when it worked back to Melton with a similar stopping goods. The irony was that a Yarmouth 2-6-0 performed exactly the same routine in reverse.

By and large the service consisted of low-classification trains - class H - that could accommodate any type of wagon likely to appear and the nearest to an express goods was the class E service which left at 17.50 but was actually a through train between Yarmouth and Peterborough. If it had less than a full load on leaving Yarmouth it could be made up with empties for Melton (where they could be exchanged for any loaded traffic that happened to be on hand) but otherwise it called simply to change crews.

Passenger traffic was very brisk for much of the day and the seventy-two passenger movements between 06.00 and 22.45 equated to a train every fourteen minutes which was a very good average for a rather basic island platform.

The basic service was one of services to and from Cromer and Norwich running in connection with the Peterborough - Yarmouth trains but there were variations such as the 08.15 Lowestoft - Birmingham which arrived with two coaches and left with five, having attached two from Cromer and one from Norwich. The procedure was reversed when the train returned in the evening.

There was also a smattering of purely local trains - mainly for school traffic - but perhaps Melton's most profitable services were the interlopers from the Great Eastern; through trains to Liverpool Street which ran via Sheringham, Cromer and Norwich Thorpe. Thanks to the vagaries of the carriage workings, they were curiously unbalanced services with three through services from Melton to London but only one in the opposite direction.

These Great Eastern trains were usually booked to D16 4-4-0's but could appear with B17 or B12 4-6-0's and the fact that in 1952 the 47' turntable at Melton was replaced by one of 70' suggests that there may have been plans for even larger engines on a regular basis.

In addition to its own needs, Melton also provided Norwich City with two D16 4-4-0's and a J67 0-6-0T; the 4-4-0's spending a rather dull exile on branch trains, with neither engine going beyond Melton Constable. The branch, however, did not rely solely on its two 4-4-0's but saw quite an interesting array of daily visitors which included a South Lynn LM4 2-6-0 that arrived with the through goods in the morning and worked a passenger trip to Melton before returning to South Lynn with the evening goods.

Although the branch gave Norwich access to the Midlands and the North of England, so did the Great Eastern and most goods moved from Norwich City were crumbs from a rich man's table combined with the fact that most traffic routings were those in force before the grouping. For all this, the M&GN did well to muster three goods trains a day from Norwich, two running largely for local - mainly agricultural - needs whilst another ran through to South Lynn.

Pleasant though a ride down the Norwich branch usually was, one felt that it could have been used to better effect. Norwich and King's Lynn, Norfolk's two principal towns, were connected by an abysmal train service - the Great Eastern ran one through train a day -

and had the M&GN devoted an engine and a set of coaches to performing a couple of return workings a day with limited stops, the result might have been profitable.

In the event the most major change came in 1957 when diesel multiple units - some services running from Norwich Thorpe to Norwich City - took over the working of the branch, killing not only the atmosphere of the line but eliminating the through coach to Birmingham. Not everyone regarded innovation as an improvement!

MELTON CONSTABLE STATION - 1952					
Train	Arrive	Loco	Stock	Depart	Destination
		D16 4-4-0 MC3	27/2	06.00	North Walsham
		LM4 2-6-0 MC4	18/4	06.36	Norwich
		D16 4-4-0 MC6	19/4	06.50	Holt
		D16 4-4-0 MC7	GE/3	07.05	Liverpool St
		D16 4-4-0 MC8	5/4	07.17	Yarmouth
06.28 Norwich	07.19	D16 4-4-0 NOR1	15/4		
		LM4 2-6-0 MC9	11/4	07.30	Peterborough
07.35 Holt	07.44	D16 4-4-0 MC6	19/4	(07.49)	(Engine change)
	(07.44)	D16 4-4-0 NOR1	19/4	07.49	Norwich
06.51 Yarmouth	08.27	B12 4-6-0 YAR4	4/4	(08.36)	
07.55 Cromer	08.30	F6 2-4-2T CB2	13/2		
07.40 Norwich	08.30	D16 4-4-0 NOR2	15/4	08.32	ECS Holt
	(08.27)	B12 4-6-0 YAR4	4/4	08.36	Peterborough
		F6 2-4-2T CB2	17/4	08.40	Cromer
09.05 Holt	09.14	D16 4-4-0 NOR2	15/4	(09.37)	
06.45 Peterborough	09.24	LM4 2-6-0 SL11	9/4+2	09.34	Yarmouth
		LM4 2-6-0 SL2	23/4	09.35	Cromer
	(09.14)	D16 4-4-0 NOR2	15/4	09.37	Norwich
09.30 Norwich	10.14	D16 4-4-0 NOR1	18,33/5		
09.40 Cromer	10.16	D16 4-4-0 MC7	35/2		
08.15 Lowestoft	10.20	D16 4-4-0 MC3	37/2	(10.28)	(Attach coaches)
(Attach coaches)	(10.20)	D16 4-4-0 MC3	33,35,37/5	10.28	Birmingham NS
09.18 Norwich (GE)	11.05	D16 4-4-0 GE	20/2&GE/3		(GE set for 16.45 LV)
10.30 Norwich	11.19	LM4 2-6-0 SL3	28/4		
11.00 Cromer	11.35	F6 2-4-2T CB2	23/4		
10.05 Yarmouth	11.38	B12 4-6-0 YAR6	5/4	11.45	Peterborough
		D16 4-4-0 GE	GE/2	11.50	Liverpool St
10.33 Peterborough	13.22	B12 4-6-0 YAR4	2/4	13.30	Yarmouth
		D16 4-4-0 NOR1	28/4	13.32	Norwich
		F6 2-4-2T CB2	28/4	13.35	Cromer
13.21 Norwich	14.09	D16 4-4-0 NOR2	15/4		
13.15 Cromer	14.12	D16 4-4-0 MC6	17/4		
12.42 Yarmouth	14.14	YAR7 4-4-0	6/4+1	(14.20)	(Engine change)
(Engine change)	(14.14)	D16 4-4-0 MC10	6/4+1	14.22	Peterborough
		D16 4-4-0 MC11	15/4	14.25	Cromer
12.55 Yarmouth (Pcls)	14.59	LM4 2-6-0 SL11	9 Vans	15.10	Peterborough
12.45 Peterborough	15.28	LM4 2-6-0 SL8	4/4	15.43	Yarmouth
		D16 4-4-0 YAR7	10,13/6	15.55	Fakenham
15.24 Cromer	15.57	D16 4-4-0 GE	15/4		
		D16 4-4-0 NOR2	17/4	16.02	Norwich
		D16 4-4-0 MC6	18/4	16.25	Corpusty
		D16 4-4-0 MC7	GE/3	16.45	Liverpool St
16.30 Fakenham	16.48	D16 4-4-0 YAR7	10,13/6	(17.02)	(Split train)
16.42 Corpusty ECS	16.50	D16 4-4-0 MC6	18/4	(17.05)	
(Split train)	(16.48)	D16 4-4-0 YAR7	13/2	17.02	North Walsham
(Split train)	(16.48)	D16 4-4-0 MC8	10/4	17.05	Norwich
		D16 4-4-0 MC6	18/4	17.05	Cromer
16.45 Cromer	17.23	D16 4-4-0 MC11	28/4		
16.50 Norwich	17.43	D16 4-4-0 NOR1	20/2		
		D16 4-4-0 GE	20/2	17.50	Cromer
13.45 Birmingham NS	18.12	B12 4-6-0 YAR6	32,36,34/5	(18.18)	(Split train)
(Split train)	(18.12)	B12 4-6-0 YAR6	34/2	18.18	Lowestoft
17.30 Norwich	18.21	D16 4-4-0 NOR2	19/4	(18.24)	(Engine change)
		D16 4-4-0 NOR1	28,32/5	18.22	Norwich
(Engine change)	(18.21)	LM4 2-6-0 MC1	19/4	18.24	Fakenham
		D16 4-4-0 MC11	34/2	18.25	Cromer
16.55 Yarmouth	18.34	D16 4-4-0 YAR2	9,27/6		
18.10 Cromer	18.46	D16 4-4-0 MC6	18/4		
17.55 King's Lynn	19.05	D16 4-4-0 MC3	3/4	(19.15)	(Engine change)
(Engine change)	(19.05)	D16 4-4-0 YAR2	3/4	19.15	Yarmouth
19.00 Fakenham ECS	19.16	LM4 2-6-0 MC1	19/4		
		D16 4-4-0 MC6	18/4	19.25	Norwich
18.15 Yarmouth	20.00	LM4 2-6-0 SL8	4,12/6	(20.07)	(Engine change)
19.25 Cromer	20.02	D16 4-4-0 MC7	GE/3		(Berth for 11.50 LV)
19.15 Norwich	20.04	D16 4-4-0 MC8	10/4+1	(20.10)	(Engine change)
	(20.00)	D16 4-4-0 MC6	12/2	20.07	Cromer
	(20.04)	LM4 2-6-0 SL8	10/4+1	20.10	King's Lynn
17.30 Liverpool St	21.32	D16 4-4-0 MC11	GE/3		(Berth for 07.05)
20.10 Peterborough	22.45	D16 4-4-0 MC10	7/4		

79

LM4 2-6-0 43160 of Yarmouth runs into Melton Constable with the 09.35 Derby - Yarmouth Beach on a summer Saturday in 1958 whilst another LM4 2-6-0 waits on the up main to crossover and work the Cromer portion of the following 09.55 Derby - Yarmouth.   Summer Saturdays saw - in 1958 as an example - nine long distance trains arrive in Yarmouth from the Midlands giving the impression that the M&GN was a great deal busier on summer Saturdays than at other times.   In fact the converse was the case since almost all goods traffic had to be abandoned in order to find engines and men for the holiday trains. (Dr Ian C. Allen/transporttreasury.co.uk)

More typical of Melton Constable was the weekday scene depicted above where a Yarmouth D16 4-4-0 runs clear of the station after arriving with the 12.42 Yarmouth - Peterborough whilst the Melton LM4 2-6-0 which has replaced it, departs with the train for Peterborough.   On the down side of the line 43068 arrives with the morning goods from Holt, much of the traffic seeming to consist of sugar beet.   (Dr Ian C. Allen/transporttreasury.co.uk)

East Anglia was not a land flowing with milk and honey, at least not so far as railway traffic was concerned, and therefore the M&GN and the Great Eastern tended to keep to their respective spheres of operation. King's Lynn was the principal exception but even here each company had its own station and yards; connections between the two being by trip services and an occasional through passenger.

The one area where the two railways met and intertwined was in the Cromer area: a group of rather select seaside resorts which were forecast to expand out of all recognition but which failed to do so.

The basic links to Cromer formed a letter 'T' with the M&GN running from West to East from Melton Constable via Sheringham to its Cromer Beach terminus whilst the Great Eastern ran from north to south from its terminus at Cromer High to Norwich via Gunton and North Walsham.

Thus by 1887 was Cromer independently served by separate two railways and the position might have continued thus had it not been for the extraordinary growth of seaside resorts and the fact that by the early twentieth century the GER and the M&GN had learned to bury their differences and work towards a common aim where circumstances indicated a mutual benefit.

This cooperation manifested itself in 1898 as the Norfolk & Suffolk Joint Committee and produced in 1903 the direct Yarmouth - Lowestoft route which not only put the growing resort of Gorleston on the railway map but reduced the distance between Yarmouth and Lowestoft by four miles.

The Committee then turned its attention to north-east Norfolk where Mundesley, Cromer and Sheringham all held promise as resorts capable of expansion.

The attraction to the Great Eastern was the possibility of access to Sheringham and through the medium of the Committee, it does appear that the Great Eastern got what it wanted for very little cost.

In 1903 the two lines were connected by a link from West Runton on the M&GN to Cromer Junction on the Great Eastern and the latter was finally able to run through from London to Sheringham.

The quid pro quo was the extension, also on 1903, of the M&GN's North Walsham - Mundesley branch to Cromer Beach although it is difficult to see how this was of significant benefit since the distance from South Lynn to Mundesley was the same via Sheringham as it was via North Walsham.

Whatever the intentions of the instigators may have been, successive generations of

F6 2-4-2T 67228 of Cromer Beach leaves Overstrand with a Cromer Beach - North Walsham working in April 1953. Three F6 engines were allocated to Melton Constable with two being outbased at Cromer Beach to work over the Norfolk & Suffolk Joint. Overstrand had once been equipped with full signalling facilities and a passing loop but was reduced to single line status in 1922; the signalling section extending from Cromer Links to Mundesley.

railwaymen were left with some interesting operating problems not the least of which was the fact that down Great Eastern trains could serve either Cromer or Sheringham but not - at least without a good deal of delay and bother - both. The reason is clear from the map and the usual course of action was for northbound trains to stop and divide at Cromer Junction, the front portion continuing forward to Cromer High whilst a second engine backed onto the rear portion and worked it the five miles to Sheringham.

Such a procedure could only be worked with northbound trains and in the opposite direction, the Sheringham coaches were worked in the normal way to Cromer Junction and then backed down, through the tunnel, into Cromer High station. This resulted in some curious diagramming which saw engines working from Norwich to Cromer High before running light to Cromer Junction to pick up the Sheringham coaches of the next down train. At Sheringham the engine would turn on the Newstead Lane angle - if it had not already done so before leaving Cromer - and then work its train through to Norwich, reversing into Cromer en route.

Between Runton West Junction and Sheringham the line was served by M&GN services from Cromer Beach to Melton Constable and services of the Great Eastern from London and Norwich. Most of the latter terminated at Sheringham but one or two ran through to Melton Constable

The joint working remained largely unchanged for half a century and even though the M&GN became part of the LNER in 1936, trains continued to run as they always had, so much so that right up to the time of closure, separate working(!) timetables were needed in order to work out the complete service between Cromer and Melton Constable.

The principal beneficiary of the 1903 alterations was, of course, the Great Eastern since they were able to persuade a proportion of their eight million-strong London market to travel via Liverpool Street to Sheringham and profited thereby. The M&GN, on the other hand, did not seem to benefit at all. It ran a couple of through coaches to Birmingham once a day - which would have operated had the Norfolk & Suffolk Joint never existed - whilst Mundesley-on-Sea stubbornly refused to develop as a seaside resort.

CROMER BEACH STATION WORKING - 1952						
Train	Arrive	Loco	Shed	Stock	Depart	Destination
		F6 2-4-2T	CB 1	NS1/2	07.00	North Walsham
07.15 ECS N. Walsham	07.40	D16 4-4-0	GE10	NS3/2		
		F6 2-4-2T	CB 2	13/2	07.55	Melton Constable
07.50 Sheringham	08.00	D16 4-4-0	GE1	NS2/2	(08.09)	
	(08.00)	D16 4-4-0	GE10	NS2/2	08.09	North Walsham
Light ex Cromer High	08.14	D16 4-4-0	MC 7	-		
08.40 Melton Constable	09.15	F6 2-4-2T	CB 2	17/4		
09.02 ECS N. Walsham	09.22	D16 4-4-0	GE10	NS2/2		
		D16 4-4-0	MC 7	35/2	09.40	Birmingham NS
		D16 4-4-0	GE1	NS2/2	09.51	Norwich GE
09.35 Melton Constable	10.15	LM4 2-6-0	SL 2	23/4		
10.05 North Walsham	10.45	F6 2-4-2T	CB 1	NS1/2		
		F6 2-4-2T	CB 2	23/4	11.00	Melton Constable
		F6 2-4-2T	CB 1	NS1/2	12.05	North Walsham
13.07 Sheringham	13.16	D16 4-4-0	GE12	NS3/2	(13.26)	
	(13.16)	D16 4-4-0	GE12	NS3/2	13.26	Norwich GE
		D16 4-4-0	MC 6	17/4	13.35	Melton Constable
13.35 Melton Constable	14.10	F6 2-4-2T	CB 2	28/4		
14.25 Melton Constable	14.59	D16 4-4-0	MC 11	15/4		
Light ex Cromer High	15.05	D16 4-4-0	GE15	-		
		D16 4-4-0	GE15	15/4	15.24	Melton Constable
16.00 N. Walsham	16.40	F6 2-4-2T	CB 1	NS1/2		
		D16 4-4-0	MC 11	28/4	16.45	Melton Constable
		F6 2-4-2T	CB 2	NS1/2	17.05	North Walsham
17.05 Melton Constable	17.37	D16 4-4-0	MC 6	18/4		
		D16 4-4-0	MC 6	18/4	18.10	Melton Constable
ECS ex Sheringham	18.52	D16 4-4-0	MC 7	GE/3		
13.45 Birmingham NS	19.02	D16 4-4-0	MC 11	34/2		
		D16 4-4-0	MC 7	GE/3	19.25	Melton Constable
19.15 N. Walsham	19.55	F6 2-4-2T	CB 2	NS1/2		
		F6 2-4-2T	CB 2	NS1/2	20.18	North Walsham
		D16 4-4-0	MC 11	-	20.30	Light to Cromer Jcn
18.15 Yarmouth	20.42	D16 4-4-0	MC 6	12/2		
		D16 4-4-0	MC 6	-	21.10	Light to Melton.
21.50 N. Walsham	22.27	F6 2-4-2T	CB 2	NS1/2		

WORKING TIMETABLE : NORWICH - MELTON CONSTABLE - SHERINGHAM - CROMER - NORTH WALSHAM (1952)

Train	06.15						07.15				07.50						06.30	09.02		06.30
From	High						Walsham				Sher	High					S. Lynn	Walsham		S. Lynn
Class	ECS	Pass	Pass	Pass	Pass	Pass	ECS	Pass		Pass	Pass	Light	ECS	Pass	Pass	Pass	Goods	ECS	Pass	Goods
Engine	GE10	GE12	GE10	MC 6	CB 1	MC 7	GE10	NR 1	CB 2	GE1	GE10	MC 7	MC 6	GE14	NR 2	CB 2	MC 6	GE10	GE3	MC 6
Class	D16	D16	D16	D16	F6 2-4-2T	D16	D16	D16	F6 2-4-2T	D16	D16	D16	D16	D16	D16	F6 2-4-2T	D16	D16	D16	D16
Carriage Wkg/Vehicles	NS3/2	GE/3	NS3/2	19/4	NS1/2	GE/3	NS3/2	15/4	13/2	NS2/2	NS2/2	-	15/4	GE/3	17/4	17/4	-	NS2/2	GE/3	-
NORWICH CITY							06.28											07.40		
Hellesdon																		07.45		
Drayton							06.37											07.50		
Attlebridge							06.46											07.59		
Lenwade							06.50											08.03		
Whitwell							06.54											08.08		
Whitwell							06.55											08.09		
Guestwick							06.59											08.18		
Hindolvestone							07.14											08.23		
MELTON CONSTABLE							07.19											08.30	(08.30)	
MELTON CONSTABLE		06.50				07.05					08.07						(08.40)	08.40	08.45	
Brininghan Jcn		06/52				07/07					08/09							08/42	08/51	
Holt		06.59				07.14					08.16							08.50	09.03	09.16
Weybourne						07.23												08.58		09.26
SHERINGHAM						07.29												09.04		
SHERINGHAM		06.20					07.32			07.50			08.20					09.06		09.20
West Runton		06.24					07.36			07.54			08.24					09.10		09.24
Runton West Jcn		06/26					07/38			07/57			08/26					09/12		09/26
Runton East Jcn							07/38			07/58		08/12						09/13	09/20	
CROMER BEACH							07.40			08.00		08.14						09.15	09.22	
CROMER BEACH						07.00				07.55	08.09									
Runton East Jcn						07/02				07/57	08/11									
Newstead Lane Jcn		06.27				07/03	07/39			08/12			08/27						09/27	
Roughton Road Jcn	06.22	06/28				07/04	07/40			08/13			08/28						09/28	
Cromer Links	06/23					07.08				08.17										
Overstrand	06.26	06.33				07.11				08.20										
Sidestrand						07.15				08.24										
Trimingham		06.39				07.19				08.28										
Mundesley-on-Sea		06.44				07.24				08.33										
Mundesley-on-Sea		06.45				07.26				08.35										
Paston						07.32				08.41										
Antingham Road Jcn		06/53				07/38				08/47										
NORTH WALSHAM		06.54				07.39				08.38										
Destination		L. St					L. St			Melton	N. Wal		L. St						Norwich	

Train	05.28		05.20	05.32		05.32	07.15	05.32		06.18	07.35		07.50			08.02	05.20		08.40	05.20
From	High		Norwich	Lynn		Lynn	Walsahm	Lynn		Norwich	Holt		Sher			High	Norwich		Melton	Norwich
Class	Light	Pass	ECS	Goods	Pass	Goods	ECS	Goods	Pass	Pass	Pass	Pass	Pass	Pass	Pass	Light	Goods	Pass	Pass	Goods
Engine	GE12	MC 4	GE1	SL 3	CB 1	SL 3	GE10	SL 3	MC 6	GE14	NR 1	CB 2	GE1	CB 1	GE10	MC 7	GE20	MC 6	CB2	GE20
Class	D16	LM 4	D16	LM 4	F6 2-4-2T	LM 4	D16	LM 4	D16	D16	D16	D16	D16	F6 2-4-2T	D16	D16	J17 0-6-0	D16	F6 2-4-2T	J17 0-6-0
Carriage Wkg/Vehicles	-	18/4	NS2/2	-	NS1/2	-	NS3/2	-	19/4	GE/3	19/4	13/2	NS2/2	NS1/2	NS2/2	-	-	15/4	17/4	-
NORTH WALSHAM							07.15								07.58			08.10		
Antingham Road Jcn															07/59			08/13		
Paston															08.05					
Mundesley-on-Sea															08.09			08.28		
Mundesley-on-Sea																		09.00		
Trimingham																		09.08		09.18
Sidestrand																				
Overstrand																				09.24
Cromer Links																				
Roughton Road Jcn							07/36				07/37							08/10		
Newstead Lane Jcn							07/37				07/38							08/11		
Runton East Jcn							07/38						07/58					08/12		09/13
CROMER BEACH							07.40						08.00					08.14		09.15
CROMER BEACH					07.00						07.55			08.09						
Runton East Jcn					07/02						07/57			08/11						
Runton West Jcn	05/39		06/42								07/39			07/58						
West Runton	05/41										07.42			08.00						
SHERINGHAM	05.45		06.47								07.45			08.03						
SHERINGHAM														08.05						
Weybourne														08.12						
Holt									07.35					08.20				09.05		
Brininghan Jcn									07.42					08/27				09/12		
MELTON CONSTABLE									07.44		(07.44)			08.30				09.14		
MELTON CONSTABLE		06.36		06/54					(07.49)		07.49							(09.37)		
Hindolvestone		06.40									07.53									
Guestwick		06.46		07.05		07.13					07.59									
Whitwell		06.53									08.06									
Whitwell		06.56					07/24				08.10									
Lenwade		07.01					07/28				08.15									
Attlebridge		07.06									08.20									
Drayton		07.15					07.46	07.54			08.29									
Hellesdon		07.21									08.35									
NORWICH CITY		07.25					08.05				08.39									

WORKING TIMETABLE : NORWICH - MELTON CONSTABLE - SHERINGHAM - CROMER - NORTH WALSHAM (1952)

Train				06.30			09.42	09.42	06.30		10.05					09.42		09.42	09.42	
From				S. Lynn			Norwich	Norwich	S. Lynn		N. Wal					Norwich		Norwich	Norwich	
Class	Pass	Pass	Pass	Goods	Pass		Goods	Goods	Goods	Goods	Pass		Goods	Pass	Pass	Goods	Pass	Goods	Goods	Pass
Engine	CB 1	MC 7	GE1	MC 6	SL 2	NR 1	MC 4	MC 4	MC 6	MC 7	CB 1	CB 2	GE20	CB 1	SL 3	MC 4	GE2	MC 4	MC 4	GE12
Class	F6	D16	D16	D16	LM 4	D16	LM 4	LM 4	D16	D16	F6	F6	J17	F6	LM 4	LM 4	D16	LM 4	LM 4	D16
Carriage Wkg/Vehicles	NS1/2	35/2	NS2/2	-	23/4	33,18/5	-	-	-	-	NS1/2	23/4	-	NS1/2	28/4	-	GE/3	-	-	NS3/2
NORWICH CITY						09.30	09.42							10.30						
Hellesdon						09.35	09.51	10.02						10.35						
Drayton						09.40		10.13						10.41		10.54				
Attlebridge														10.50		11.10		11.20		
Lenwade						09.51								10.54				11.32	11.52	
Whitwell						09.56								10.59					12.02	
Whitwell						09.57								11.00					12.22	
Guestwick						10.04								11.09						
Hindolvestone														11.14						
MELTON CONSTABLE						10.14								11.19						12.55
MELTON CONSTABLE					09.35	To			10.32						11.50					
Briningham Jcn					09/37	B'ham			10/38						11/51					
Holt					09.45				10.48						12.00					
Weybourne				09.38	09.57										12.08					
SHERINGHAM				09.46	10.04				(09.46)						12.14					
SHERINGHAM				(10.29)	10.05			10.29					11.28		12.20					13.07
West Runton					10.09			10.33					11.33		12.24					13.11
Runton West Jcn					10/12			10/35					11/35		12/26					13/13
Runton East Jcn					10/13			10/37		10/43										13/14
CROMER BEACH					10.15			10.39		10.45										13.16
CROMER BEACH		09.40	09.51								11.00			12.05						
Runton East Jcn		09/42	09/53								11/02			12/07						
Newstead Lane Jcn			09/54										11/37	12/08		12/27				
Roughton Road Jcn			09/55										11/39	12/09		12/28				
Cromer Links			09.59											12.13						
Overstrand			10.02											12.16						
Sidestrand			10.06											12.20						
Trimingham			10.10											12.24						
Mundesley-on-Sea			10.15											12.29						
Mundesley-on-Sea	09.37		10.17											12.36						
Paston	09.43		10.23											12.42						
Antingham Road Jcn	09/49		10/29											12/48						
NORTH WALSHAM	09.50		10.30											12.49						
Destination		B'ham	Nor								Melton	Nor			L. St					N. Wal

Train	09.02			05.20		09.35	09.18	08.45		09.10			09.10	12.35	09.10	09.30			13.07	09.10
From	Walsham			Norwich		Melton	Norwich	Melton		Lynn			Lynn	High	Lynn	L. St			Sher	Lynn
Class	ECS	Pass	Pass	Goods	Pass	Pass	Goods	Goods	Pass	Goods	Pass	Pass	Goods	Pass	Goods	XP	Goods	Pass	Pass	Goods
Engine	GE10	NR 2	MC 7	GE20	GE1	SL 2	GE2	MC 6	CB 1	MC 1	CB 2	CB 1	MC 7	MC 1	GE12	MC 1	GE14	GE20	GE12	MC 1
Class	D16	D16	D16	J17	D16	LM 4	D16	D16	F6	LM 4	F6	F6	D16	LM 4	D16	LM 4	D16	J17	D16	LM 4
Carriage Wkg/Vehicles	NS2/2	15/4	35/2	-	NS2/2	23/4	20/2GE/3	-	NS1/2	-	23/4	NS1/2	-	-	NS3/2	-	GE/3	-	GE/2	-
NORTH WALSHAM	09.02							10.05							12.26	12.50				
Antingham Road Jcn								10/06							12/27	12/53				
Paston								10.12												
Mundesley-on-Sea								10.16							12.35	13.20				
Mundesley-on-Sea								10.18							12.37					
Trimingham								10.24							12.43					
Sidestrand								10.28												
Overstrand						09.34		10.32							12.49					
Cromer Links								10.36												
Roughton Road Jcn	09/18					09/43	10/26	10/41							12/55					
Newstead Lane Jcn	09/19					09/45	10/27	10/42							12/57					
Runton East Jcn	09/20				10/13		10/37	10/43											13/14	
CROMER BEACH	09.22				10.15		10.39	10.45											13.16	
CROMER BEACH			09.40	09.51							11.00		12.05							
Runton East Jcn			09/42	09/53							11/02		12/07							
Runton West Jcn			09/43	09/52	(To		10/28				11/03			12/41				12/59		
West Runton			09.45	09/55	Norwich)		10.31				11.05			12.42				13.02		
SHERINGHAM			09.48	10.00			10.34				11.09			12.45				13.05		
SHERINGHAM			09.50				10.40				11.10									
Weybourne			09.57				10.48				11.18									
Holt			10.07				10.56				11.26		12.30							
Briningham Jcn			10/14				11/03				11/33		12/42							
MELTON CONSTABLE	(09.14)		10.16				11.05		(11.01)		11.35		12.45							
MELTON CONSTABLE			09.37	To						11.25										
Hindolvestone			09.42	B'ham																
Guestwick			09.48							11.40			11.55							
Whitwell			09.55										12.10							
Whitwell			09.58										12.35							
Lenwade			10.03										12.45	12.55						
Attlebridge			10.08																	
Drayton			10.17													13.19				13.35
Hellesdon			10.23																	
NORWICH CITY			10.27																	13.51

Upper table

Station / Detail	1	2	3	4	5	6	7	8	9	10	11	12	13	14	15	16	17	18	19	20
Train From								14.50 High Light					16.00 Walsham				17.00 High Light			
Class	Pass	Pass	EBV	Goods	Pass	Pass	Pass	Light	Pass	Pass	Pass	Pass	Goods	Pass	ECS	Pass	Light	Pass	Pass	Pass
Engine	GE12	MC 6	GE20	SL 2	CB 2	NR 2	MC 11	GE15	GE15	GE13	CB 1	GE16	MC 1	CB1	GE3	MC 11	GE10	CB 2	MC 7	MC 6
Class	D16	D16	J17	F6	D16	D16	D16	D16	D16	D16	F6	D16	LM 4	F6	D16	D16	D16	F6	D16	D16
Carriage Wkg/Vehicles	NS3/2	17/4	-	-	28/4	15/4	15/4	-	15/4	GE/3	NS1/2	GE/3	-	NS1/2	GE/3	28/4	-	NS1/2	GE/3	18/4
NORWICH CITY						13.21							15.26							
Hellesdon						13.26														
Drayton						13.32							15/39							
Attlebridge						13.41														
Lenwade						14.45							15/57							
Whitwell						13.50							16.04							
Whitwell						13.51							16.12							
Guestwick						14.00														
Hindolvestone						14.05														
MELTON CONSTABLE						14.09	(14.09)						16.39							
MELTON CONSTABLE					13.35	(14.25)	14.25												16.45	17.03
Brininghan Jcn					13/37		14/27												16/47	17/05
Holt					13.45		14.35												16.55	17.13
Weybourne					13.53		14.43												17.05	17.21
SHERINGHAM					13.59		14.49												17.11	17.27
SHERINGHAM					14.01		14.50			15.20		16.20		16.35					17.20	17.28
West Runton					14.05		14.54			15.24		16.24		16/38					17.24	17.32
Runton West Jcn					14.07		14.56			15/26		16/26		16/40					17/26	17/34
Runton East Jcn					14/08		14/57	15/03						16/38						17/35
CROMER BEACH					14.10		14.59	15.05						16.40						17.37
CROMER BEACH	13.26	13.35		14.10				15.24								16.45		17.05		
Runton East Jcn	13/28	13/37		14/12				15/26								17/47		17/07		
Newstead Lane Jcn	13/29									15/27		16/27		16/41				17/08	17/27	
Roughton Road Jcn	13/30									15/28		16/28		16/42				17/09	17/28	
Cromer Links	13.34																	17/12		
Overstrand	13.37																	17.15		
Sidestrand																		17.19		
Trimingham																		17.23		
Mundesley-on-Sea	13.46																	17.28		
Mundesley-on-Sea	13.47		14.00									15.37						17.30		
Paston	13.53											15.43						17.36		
Antingham Road Jcn	13/59		14/12									15/49						17/42		
NORTH WALSHAM	14.00		14.15									15.50					17.17	17.43		
Destination	Norwich	Melton		Melton				Melton	L. St		L. St			High	Melton				L. St	

Lower table

Station / Detail	1	2	3	4	5	6	7	8	9	10	11	12	13	14	15	16	17	18	19	20
Train From				12.45 Lynn		13.35 Melton		10.30 L. St	14.25 Melton	14.50 Hugh		15.30 High	12.45 Lynn		12.30 L. St					
Class	Pass	Pass	Pass	Goods	Goods	Pass	Pass	XP	Pass	Light	Pass	Light	Goods	Pass	XP	Pass	Goods	Pass	Pass	Pass
Engine	GE12	NR 1	MC 6	SL 3	SL 2	CB 2	CB 1	GE13	MC 11	GE15	GE15	GE 16	SL 3	NR2	GE3	CB 1	SL 2	MC 8	MC 11	CB 2
Class	D16	D16	D16	LM 4	LM 4	F6	F6	D16	D16	D16	D16	D16	LM 4	D16	D16	F6	F6	D16	D16	F6
Carriage Wkg/Vehicles	NS3/2	20/2	17/4	-	-	28/4	NS1/2	GE/3	15/4	-	15/4	-	-	17/4	GE/3	NS1/2	-	10/4	28/4	NS1/2
NORTH WALSHAM							14.20								16.00					
Antingham Road Jcn							14/21								16/01					
Paston							14.27								16.07					
Mundesley-on-Sea							14.31								16.11					
Mundesley-on-Sea															16.13					
Trimingham															16.19					
Sidestrand															16.23					
Overstrand															16.27					
Cromer Links															16.31					
Roughton Road Jcn								14/40							16/36					
Newstead Lane Jcn								14/41							16/37					
Runton East Jcn						14/08			14/57	15/03					16/38					
CROMER BEACH						14.10			14.59	15.05					16.40					
CROMER BEACH	13.26		13.35		14.10						15.24							16.45	17.05	
Runton East Jcn	13/28		13/37		14/12						15/26							17/47	17/07	
Runton West Jcn	To		13/38		14/18			14/42			15/27			16/00				16/48		
West Runton	North		13.40		14.21			14.45			15.29			16.03				16.50		
SHERINGHAM	W'sham		13.43		14.24			14.48			15.32	15.45		16.06				16.53		
SHERINGHAM			13.44		15.32						15.33							16.57		
Weybourne			13.51		15/41						15.40							17.04		
Holt			14.03		15.52						15.48					16.32		17.14		
Brininghan Jcn			14/10								15/55					16/46		17/21		
MELTON CONSTABLE			14.12								15.57					16.50		17.23		
MELTON CONSTABLE		13.32		14.46										16.02					17.05	
Hindolvestone		13.36												16.06					17.09	
Guestwick		13.42		14/59										16.12					17.15	
Whitwell		13.49												16.19					17.22	
Whitwell		13.52		15/09										16.20					17.23	
Lenwade		13.57		15/14										16.25					17.28	
Attlebridge		14.02												16.30					17.33	
Drayton		14.11		15.35									15.52	16.39					17.42	
Hellesdon		14.17												16.45					17.48	
NORWICH CITY		14.21												16.49	16.08				17.52	

WORKING TIMETABLE : NORWICH - MELTON CONSTABLE - SHERINGHAM - CROMER - NORTH WALSHAM (1952)

							13.45 B'ham				19.15 Walsham			18.15 Yar				21.50 Walsham	
Class	Pass	Pass	Pass		Pass	ECS	XP	Light	Pass	Pass	Pass	Pass	Pass	Pass	LE	Goods	Light	Pass	Light
Engine	NR1	MC6	CB2	GE15	NR2	MC7	MC11	GE14	MC7	CB2	MC8	CB2	MC6	GE10	MC11	SL3	MC6	CB2	GE16
Class	D16	D16	F6	D16	D16	D16	D16	D16	D16	F6	D16	F6	D16	D16	D16	LM4	D16	F6	D16
Carriage Wkg/Vehicles	20/2	18/4	NS1/2	20/2	19/4	GE/3	34/2	-	GE/3	NS1/2	10/4	NS1/2	12/2	GE/3	-	-	-	NS1/2	-
NORWICH CITY	16.50				17.30						19.15						19.45		
Hellesdon	16.55				17.35														
Drayton	17.01				17.43						19.25						20/05		
Attlebridge	17.10				17.52						19.34								
Lenwade	17.14				17.56						19.38						20/17		
Whitwell	17.19				18.01						19.42								
Whitwell	17.24				18.02						19.45						20/22		
Guestwick	17.33				18.11						19.54						20/34		
Hindolvestone	17.38				18.16						19.59								
MELTON CONSTABLE	17.43				18.21						20.04						20.53		
MELTON CONSTABLE				17.50	18.24		18.25				(20.10)			20.07			(21.02)		
Briningham Jcn				17/51	To		18/27				To			20/09			To		
Holt				18.00	F'ham		18.35				Kings			20.17			South		
Weybourne				18.08	West		18.45				Lynn			20.25			Lynn		
SHERINGHAM				18.14			18.51							20.31					
SHERINGHAM				18.20		18.42	18.53	19.10						20.33	20.26				22.30
West Runton				18.24		18/45	18.57	19/13						20.37	20.30				22.36
Runton West Jcn				18/26		18/50	18/59	19/16						20/39	20/32				22/38
Runton East Jcn						18/51	19/01				19/53			20/40				22/23	
CROMER BEACH						18.52	19.02				19.55			20.42				22.27	
CROMER BEACH		18.10								19.25	20.18				20.30		21.10		
Runton East Jcn		18/12								19/27	20/20				20/32		21/12		
Newstead Lane Jcn		18/27							19/17		20/21			20/33	20/34				22/39
Roughton Road Jcn		18/28							19/18		20/22			20/34	20/35				22/40
Cromer Links															To				
Overstrand											20.28				Cromer				
Sidestrand															Jcn)				
Trimingham											20.35								
Mundesley-on-Sea											20.40								
Mundesley-on-Sea			18.40								20.41								
Paston			18.46								20.47								
Antingham Road Jcn			18/52								20/53								
NORTH WALSHAM			18.53								20.54								
Destination		Melton		High			High		Melton					Norwich				Melton	High

Train From	17.03 Melton	13.30 L.St	13.45 B'ham			17.25 Norwich	18.42 Sher	15.30 L.St	13.45 B'ham					18.15 Yar	17.30 L.St		21.05 Norwich		
Class	Pass	XP	XP	Pass	Pass	Pass	ECS	XP	XP	Pass	Pass	Pass	Light	Pass	Pass	Light	Pass	Pass	Pass
Engine	MC6	GE14	NR1	MC6	CB2	MC7	MC7	GE10	MC11	NR2	MC7	CB2	CB2	MC11	MC6	MC11	MC6	GE16	CB2
Class	D16	D16	D16	D16	F6	D16	D16	D16	D16	D16	D16	F6	F6	D16	D16	D16	D16	D16	F6
Carriage Wkg/Vehicles	18/4,23/4	GE/3	28,32/5	18/4	NS1/2	GE/3	23/4	GE/3	34/2	18/4	GE/3	NS1/2	NS1/2	-	12/2	GE/3	-	GE/3	NS1/2
NORTH WALSHAM						18.05			18.25					19.15					21.50
Antingham Road Jcn						18/06			18/26					19/16					21/51
Paston						18.12								19.22					21.57
Mundesley-on-Sea						18.16			18.34					19.26					22.01
Mundesley-on-Sea									18.36					19.28					22.02
Trimingham									18.42					19.34					22.08
Sidestrand									18.46					19.38					22.12
Overstrand									18.50					19.42					22.16
Cromer Links									18/53					19.46					22/19
Roughton Road Jcn		17/47				18/26			18/55						20/58		22/10		22/21
Newstead Lane Jcn		17/48				18/27			18/58			19/52			20/59		22/12		22/22
Runton East Jcn	17/35						18/51			19/01		19/53			20/40				22/23
CROMER BEACH	17.37						18.52			19.02		19.55			20.42				22.27
CROMER BEACH				18.10						19.25	20.18	20.30					21.10		
Runton East Jcn				18/12						19/27	20/20	20/32					21/12		
Runton West Jcn		17/49		18/13		18/28		19/00		19/28					21/00		21/13	22/12	
West Runton		17.52		18.15		18.31		19.03		19.30					21.03			22.15	
SHERINGHAM		17.55		18.18		18.34		19.07		19.33					21.06			22.18	
SHERINGHAM				18.19						19.37					21.08	21/19			
Weybourne				18.26						19.44					21.14				
Holt				18.37						19.53					21.23				
Briningham Jcn				18/44						20/00					21/30				
MELTON CONSTABLE				18.46						20.02					21.32	21.41			
MELTON CONSTABLE			18.22							19.25									
Hindolvestone										19.29									
Guestwick			18/28							19.35									
Whitwell			18.34							19.43									
Whitwell			18.36							19.44									
Lenwade			18.41							19.49									
Attlebridge										19.54									
Drayton			18.52							20.06									
Hellesdon										20.12									
NORWICH CITY			19.00							20.16									

CROMER BEACH LOCO DIAGRAMS : 1952

1: F6 2-4-2T				2: F6 2-4-2T			
	Cromer Beach Loco	06.50	Light		Cromer Beach Loco	07.45	Light
06.55	Cromer Beach	07.00	Pass	07.50	Cromer Beach	07.55	Pass
07.39	N. Walsham	07.58	Pass	08.30	Melton Constable	08.40	Pass
08.09	Mundesley	09.37	Pass	09.15	Cromer Beach	11.00	Pass
09.50	N. Walsham	10.05	Pass	11.35	Melton Constable	13.35	Pass
10.45	Cromer Beach	12.05	Pass	14.10	Cromer Beach	14.15	Light
12.49	N. Walsham	14.20	Pass	14.20	Cromer Beach Loco	16.55	Light
14.31	Mundesley	15.27	Pass	17.00	Cromer Beach	17.05	Pass
15.50	N. Walsham	16.00	Pass	17.43	N. Walsham	18.05	Pass
16.40	Cromer Beach	16.50	Light	18.16	Mundesley	18.40	Pass
17.00	Cromer Beach Loco			18.53	N. Walsham	19.15	Pass
				19.55	Cromer Beach	20.18	Pass
				20.54	N. Walsham	21.50	Pass
				22.27	Cromer Beach	22.35	Light
				22.45	Cromer Beach Loco		

The principal mystery - to which no answer has ever been given - is why the Great Eastern did not abandon Cromer High in 1903 and transfer its operations to Cromer Beach. Whatever rents it would have to pay the M&GN were bound to be much less than the cost of maintaining a full station and several signalboxes. Perhaps the answer lies in the amount of rebuilding that would have been necessary to transform Cromer Beach into a station able to deal with two train services but more probably it was a result of the stagnation that tended to grip railway boardrooms as the twentieth century took hold.

With only 15 arrivals and departures a day, the Cromer Beach of early BR days was a place of charm rather than bustle. Possessing one platform that could take twelve coaches and a bay that could deal with five - far in excess of normal requirements - it also had a small locomotive depot that housed a pair of F6 2-4-2T's. Ostensibly belonging to Melton Constable, these engines had until the time of nationalisation been holding their own with the London suburban but, driven out by L1 2-6-4T's and electrification, they had been put out to grass in North Norfolk; working a couple of Melton trains in the morning and holding the fort on the Norfolk & Suffolk Joint where a typical sortie involved a train to North Walsham, a return from Walsham to Mundesley and the run back to Cromer Beach. The time taken varied from three to five hours and if the exercise seemed a trifle old-fashioned, at least the guards issued and collected tickets which is more than they could be persuaded to do on the main line. It was also a precursor of working practices that lay in the future.

The Cromer F6's were not the only trains seen on the Norfolk and Suffolk Joint since the Great Eastern maintained its share in the working by operating a handful of stopping trains and, more importantly, the Sheringham sections of the 09.30 and 15.30 expresses from Liverpool Street which ran via Mundesley and Runton West Junction. For some reason there were no corresponding up trains to Liverpool Street via Mundesley and the return workings ran via Cromer High and Gunton.

In a world where timetables remained all but unchanged, year upon year, the Cromer corner of Norfolk was rather more dynamic than the rest of the system and changes of one sort or another punctuated successive postwar timetables. Much of this instability had its roots in the Great Eastern's changes to its London - Norwich main line which rippled through to North Norfolk. In some years trains that had terminated at Sheringham would be extended to Melton Constable whilst in others the Sheringham section of the 15.40 from Liverpool Street would run through to Holt - five miles short of Melton - where the engine would run-round and take the stock back to Sheringham. Perhaps someone in the bowels of the timing office at Liverpool Street - idly supposed to be removed from reality - had some idea that to extend the train through to Melton would constitute some sort of unfair competition with the 15.10 from King's Cross (which ceased running in 1939) and invoke a civil action. (Old terrors died hard on British Railways - thirty years after nationalisation there were still plenty of railwaymen who would tell you that the Railway's losses were the result of money still paid to shareholders..........).

Goods trains were interesting rather than frequent with the area being served by both the M&GN and the Great Eastern. The M&GN train ran through from South Lynn, starting out behind an LMS 2-6-0 but changing it at Melton Constable for a D16 4-4-0. It served most of the stations on the way down and terminated at Cromer Beach four hours after leaving South Lynn.

After shunting out its traffic, the train returned to Melton Constable; not with its D16 4-4-0 but, coincidentally, by same 2-6-0 that had worked it from South Lynn to Melton.

The Great Eastern had a more complex method of working which involved a pair of J17 0-6-0's from Norwich Loco. The first left Norwich at 05.20 and ran via Overstrand to Sheringham. After an hour and a half, it reversed and ran via Gunton to North Walsham where it terminated. The engine then ran a trip to Mundesley - its second visit of the day - taking traffic left by the 08.35 Norwich - Cromer goods.

After three hours shunting the yard, the J17 departed with the 17.42 express (class E) goods for Norwich, the connection with the 21.00 Norwich - Spitalfields goods.

The second J17 followed a more conventional path by leaving Norwich at 08.35 and returning at 19.19 after working to Cromer High and back, serving all intermediate points via Gunton.

Arguably the best memories of Cromer Beach are those of the early 1950's when it was the town's second station and slumbered in the shadow of Cromer High 'from where the London trains ran'. The resident F6's fussed around with local trains for North Walsham and the odd service to Melton Constable whilst D16 'Claud' 4-4-0's looked after the station's only express, the through service to Birmingham New Street. Other Clauds worked in from Melton and Norwich with much speculation attending the latter workings which were occasionally covered by using large engines with time to kill. B1's, B12's and B17 4-6-0's were not unfamiliar sights whilst it was not unknown at times of forgetfulness for Norwich to send a Britannia to Sheringham.

Eventually, after half a century, the economic penny dropped and in September 1954 Cromer High ceased to deal with passenger traffic, all trains running henceforth to Cromer Beach together with the closure of the Norfolk & Suffolk Joint as far as Mundesley.

Later in the decade the diesel multiple-unit arrived and put paid to the through coaches between London, Cromer and Sheringham but at this point a curtain shall be pulled over the subsequent history of the Cromer corner, leaving the thoroughly depressing story of its further decline to other pens.

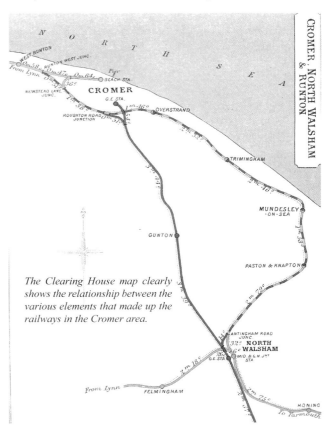

The Clearing House map clearly shows the relationship between the various elements that made up the railways in the Cromer area.

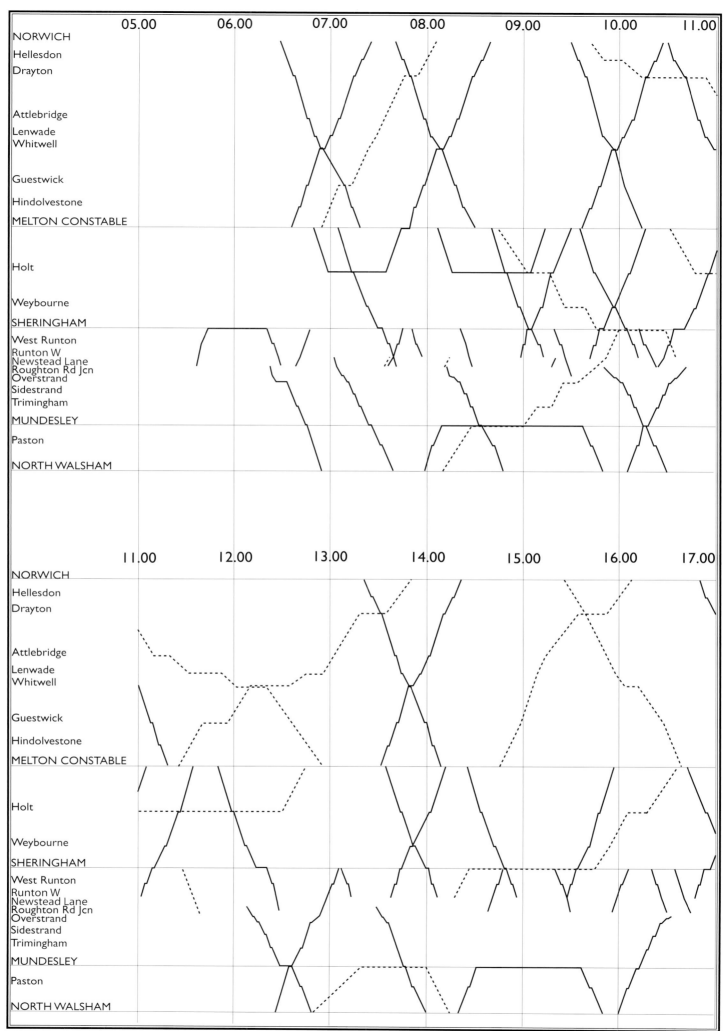

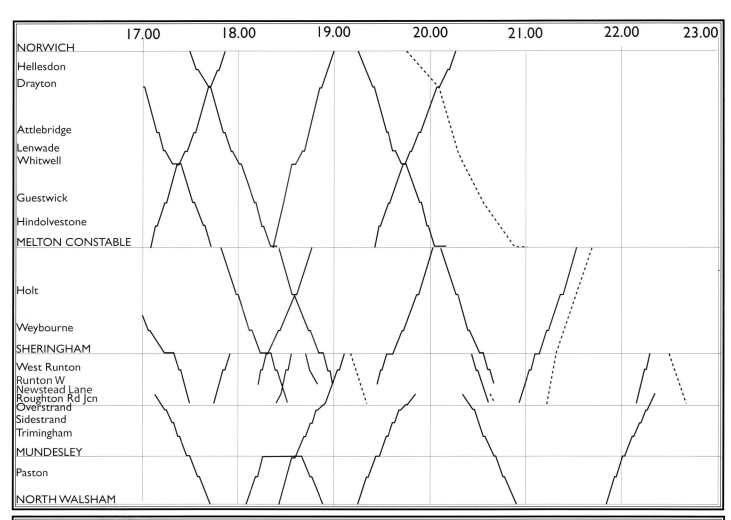

	17.00	18.00	19.00	20.00	21.00	22.00	23.00
NORWICH							
Hellesdon							
Drayton							
Attlebridge							
Lenwade							
Whitwell							
Guestwick							
Hindolvestone							
MELTON CONSTABLE							
Holt							
Weybourne							
SHERINGHAM							
West Runton							
Runton W							
Newstead Lane							
Roughton Rd Jcn							
Overstrand							
Sidestrand							
Trimingham							
MUNDESLEY							
Paston							
NORTH WALSHAM							

YARMOUTH BEACH

Yarmouth was relatively late in receiving an allocation of LMS 2-6-0's and it was not until mid-1952 that they arrived in sufficient numbers to replace the D16 4-4-0's and J17 0-6-0's that up to then had shouldered most of the shed's main line workings. LM4 2-6-0 43144 of South Lynn pulls away from Yarmouth Beach with the 18.15 Yarmouth - Melton Constable on Tuesday 21 May 1957. (R C Riley/transporttreasury.co.uk)

When arriving in Yarmouth from Liverpool Street, one felt a long way from London but when doing the journey via Peterborough - the author was one of the few to complete the marathon - one had the sensation of being in a different country.

In several of his novels set in the immediate pre-railway years, Charles Dickens noted that many of those who could not afford the coach fare cheerfully walked from London to Yarmouth and thought little of it. Walking at a good but not excessive pace, the journey would

J68 0-6-0T 68651 had a long spell at Yarmouth Beach where it covered the station and yard pilot; a working that involved shunting from six in the morning until eleven at night. The engine is seen moving a passenger vehicle from one end of Yarmouth Beach to the other on 21 May 1957, the type of duty it performed until May 1958 when it was replaced by diesel shunter 11174. (R C Riley/transporttreasury.co.uk)

take about twenty-four hours plus time spent dining but it is a fair bet than none of them went via North Norfolk and Peterborough 'just for the fun of it'. For them, the railways with their faster times and much lower fares than the stage coaches came as a Godsend that reduced the time taken whilst the fare was less than the cost of food consumed on foot.

Consisting of three platforms capable of accommodating a total of thirty-one coaches - platform three could hold an engine and thirteen coaches whilst the other two could each take an engine and nine - the facilities were far greater than anything that the ordinary weekday service called for. Indeed, the only time the resources of the station came close to being fully utilised was on Summer Saturdays when the station received and despatched ten services to and from the Midlands and North of England. This holiday traffic was operated at the expense of almost the entire goods service and had an importance that tends to be exaggerated.

For the greater part of the year Yarmouth Beach was rather a quiet spot - a cynic's description 'a rural Marylebone' was not very far off the mark - where the trains rarely exceeded four coaches and tended to be few and far between.

The normal service consisted of fourteen arrivals and twelve departures, the most important being the morning train to Birmingham and three departures for Peterborough. As though to emphasise Yarmouth's isolation from London, which via the M&GN was five miles greater than the distance from King's Cross to York, the last train to Peterborough for King's Cross left at

YARMOUTH (BEACH) LOCO DIAGRAMS : 1952

1: LMS 4MT 2-6-0

	Location	Time	Type	Notes
	Loco	06.52	Light	
	Yarmouth	07.02	Goods	
13.28	Melton C	13.30	Light	
13.40	Melton Loco	(06.35)		

2: D16 4-4-0

	Location	Time	Type	Notes
	Loco	06.25	Light	
	Yarmouth	06.35	Trip	
06.40	White Swan Yard	06.55	Trip	
07.00	Yarmouth	11.15	Pass	
11.47	Lowestoft	12.33	Pass	
13.06	Yarmouth	13.10	Light	
13.15	Beach Loco	16.45	Light	
16.50	Yarmouth	16.55	Pass	
18.34	Melton C	19.15	Pass	17.55 ex Kings Lynn
20.47	Yarmouth	21.00	Light	
21.10	Loco			

3: F6 2-4-2T

	Location	Time	Type	Notes
	Loco	06.35	Light	
	Yarmouth	06.45	Pass	
07.18	Lowestoft	08.15	Pass	Birmingham
08.50	Yarmouth	10.35	Pass	
11.08	Lowestoft	11.40	Pass	
12.13	Yarmouth	12.20	Light	
12.30	Beach Loco	15.15	Light	
15.20	Yarmouth	15.25	Pass	
15.58	Lowestoft	17.30	Pass	
18.03	Yarmouth	19.40	Pass	13.45 ex Birmingham
20.11	Lowestoft	20.50	Pass	
21.21	Yarmouth	21.30	Light	
21.40	Loco			

4: B12 4-6-0

	Location	Time	Type	Notes
	Loco	06.41	Light	
	Yarmouth	06.51	Pass	Peterborough
08.27	Melton C	08.36	Pass	
09.45	South Lynn	12.15	Pass	10.33 ex Peterborough
13.22	Melton Loco	13.30	Pass	
15.00	Yarmouth	15.10	Light	
15.20	Loco			

5: F6 2-4-2T

	Location	Time	Type	Notes
	Loco	07.35	Light	
	Yarmouth	07.45	Pass	
08.50	N. Walsham	08.51	Pass	
09.01	Aylsham	09.16	Pass	
09.28	N. Walsham	09.30	Pass	
10.30	Yarmouth	10.40	Light	
10.50	Loco			

6: B12 4-6-0

	Location	Time	Type	Notes
	Loco	09.55	Light	
	Yarmouth	10.05	Pass	Peterborough
11.38	Melton C	11.45	Pass	
12.53	South Lynn	12.55	Light	
13.00	S. Lynn Loco	17.10	Light	
17.15	South Lynn	17.24	Pass	13.45 ex Birmingham
18.12	Melton C	18.18	Pass	
19.30	Yarmouth	19.40	Light	
19.50	Loco			

7: D16 4-4-0

	Location	Time	Type	Notes
	Loco	12.32	Light	
	Yarmouth	12.42	Pass	Peterborough
14.14	Melton C	15.55	Pass	
16.13	Fakenham	16.30	Pass	
16.48	Melton C	17.02	Pass	
17.37	N. Walsham	18.08	Pass	
19.04	Yarmouth	19.10	Light	
19.20	Loco			

8: J68 0-6-0T

	Location	Time	Type
	Loco	05.50	Light
06.00	Yarmouth	23.00	
23.10	Loco		

9: J17 0-6-0

	Location	Time	Type
	Loco	07.00	Light
	Yarmouth	07.20	Goods
09.43	Lowestoft	11.45	Goods
13.46	Yarmouth	13.50	Light
14.00	Loco		

lunchtime. The rest of the main line service consisted of local trains to North Walsham and Melton Constable.

Passenger-rated goods traffic was an important line of business for the M&GN and to cater for it a parcels train ran from Yarmouth Beach at 12.55 conveying vans for both Peterborough and Spalding. Interestingly it was paralleled by the 13.20 Yarmouth (Vauxhall) to Spalding which ran via Dereham and King's Lynn to join the M&GN at South Lynn.

Yarmouth Beach was also the station for the Norfolk & Suffolk Joint service to Lowestoft; the line branching from the M&GN proper immediately outside the station and making a 180-degree turn to make a trailing connection at Gorleston Junction with the Great Eastern's branch from Yarmouth South Town. The two-mile stretch from Yarmouth Beach included the impressive Breydon Swing Bridge over the river Yare.

There were ten daily services from Lowestoft Central to Yarmouth, five to South Town and five to Yarmouth Beach, the latter including the 08.15 which was a through service to Leicester and Birmingham, New Street. The services to and from Yarmouth Beach were all worked by F6 2-4-2T's whilst those from South Town were more varied and ranged from D16 4-4-0's to the Beccles push and pull. The line was served by a daily goods service which was based at Yarmouth Beach and worked by a J17 0-6-0.

Workings were slightly more varied at the Yarmouth end of the line since the Yarmouth Union Line branched off at Caister Road Junction to make a connection with the GER quayside line from Yarmouth Vauxhall. The general method of operation was for the GER to work the Quays and to deposit all traffic for the M&GN at White Swan Yard. The M&GN sent out two trips a day - one behind a D16 4-4-0 and the other with an LMS 4MT 2-6-0 - taking coal and salt to White Swan and fish and coal empties out.

The passenger working at Yarmouth was a little less static than it was in the rest of the system and in the summer the rather desultory service was enriched by the Tantivy: a working that shuttled between Yarmouth Beach and Potter Heigham, performing eight return trips - almost the equivalent of a return run to Peterborough - between eight in the morning and midnight. The main purpose of the working - which did not run on Saturdays - was to serve the several holiday halts which littered the route for a dozen miles out of Yarmouth.

Another curiosity of Yarmouth - one that operated all the year round - were the early closing day and market day trains which remained in the timetable long after most farming people had become car owners.

One of these workings was the 12.00 Yarmouth to Stalham and its 12.59 return which ran on Wednesdays and Saturdays and employed the F6 2-4-2T that had earlier worked the 07.45 Yarmouth - North Walsham. On Thursdays the train left Yarmouth Beach at 13.20 using the same F5 but returned empty from Stalham.

On Wednesdays and Saturdays, the F5 put in a late turn with another of these odd-day workings, the 21.00 Yarmouth to North Walsham and the 22.10 return.

If Yarmouth Beach goods yard did not always seem to be particularly active, it was almost certainly more profitable than the adjacent passenger station; the value of goods taken by the 16.00 express goods to Peterborough alone - potato crisps, lemonades, cardboard packaging and frozen foods - probably paid the staff wages up the line as far as Corpusty.

The remainder of the main line service was a pair of rather everyday services which worked their way up the line to Melton Constable, dropping off empties and collecting loaded traffic as they went along.

As with the M&GN generally, Yarmouth eventually found most of its trains being worked by LMS 2-6-0's although, being at the end of the queue for the new engines, managed to retain a pre-grouping air for rather longer than the rest of the system. Prior to the arrival of the 2-6-0's, Yarmouth had an allocation of 17 engines, main line passenger work being covered by three B12 4-6-0's and four D16 4-4-0's whilst five F6 2-4-2T's handled the local workings leaving a trio of J17 0-6-0's to look after the goods traffic.

The first casualties at Yarmouth were the D16 4-4-0's which disappeared as soon the shed's half a dozen 2-6-0's had established themselves and the second were the five F5 2-4-2T's which were transferred away shortly after the closure of the branch to Lowestoft. (The closure was prompted by the state of the Breydon bridge and did not affect the services between Yarmouth South Town and Lowestoft which continued for seventeen years after the closure of the M&GN link).

It is a matter of record that the M&GN's position in regard to suitable motive power all but reached crisis point during the early BR years but much of the drama went, alas, unrecorded which is a great shame since late 1950 saw Yarmouth Beach having three of its four B12 4-6-0's wrested from it, leaving the eastern end of the M&GN highly vulnerable to failures or mechanical problems. Precisely what took place is unknown but the decision to transfer K3 2-6-0 61971 to Yarmouth from Norwich suggests an element of panic somewhere: a suspicion founded on the fact that there was not an inch of the M&GN that a K3 could lawfully pass!

It is quite possible that the error was spotted in time and that the K3 never actually arrived in Yarmouth but the Lord giveth and the Lord taketh away and as the order for 61971 was rescinded, Yarmouth's sole K2 2-6-0, 61747, that had only just arrived from Peterborough was also spirited away leaving the shed facing 1951 in a very grim position indeed.

One would dearly like to know what representations were made but it was not until Easter that the position eased with the gift of a pair of B12 4-6-0's; engines made available following the displacement of B1 4-6-0's by Britannia Pacifics.

Once the LMS 2-6-0's had bedded down, little further change of note took place except that in the summer of 1956 Yarmouth Beach received its first postwar allocation of a restaurant car. This was car E668 which for some time had been based at King's Lynn but spent the weekends at Yarmouth when it worked to Leicester in the 09.00 Birmingham, returning the same day in the 19.34 arrival. During the remainder of the week the car worked only between South Lynn and Leicester, being extended back to Yarmouth when the change of engines was moved from South Lynn to Spalding.

Goods and passenger receipts from stations east of Melton Constable had long been a source of worry but the arrival of new engines and the permanent allocation of a restaurant car seemed to suggest a promising future and few in 1956 ever dreamt that within four years neither Yarmouth Beach nor its railway would exist.

YARMOUTH BEACH YARD : 1952				
Train	Arrive	Loco	Depart	Destination
		D16/YAR2	06.35	White Swan
06.55 White Swan	07.00	D16/YAR2		
		LM4/YAR1	07.02	Melton Constable
		J17/YAR9	07.20	Lowestoft
		D16/MC8	10.30	Melton Constable
06.45 Melton Constable	13.22	LM4/MC5		
11.45 Lowestoft	13.46	J17/YAR9		
		LM4/SL15B	14.00	White Swan
14.30 White Swan	14.35	LM4/SL15B		
		LM4/SL15B	16.00	Peterborough
14.35 South Lynn	20.23	LM4/SL15A		

YARMOUTH (BEACH) : 1952						
Train	Arrive	Loco	Shed	Stock	Depart	Destination
		F6 2-4-2T	YAR 3	37/2	06.45	Lowestoft
		B12 4-6-0	YAR 4	4/4	06.51	Peterborough
06.40 North Walsham	07.41	D16 4-4-0	MC 3	27/2		
		F6 2-4-2T	YAR 5	6/4	07.45	Aylsham
07.17 Melton Constable	08.46	D16 4-4-0	MC 8	5/4		
08.15 Lowestoft	08.50	F6 2-4-2T	YAR 3	37/2	(09.00)	
		D16 4-4-0	MC 3	37/2	09.00	Birmingham NS
		B12 4-6-0	YAR 6	5/4	10.05	Peterborough
09.16 Aylsham	10.30	F6 2-4-2T	YAR 5	6/4		
		F6 2-4-2T	YAR 3	27/2	10.35	Lowestoft
06.45 Peterborough	11.05	LM4 2-6-0	SL 11	9/4+2		
		D16 4-4-0	YAR 2	12/2	11.15	Lowestoft
11.40 Lowestoft	12.13	F6 2-4-2T	YAR 3	27/2		
		D16 4-4-0	YAR 7	6/4+1	12.42	Peterborough
		LM4 2-6-0	SL 11	9 Vans	12.55	Pcls Peterborough
12.33 Lowestoft	13.06	D16 4-4-0	YAR 2	12/2		
10.33 Peterborough	15.00	B12 4-6-0	YAR 4	2/4		
		F6 2-4-2T	YAR 3	12/2	15.25	Lowestoft
		D16 4-4-0	YAR 2	9,27/6	16.55	Melton Constable
12.45 Peterborough	17.20	LM4 2-6-0	SL 8	4/4		
17.30 Lowestoft	18.03	F6 2-4-2T	YAR 3	12/2		
		LM4 2-6-0	SL 8	4,12/6	18.15	Cromer
18.08 North Walsham	19.04	D16 4-4-0	YAR 7	13/2		
13.45 Birmingham NS	19.34	B12 4-6-0	YAR 6	36/2		
		F6 2-4-2T	YAR 3	36/2	19.40	Lowestoft
17.50 King's Lynn	20.47	D16 4-4-0	YAR 2	3/4		
		F6 2-4-2T	YAR 5	8/4	21.00	North Walsham (Th.O)
20.50 Lowestoft	21.12	F6 2-4-2T	YAR 3	36/2		
22.10 N. Walsham (Th.O)	23.07	F6 2-4-2T	YAR 5	8/4		

YARMOUTH 1

	On Duty	05.20		
	Prepare			YAR2/D16
	Beach Loco	06.25	Light	YAR2/D16
	Yarmouth	06.35	Trip	YAR2/D16
06.40	White Swan Yard	06.55	Trip	YAR2/D16
07.00	Yarmouth	11.15	Pass	YAR2/D16
11.47	Lowestoft	12.33	Pass	YAR2/D16
13.06	Yarmouth	13.10	Light	YAR2/D16
13.15	Beach Loco			
13.2	Off Duty			

YARMOUTH 2

	On Duty	05.50		
	Prepare			YAR3/F6
	Beach Loco	06.35	Light	YAR3/F6
	Yarmouth	06.45	Pass	YAR3/F6
07.18	Lowestoft	08.15	Birmingham	YAR3/F6
08.50	Yarmouth	10.35	Pass	YAR3/F6
11.08	Lowestoft	11.40	Pass	YAR3/F6
12.13	Yarmouth	12.20	Light	YAR3/F6
12.30	Beach Loco			
13.50	Off Duty			

YARMOUTH 3

	On Duty	05.52		
	Prepare			YAR1/LM4
	Beach Loco	06.52	Light	YAR1/LM4
	Yarmouth	07.02	Melton Goods	YAR1/LM4
10.17	Stalham	11.00	06.45 ex Melton	MC5/LM4
13.22	Yarmouth	13.30	Light	MC5/LM4
13.35	Beach Loco			
13.52	Off Duty			

YARMOUTH 4

	On Duty	06.25		
	Prepare			YAR4/B12
	Beach Loco	06.41	Light	YAR4/B12
	Yarmouth	06.51	P'boro Pass	YAR4/B12
08.27	Melton C	08.36	P'boro Pass	YAR4/B12
09.45	South Lynn	12.15	10.33 ex P'boro	YAR4/B12
13.22	Melton Loco	13.30	10.33 ex P'boro	YAR4/B12
15.00	Yarmouth		Relieved	
15.10	Off Duty			

YARMOUTH 5
MONDAY, TUESDAY, FRIDAY ONLY

	On Duty	06.50		
	Prepare			YAR5/F6
	Beach Loco	07.35	Light	YAR5/F6
	Yarmouth	07.45	Pass	YAR5/F6
08.50	N. Walsham	08.51	Pass	YAR5/F6
09.01	Aylsham	09.16	Pass	YAR5/F6
09.28	N. Walsham	09.30	Pass	YAR5/F6
10.30	Yarmouth	10.40	Light	
10.45	Beach Loco			
	Prepare			SL15/LM4
14.50	Off Duty			

YARMOUTH 5
WEDNESDAY, SATURDAYS ONLY

	On Duty	06.50		
	Prepare			YAR5/F6
	Beach Loco	07.35	Light	YAR5/F6
	Yarmouth	07.45	Pass	YAR5/F6
08.50	N. Walsham	08.51	Pass	YAR5/F6
09.01	Aylsham	09.16	Pass	YAR5/F6
09.28	N. Walsham	09.30	Pass	YAR5/F6
10.30	Yarmouth	10.40	Light	YAR5/F6
10.45	Beach Loco	11.45	Light	YAR5/F6
11.50	Yarmouth	12.00	Passenger	YAR5/F6
12.40	Stalham	12.59	Passenger	YAR5/F6
13.43	Yarmouth	13.50	Light	YAR5/F6
13.55	Beach Loco			
14.50	Off Duty			

YARMOUTH 5
THURSDAY ONLY

	On Duty	06.50		
	Prepare			YAR5/F6
	Beach Loco	07.35	Light	YAR5/F6
	Yarmouth	07.45	Pass	YAR5/F6
08.50	N. Walsham	08.51	Pass	YAR5/F6
09.01	Aylsham	09.16	Pass	YAR5/F6
09.28	N. Walsham	09.30	Pass	YAR5/F6
10.30	Yarmouth	10.40	Light	YAR5/F6
10.45	Beach Loco	13.10	Light	YAR5/F6
13.15	Yarmouth	13.20	Passenger	YAR5/F6
13.42	Martham	13.52	Passenger	YAR5/F6
14.12	Yarmouth	14.20	Light	YAR5/F6
14.25	Beach Loco			
14.50	Off Duty			

YARMOUTH 6

	On Duty	08.50		
	Prepare			YAR6/B12
	Beach Loco	09.55	Light	YAR6/B12
	Yarmouth	10.05	P'boro Pass	YAR6/B12
11.38	Melton C	11.45	P'boro Pass	YAR6/B12
12.53	South Lynn	12.55	Light	YAR6/B12
13.00	S. Lynn Loco			
	S. Lynn	14.19		pass
17.20	Yarmouth			
17.30	Off Duty			

YARMOUTH 7

	On Duty	11.32		
	Prepare			YAR7/D16
	Beach Loco	12.32	Light	YAR7/D16
	Yarmouth	12.42	P'boro Pass	YAR7/D16
14.14	Melton C	15.55	Pass	YAR7/D16
16.13	Fakenham	16.30	Pass	YAR7/D16
16.48	Melton C	17.02	Pass	YAR7/D16
17.37	N. Walsham	18.08	Pass	YAR7/D16
19.04	Yarmouth	19.10	Light	YAR7/D16
19.20	Beach Loco			
19.32	Off Duty			

YARMOUTH 8

	On Duty	12.22		
	Yarmouth	12.42		Pass
15.28	South Lynn			
13.00	S. Lynn Loco	17.10	Light	YAR6/B12
17.15	South Lynn	17.24	13.45 ex B'ham	YAR6/B12
18.12	Melton C	18.18	13.45 ex B'ham	YAR6/B12
19.30	Yarmouth	19.40	Light	YAR6/B12
19.50	Loco			
20.22	Off Duty			

YARMOUTH 9

	On Duty	13.30		
	Yarmouth Loco	13.50	Light	SL15B/LM4
	Yarmouth Beach	14.00	Goods	SL15B/LM4
14.05	White Swan Yard	14.30	Goods	SL15B/LM4
14.35	Yarmouth Beach	16.00	P'boro Goods	SL15B/LM4
17.21	Melton C	17.34	S. Lynn Goods	SL15A/LM4
20.23	Yarmouth Beach	20.25	Light	SL15A/LM4
20.30	Yarmouth Loco			
21.30	Off Duty			

YARMOUTH 10

	On Duty	14.30		
	Prepare			YAR3/F6
	Beach Loco	15.15	Light	YAR3/F6
15.20	Yarmouth	15.25	Pass	YAR3/F6
15.58	Lowestoft	17.30	Pass	YAR3/F6
18.03	Yarmouth	19.40	13.45 ex B'ham	YAR3/F6
20.11	Lowestoft	20.50	Pass	YAR3/F6
21.21	Yarmouth	21.30	Light	YAR3/F6
21.40	Loco			
22.30	Off Duty			

YARMOUTH 11

	On Duty	14.40		
	Prepare			YAR2/D16
	Beach Loco	16.45	Light	YAR2/D16
16.50	Yarmouth	16.55	Pass	YAR2/D16
18.34	Melton C	19.15	17.55 ex K Lynn	YAR2/D16
20.47	Yarmouth	21.00	Light	YAR2/D16
21.10	Loco			
22.40	Off Duty			

YARMOUTH 12

	On Duty	18.30		
	Dispose			YAR7/D16

WEDNESDAY, SATURDAYS ONLY

	Beach Loco	20.50	Light	YAR5/F6
20.55	Yarmouth	21.00	Passenger	YAR5/F6
21.59	N. Walsham	22.10	Passenger	YAR5/F6
23.07	Yarmouth	23.10	Light	YAR5/F6
23.20	Beach Loco			
02.30	Off Duty			

YARMOUTH 13

	On Duty	22.00		
	As Ordered			
06.00	Off Duty			

YARMOUTH 14

	On Duty	04.05		
	Prepare			YAR8/J68
	Beach Loco	06.00	Light	YAR8/J68
	Yarmouth		Pilot	YAR8/J68
10.45	Relieved			
12.05	Off Duty			

YARMOUTH 15

	On Duty	10.35		
10.45	Yarmouth		Pilot	YAR8/J68
18.10	Relieved			
18.35	Off Duty			

YARMOUTH 16

	On Duty	18.00		
18.10	Yarmouth	23.00	Pilot	YAR8/J68
23.10	Beach Loco			
02.00	Off Duty			

YARMOUTH 17

	On Duty	14.00		
	Shed duties			
22.00	Off Duty			

YARMOUTH 18

	On Duty	06.10		
	Prepare			YAR9/J17
	Loco	07.00	Light	YAR9/J17
07.05	Yarmouth	07.20	Goods	YAR9/J17
09.43	Lowestoft	11.45	Goods	YAR9/J17
13.46	Yarmouth	13.50	Light	YAR9/J17
14.00	Loco			
14.10	Off Duty			

Despite its position at the end of the line, most Yarmouth turns were either local or worked across the Norfolk & Suffolk Joint to Lowestoft and only three workings took Yarmouth men west of Melton Constable. The shed lost its most prestigious turns - the through express to and from Birmingham - in June 1956 when the working was altered to run via Spalding, where engines were changed. Under the revised arrangements, Yarmouth crews worked the train only as far as Melton Constable.

It is interesting to note how seldom Yarmouth men worked on foreign engines.

M&GN CARRIAGE WORKINGS : 1952

Listed in order of cyclical working and not strict numerical order.

1 PUSH & PULL SET
2 NON-CORRIDOR C(2-6), BT(4)
CW 1

	King's Lynn	08.00
08.05	South Lynn	08.15
08.20	King's Lynn	08.33
08.38	South Lynn	08.45
08.50	King's Lynn	09.44
09.49	South Lynn	09.55
10.00	King's Lynn	10.30 ECS
10.35	South Lynn	11.13
11.18	King's Lynn	11.55
12.00	South Lynn	12.11
12.16	King's Lynn	12.50
12.55	South Lynn	13.05
13.10	King's Lynn	14.09
14.14	South Lynn	14.20
14.25	King's Lynn	15.25
15.30	South Lynn	15.40
15.45	King's Lynn	17.05
17.10	South Lynn	17.22
17.27	King's Lynn	17.43
18.41	Dereham	19.11
20.11	King's Lynn	21.25
21.30	South Lynn	21.45
21.50	King's Lynn	(08.00)

4 CORRIDOR SET (LNER)
TK(7), TK(7), CK(2-4), BTK(3)
Cycle 1
CW 2

	Peterborough N	05.10	
06.28	King's Lynn	06.53	ECS
06.58	South Lynn	07.08	
08.26	Peterborough N	10.00	
15.00	Yarmouth	)06.51)	

CW 4

	Yarmouth	06.51	
11.07	Peterborough N	12.45	
17.20	Yarmouth	18.15	RP
20.00	Melton Constable	(07.17)	

CW 5

	Melton Constable	07.17
08.46	Yarmouth	10.05
14.08	Peterborough N	15.40
17.15	King's Lynn	17.50
20.47	Yarmouth	(07.45)

CW 8

| | Spare Yarmouth | |

CW 6

	Yarmouth	07.45
09.01	Aylsham	09.16
10.30	Yarmouth	12.45
16.40	Peterborough N	(05.10)

4 CORRIDOR SET (LNER)
TK(7), TK(7), CK(2-4), BTK(3)
Cycle 2
CW 3

	King's Lynn	17.55
19.38	Peterborough	(06.45)

CW 9

	Peterborough	06.45
11.05	Yarmouth	16.55
18.34	Melton Constable	(07.30)

CW 11

	Melton Constable	07.30
10.21	Peterborough	22.45
23.59	King's Lynn	(10.13)

CW 7

	King's Lynn	10.13	ECS
10.18	South Lynn	14.45	Pcls
15.56	Wisbech N.	16.25	
17.20	Peterborough	20.10	
22.45	Melton Constable	(15.55)	

CW 10

	Melton Constable	15.55
16.13	Fakenham	16.30
16.48	Melton Constable	17.05
17.50	Norwich City	19.15
21.30	King's Lynn	(17.55)

2 CORRIDOR SET (LNER)
BTK(3), CK(2-5)
CW 12

	Yarmouth	11.15	
11.47	Lowestoft Central	12.33	
13.06	Yarmouth	15.25	
1558	Lowestoft Central	17.25	
17.58	Yarmouth	18.15	FP
20.00	Melton Constable	20.07	
20.42	Cromer	(07.55)	

CW 13

	Cromer	07.55
08.30	Melton Constable	15.55
16.13	Fakenham	16.30
16.48	Melton Constable	17.05
17.37	North Walsham	18.08
19.03	Yarmouth	(11.15)

4 CORRIDOR SET (M&GN)
CK(2-5), TK (7), TK(7), BZ
Cycle 3
CW 15

	Norwich City	06.28	
07.19	Melton Constable	08.07	ECS
08.16	Holt	09.05	
09.14	Melton Constable	09.37	
10.27	Norwich City	13.21	
14.09	Melton Constable	14.25	
14.59	Cromer Beach	15.24	
15.57	Melton Constable	(09.35)	

CW 23

	Melton Constable	09.35
10.15	Cromer Beach	11.00
11.35	Melton Constable	(06.36)

CW 18

	Melton Constable	06.36	
07.25	Norwich City	09.30	
10.14	Melton Constable	16.25	
16.33	Corpusty	16.42	ECS
16.50	Melton Constable	17.03	
17.37	Cromer Beach	18.10	
18.46	Melton Constable	19.25	
20.16	Norwich City	(06.28)	

4 CORRIDOR SET (M&GN)
CK(2-5), TK (7), TK(7), BZ
CW 17

	Norwich City	07.40
08.30	Melton Constable	08.40
09.15	Cromer Beach	13.35
14.12	Melton Constable	16.02
16.49	Norwich City	(07.40)

4 CORRIDOR SET (M&GN)
CK(2-5), TK (7), TK(7), BZ
CW 19

	Melton Constable	06.50	
06.59	Holt	07.35	
07.44	Melton Constable	07.49	
08.39	Norwich City	17.30	
18.21	Melton Constable	18.27	
18.45	Fakenham	19.00	ECS
19.16	Melton Constable	(06.50)	

2 CORRIDOR SET (M&GN)
BTK(5), CK(2-4)
CW 20

	Norwich (GE)	09.18
10.18	Cromer Jcn	10.21
11.05	Melton Constable	13.32
14.21	Norwich City	16.50
17.43	Melton Constable	17.50
18.37	Cromer High	18.45
19.44	Norwich (GE)	(09.18)

3 CORRIDOR SET (M&GN)
BTK(3), TK(7), CK(2-4)
CW 21

	Sutton Bridge	09.15
09.58	Spalding	11.45
12.06	Bourne	12.38
13.18	Saxby	13.45
14.46	Spalding	16.08
16.29	Bourne	16.35
16.56	Spalding	17.45
18.25	Sutton Bridge	(09.15)

3 CORRIDOR SET (M&GN)
BTK(3), TK(7), CK(2-5)
CW 22

	Sutton Bridge	08.00
08.41	Spalding	16.00
16.40	Sutton Bridge	(08.00)

3 CORRIDOR SET (M&GN)
BTK(3), TK(7), CK(2-4)
CW 25

	Bourne	07.40	
08.00	Spalding	08.15	
09.26	King's Lynn	10.13	ECS
10.18	South Lynn	13.50	ECS
14.40	Sutton Bridge	18.43	Pcls
19.23	Spalding	20.36	
20.57	Bourne	(07.40)	

2 CORRIDOR SET (M&GN)
BTK(5), CK(2-4)
CW 27

	Melton Constable	06.00	ECS
06.36	N. Walsham	06.40	
07.41	Yarmouth	10.35	
11.08	Lowestoft Central	11.35	
12.08	Yarmouth	16.55	
18.34	Melton Constable	(06.00)	

4 CORRIDOR SET (M&GN)
CK(2-5), TK (7), BZ, BZ
CW 28

	Norwich City	10.30
11.19	Melton Constable	13.35
14.10	Cromer Beach	16.00
17.23	Melton Constable	18.22
19.00	Norwich City	(10.30)

3 CORRIDOR SET (LMS)
BTK(5), CK(3-4), BTK(4)
CW 29

	King's Lynn	06.45
10.24	Nottingham	16.20
19.57	King's Lynn	(06.45)

3 CORRIDOR SET (LMS)
BTK(5), CK(3-4), BTK(4)
CW 30

	Nottingham	08.40
09.24	Saxby	09.55
12.36	King's Lynn	16.21
20.00	Nottingham	(08.40)

3 CORRIDOR SET (LMS)
BTK(5), CK(3-4), BTK(4)
CW 31

	Spalding	12.20
13.05	Sutton Bridge	13.35
14.20	Spalding	16.08
18.06	Nottingham	19.42
21.26	Spalding	(12.20)

1 CORRIDOR SET (LMS)
BCK(2-4)
CW 32

	Norwich City	09.30	
10.14	Melton Constable	10.28	
15.39	Birmingham NS	15.46	ECS
16.00	King's Norton	(12.37)	

1 CORRIDOR SET (LMS)
BCK(2-4)
CW 33

	King's Norton	12.37
12.53	Birmingham	13.45
18.12	Melton Constable	18.22
19.00	Norwich City	(09.30)

2 CORRIDOR SET (LMS)
BCK(2-4), TK(7)
CW 34

	King's Norton	12.37
12.53	Birmingham	13.45
18.12	Melton Constable	18.25
19.02	Cromer Beach	(09.40)

2 CORRIDOR SET (LMS)
BCK(2-4), TK(7)
CW 35

	Cromer Beach	09.40	
10.16	Melton Constable	10.28	
15.39	Birmingham NS	15.46	ECS
16.00	King's Norton	(12.37)	

2 CORRIDOR SET (LMS)
BCK(2-4), TK(7)
CW 36

	King's Norton	12.37
12.53	Birmingham	13.45
20.11	Lowestoft	(08.15)

2 CORRIDOR SET (LMS)
BCK(2-4), TK(7)
CW 37

	Lowestoft	08.15
15.39	Birmingham	15.46
16.00	King's Norton	(12.37)

3 CORRIDOR SET (LMS)
BTK(3), TK(7), CK(2-5)
CW 38

	King's Lynn	11.13
12.46	Peterborough	17.55
19.27	King's Lynn	(11.13)

1 CORRIDOR SET (LNER)
RESTAURANT BUFFET
CW 39

	King's Lynn	10.13	ECS
10.18	South Lynn	11.22	
13.40	Leicester LR	15.15	
17.16	South Lynn	21.25	ECS
21.30	King's Lynn	(10.13)	